06/08

DUSTY WARRIORS

DUSTY WARRIORS

MODERN SOLDIERS AT WAR

RICHARD HOLMES

HarperPress

An Imprint of HarperCollinsPublishers

Harper Press
An imprint of HarperCollins*Publishers*
77–85 Fulham Palace Road
Hammersmith, London, W6 8JB
www.harpercollins.com

Published by Harper Press in 2006

3

A catalogue record for this book
is available from the British Library

ISBN-13 978 0 00 721284 2
ISBN-10 0 00 721284 4

Maps by John Gilkes

Set in PostScript Linotype Baskerville
with Bulmer and Gresham display by
Rowland Phototypesetting Ltd, Bury St Edmunds, Suffolk

Printed and bound in Great Britain by
Clays Ltd, St Ives plc

This is for JD, Scoots, Bellies, Sugar Ray, Corkie, Solid, Waterkid, Nasty Nick, Obersturmgruppenführer Brooksmong, Nicky T, Bagpuss, Doilie, Stanley, various Rats, Cannibal, Barnie, Ains, the Falcon, the Wise Man, General Brodie, Officer Dribble, the Tobinator, the Australian Cultural Attaché, Warlock, Dark Lord, Chalky, Jonah, all the Dazzes, Brownstar, Llewy, B, Passmong, TJ, Stiffler, Baz, Mogg, Rosco, Stick, Vola, Duk, Max, Alf, Taddie, Eddie Bloom, Thomo, Sammy, Big Badge, Good Bloke Knick-knack Head Brinx Matt von Felz, Sideshow Bob, Jarine, Golley, Featherbrain, Jono, Wolfie, the Princess Royal, Silverback, Murph, Goose, Combat Carrot, Amos, the Thug, Obby, Moley, Dog, Pearsie, Vin Diesel, Blinky 1 and 2, Horse, Rasher and Smudge.

All the Bods, Lance Jacks, Screws, Colours, Staffs and Qs . . . and Basher 75.

But above all to Ray, Lee and Little Steve, who didn't make it.

CONTENTS

ILLUSTRATIONS

The author received the photographs in this book on disc, which makes tracing their precise provenance difficult. However, most were taken by members of 1st Battalion The Princess of Wales's Royal Regiment. The pictures on page 5 of the plate section of a stand-off in Al Amarah and on page 213 of a baton gunner engaging a rioter were taken by 1st Battalion The Light Infantry, and that on page 27 of A Company 1 RWF on border patrol by members of A Company 1st Battalion The Royal Welsh Fusiliers. The photographs on page 243 of Danny Boy veterans and on page 335 of Major Justin Feather-stone holding Tigris are copyright NI Syndication.

PLATE SECTION

C Company canoeing on adventure training in Bavaria.
A recce platoon patrol on the Tigris.

WO2 Falconer (*centre*).
View from the roof of CIMIC House.

Training for a petrol-bomb attack.
View from the top sangar of CIMIC House, looking east.

Night fighting from the roof of CIMIC House, August 2005.
An 81mm mortar in action.

Stand-off in Al Amarah. This photograph probably shows 1 LI, from whom 1 PWRR took over in April 2004.

Major James Coward QRL and an Iraqi policeman.
Corporal Palmer QRL training Iraqi police recruits.
Iraqi police.

Hearts and minds.
Private Lee O'Callaghan's body is repatriated from Basra.

Major Coote and WO2 Falconer of C Company.

While every effort has been made to trace the owners of copyright material reproduced herein, the publishers would like to apologise for any omissions and will be pleased to incorporate missing acknowledgements in any future editions.

MAPS

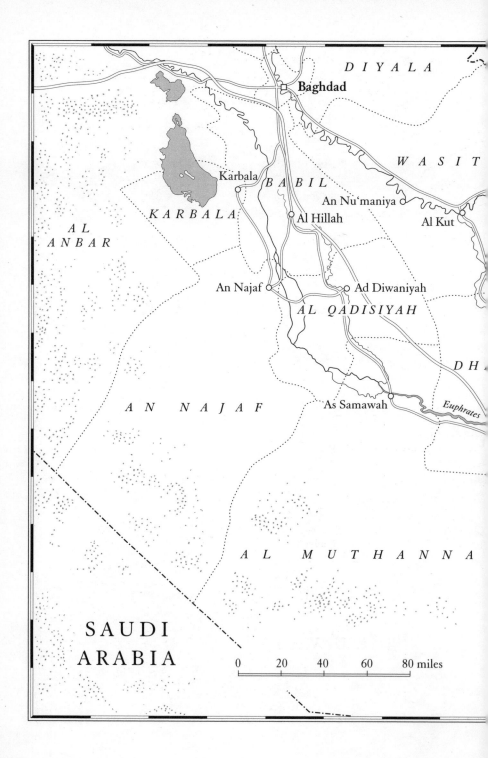

DIYALA

Baghdad

WASIT

Karbala

BABIL

An Nu'maniya

Al Kut

KARBALA

AL
ANBAR

Al Hillah

An Najaf

Ad Diwaniyah

AL QADISIYAH

DH

AN NAJAF

As Samawah

Euphrates

AL MUTHANNA

SAUDI
ARABIA

0   20   40   60   80 miles

Southern Iraq

KUWAIT

IRAN

'Ali al
Gharbi

MAYSAN

Al Amarah

Al Majar
al Kabir

)AR

An Nasiriyah

Tigris

Shatt al Arab

Ahvaz

Basra

Shaiba

Abadan

AL   BASRYAH

Umm Qasr

KUWAIT

Kuwait

Persian
Gulf

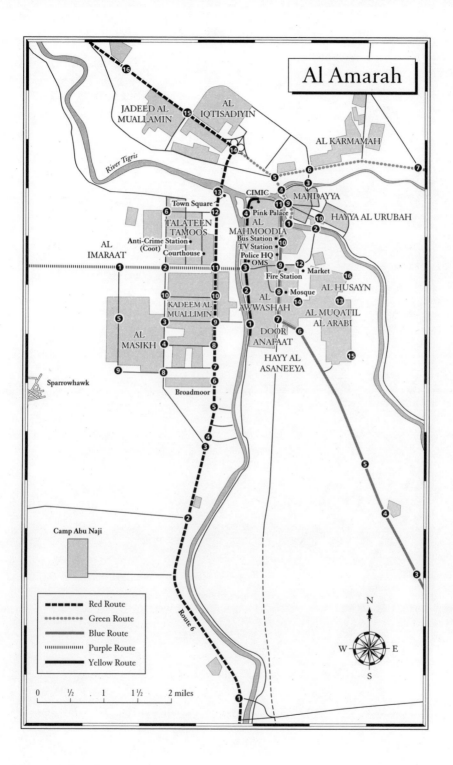

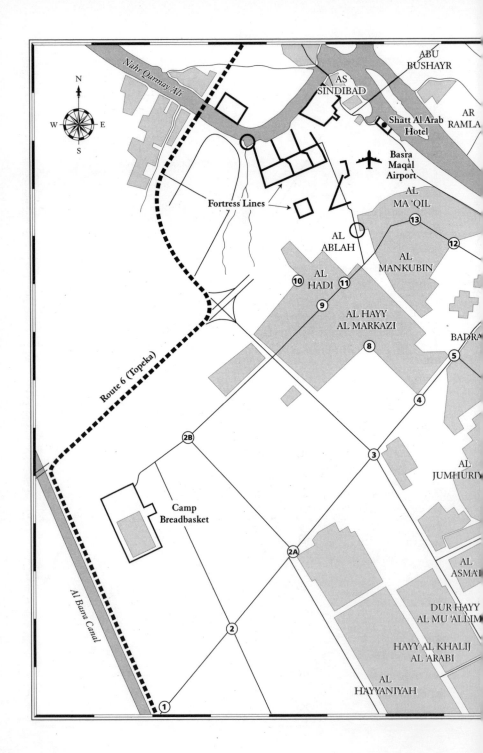

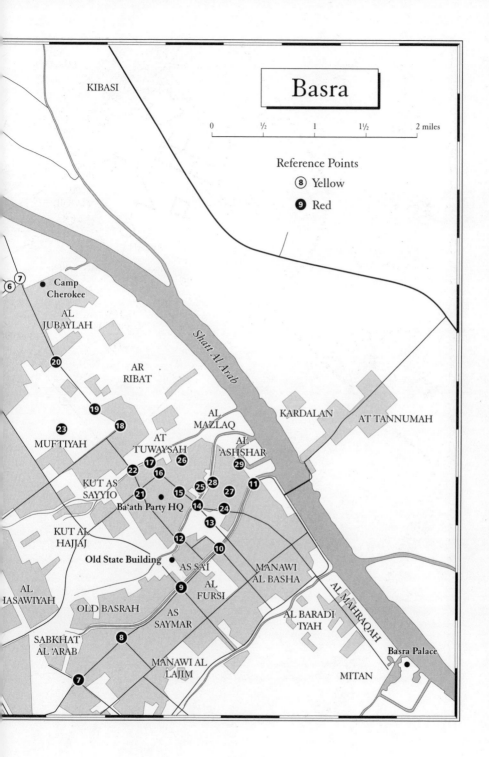

INTRODUCTION

This book was never part of a long-term literary plan, although in one sense it fits neatly onto my recent trilogy (*Redcoat, Tommy* and *Sahib*) about the experience of the British soldier across history. In September 2004 I returned from a brief visit to 1st Battalion The Princess of Wales's Royal Regiment, 1 PWRR in the army's armour-plated abbreviation and 'the Tigers' by nickname. As I drove through the Oxfordshire lanes from RAF Brize Norton in my all too evidently sweaty combat kit I felt guilty, relieved and angry. Guilty because I was safe home and too many of my friends were not; relieved because my exit from the desert had been a white-knuckle switch-back of a flight, and it was lung-fillingly good to be alive; and cross because few of my countrymen seemed to have the least idea of what British soldiers were actually doing in Iraq, although that did not stop them from speaking and writing, then as now, a good deal of tosh about it.

I knew then that I had to write about it, although it was clear, even before I started to tap out a synopsis on this machine, that this book would inevitably sit on that windswept headland somewhere between journalism and history. It is history in the sense that I deal, as accurately as I can, with past events, and that I use the written or spoken accounts of participants to help me make sense of them. It is journalism too, in that it tries to explain contemporary events to a non-expert audience, and so brings the risk of descending into journalese and meeting my dictionary's sniffy definition of a 'style of language said to be characteristic of (hasty or inferior) newspaper writing'. However, it can be neither objective history nor balanced journalism, for my sources, fresh and abundant though they are, come from one team playing in a particular match, and pay little regard to their opponents, the remainder of the league, or to events outside the stadium. And although I have not abrogated the critical function which lies at the heart of good history and journalism alike, most of the accounts in this book are written by folk I am proud to call my friends.

I see the events of 2004 in Iraq's Maysan province, and to a lesser extent in the country's second city Basra, through the eyes of a small community of British soldiers. They were men and women with an average age of twenty-one, recruited, for the most part, in south-east England but with a substantial slice of overseas soldiers, and that rich smattering of Jocks, Taffs, Scousers, Geordies, Micks and Brummies that helps give the army its rich and, to an outsider, often puzzling patina. Most were professional soldiers, though there were not a few members of the part-time Territorial Army who had been mobilized for full-time service. All risked their lives in the longest period of sustained fighting in which the army has been involved since the Korean War. Mercifully few were killed, thanks to the excellence of Kevlar helmets, combat body armour, the redoubtable Warrior armoured vehicle, prompt medical assistance, solid professional skills and, it must be said, a huge quantity of luck. But two members of 1 PWRR and another soldier in an attached company paid the ultimate price, and there are young men now in their teens who may live for another sixty years but will carry the scars of Maysan province with them to their graves.

Few of them were much concerned with the rights and wrongs of the government's decision to invade Iraq, and so, inasmuch as this book is concerned, neither am I. They were, as one officer put it, 'apolitical – not amoral'. Despite the manifest difficulties of their task they wanted to make a difference and to leave a better Iraq behind them. They believed that Saddam Hussein had been a monstrous tyrant and were glad that he had gone, and when they were critical of the government it was far less for sending the army there in the first place than for paying insufficient attention to the requirements of a complex campaign waged of necessity, amongst the people. Few, given the chance, would not have gone to Iraq, and the overwhelming majority were proud of what they had done there.

They were clannish and introspective, the expression REMF (borrowed from the US army in the Vietnam War and explained in the Glossary) defining for them those who lay outside their tight little circle. Much of this partisan view has soaked into my account, and you must not blame me for it. For instance, I am sure that the RAF air transport staff and Joint Service Movements Staff are neither incompetent nor callous, but they are held in disdain by many of those who attend (often at length) upon their kindly mercies. While there was what I term 'creative tension' between the PWRR battalion and its attached company of Royal Welch Fusiliers, it was constrained by mutual respect and, dare I say, affection. Relations with the attached military police platoon were not always as good, and in reporting the fact I acknowledge that there are two sides to every story, and I am telling only one of them.

It will be some time before any historian can hope to trace the reverse of this medal by interviewing Iraqi civilians, militiamen and police who also played their parts in this drama. They emerge in these pages as many things: abused turned abusers, mafioso hoods, religious enthusiasts, frustrated boys seeking jobs, generous tribal leaders, uppity local politicians, despairing folk trying to get on with their lives in safety and often – across nearly a thousand separate armed clashes that the army calls 'contacts' – determined adversaries. It is, I think, fair to say that the British army at least makes a start in understanding local language and culture, but it is no less true that the small change of counter-insurgency, polished by the army's long use over a dozen campaigns, is paid out less often in Iraq than we might like to imagine. The Americans are not universally trigger-happy, and the British do not always make their way on foot, doling out smiles for the adults and sweets for the children. Iraq is dangerous, unpredictable, and its stark, shocking violence is binary, full on or full off, often with little warning that the switch has flicked.

This book taught me more than I thought I needed to know about the writing of military history. Most participants saw action through blinkers, often with little idea of what was happening even a short distance away, and when they recalled events they some-times reassembled them in the wrong order, like an editor hap-hazardly reassembling film from the cutting-room floor. Dates and times sometimes came hard, but recalling the firework whoosh of the rocket-propelled grenade (RPG) or the heartening clatter of the Warrior's chain gun (that best of all sounds to so many of my contributors) came very easy. Even though I could telephone or email to check or question accounts, it was occasionally difficult to reconcile four versions of what happened at the same place and the same time. If it was hard for an hour-long battle at the road junction known as Yellow 3 in Al Amarah, then it must have been correspondingly more difficult for the retreat from Moscow or the Battle of the Somme.

I was dependent throughout on what people wanted to tell me, and had no access to official records: the battalion's War Diary will, I presume, remain closed for thirty years. I relied instead upon accounts from soldiers of all ranks, from the Commanding Officer, Lieutenant Colonel Matt Maer, to recently joined private soldiers. Some of these were elegant and reflective pieces, publishable in their own right, and others were one-pagers, written in pencil on paper torn from a notebook. They were often compiled while operations were in progress, by men who did not know that they would live to come safe home, and they sometimes embody judgements that their writers might regret in quieter times. My account is stronger in some areas than it is in others: B and C Company 1 PWRR are much better represented than are those armoured gypsies of A Company. They formed the brigade reserve and were so often on the move, though Operation Waterloo could scarcely have been fought without them. I will inevitably have devoted more time to good talkers than I have to strong, silent types who may have had a better story to tell but declined to tell it. There will be moments when participants may either disagree with my description of events, or lament a balance that pays more attention to one operation than to another. Had I waited another three years then my story would have been more complete, but the moment for its telling might have passed.

I could not have begun this book without the assistance and support of Matt Maer, whose openness made the most positive contribution to my task. Captain James Rands was my main point of contact with the officers and men who chose to contribute their accounts and reflections, and I owe a great deal to his nose for a story and ability to sieve wheat from chaff. Errors of omission or inclusion are mine alone. The real hero of my tale is, of course, the British private soldier. If I can begin to persuade you how good he is, how durable and enduring, then wedging the writing of the book into a diary that already seemed full will have been well worth it.

RICHARD HOLMES
Ropley
October 2005

CHAPTER 1

Thin Red Line

SAND, SWEAT AND POLITICS

It HAD NOT BEEN a restful night. I had spent four hours on a camp bed in what was in happier times (if any times were really much happier in that blighted place) the VIP waiting-room of Basra International Airport, but was now filled with military transit passengers of one sort or another, some sprawled out across chairs, others lying on the floor, in a welter of Kevlar helmets, body armour and Bergens. There were frequent power cuts, and the air-conditioning would clunk resoundingly into life each time the electricity came back on. I was glad enough when my alarm clock beeped to let me know that it was 0500, and as I sat up I could see my two companions, Captain Bob Wells, who had flown out from England with me, and Captain Simon Doyle, who had come down from Al Amarah to collect us, lacing up their boots and getting their kit together. There was no question of even a quick wash and shave – the 'facilities' were forlorn Portaloos just behind the building – and soon we were walking through the stifling airport corridors, a tacky mixture of plastic veneer, dilapidated mosaic and bilingual signs pointing nowhere, past more sleeping bodies, into a pleasantly cool Iraqi morning for the short walk to the helicopter base.

Dawn roared up like an express train as we arrived. One moment it was dark, with ground crew preparing helicopters in splashes of electric light, and the next it was bright enough for me to get my first real glimpse of Iraq: desert broken up by long, straight sand berms, with the airport and the airport hotel – the latter housing the headquarters of the British-commanded Multinational Division South-East – rising incongruously out of a bleached landscape. I climbed into the back of an Army Air Corps Lynx helicopter whose two helmeted pilots were already clicking through their pre-flight checks, shoved my kit beneath the canvas seat and strapped myself in, while the gum-chewing gunner, his general-purpose machine gun (GPMG) jutting out through the open door, looked left and right as we took off.

We were the second of two helicopters, flying above and just behind the leading aircraft as it clattered northwards beneath a sun now bright enough to give it a sharp shadow, over desert still strewn with the debris of the Iran–Iraq War and the Iraqi defeats of two Gulf Wars. There were wrecked and rusting tanks and armoured personnel carriers, defensive positions laid out according to the best precepts of some long-discarded manual, first stripped naked before the scourge of air power, and then drowned beneath the coalition's armoured torrent. There was battlefield beneath us for perhaps twenty minutes, and then suddenly, instead of desert there was marsh: vast reed-beds intersected with canals and splashed with lakes, with small villages on the banks, the smoke of early-morning cooking fires pointing straight into the sky. Fishermen were already at work in the canals. Some looked up and waved, but most simply got on with their work, for there was nothing even remotely remarkable about low-flying helicopters in this part of southern Iraq.

It took us about an hour to reach our destination, Camp Abu Naji, 5 kilometres south of the town of Al Amarah, capital of Maysan province, on the Tigris roughly a third of the way from Basra and Baghdad. From the air it was evident that the camp, a mixture of single-storey, flat-roofed buildings, tents and containers, stood in what had once been a very much larger military area. Around it lay a wilderness of trashed bunkers and flattened buildings, the wreckage of what had once been an Iraqi corps headquarters, for this was vital ground on a dangerous frontier, with the Iranian towns of Dezful and Ahvaz rather closer than Basra, itself 130 kilometres away.

There had been heavy fighting nearby during the Iran–Iraq War, and since 1988 the Marsh Arabs, Shi'a tribesmen who lived in the southern marshes, had been targets of determined repression by Saddam Hussein's regime. Beginning in the early 1950s, the government had set about draining the marshes, a process that accelerated as Saddam Hussein sought to rid the area of army deserters and to quell dissent amongst his Shi'a opponents. In 2003 Human Rights Watch estimated that, of a population of some 250,000 in 1991, only 40,000 Marsh Arabs remained in their ancestral homeland. Marsh Arabs had joined the 1991 rebellion against the Baghdad government, and the response had been predictably harsh: in August–November 1998, for instance, infantry, backed by armour and artillery, had mounted large-scale operations around Basra, Al Amarah and Nasiriya. Whole villages were destroyed and their populations killed or exiled. In February 1999 the prominent Shi'a cleric Ayatollah Mohammed Sadiq al-Sadr, with two of his sons, was shot dead in Najaf. Although the government maintained that the murderers had been arrested and executed, there was widespread suspicion that the hand of Baghdad was behind the crime.

Many Marsh Arabs had moved into refugee camps in Iran or settled, often in depressing misery belts, on the edges of towns in Iraq. But some had fought on in the marshes, and the most notable of the guerrilla leaders, Abu Hatim, had spent thirteen years struggling on at the head of his Iraqi Hizbollah, assuming the title Lord of the Marshes. Some dispossessed Marsh Arabs slipped easily into relying on crime for their livelihood. Indeed, crime has always been something of a traditional industry in Maysan, with the robbing of Shi'a pilgrims on their way to the shrines at Najaf and Karbalah. Smuggling, too, has long been a natural part of life. The border with Iran is long and porous, and domestic goods, antiquities, money and weapons move easily across it: a single load of 352kg of cannabis resin, discovered in Maymunah just before I arrived, probably originated in Afghanistan.

As I was soon to discover, few things in Iraq are quite as they seem, and the fact that the inhabitants of Maysan province had not much liked Saddam Hussein did not necessarily imply that they welcomed coalition forces. But nor, for that matter, did it mean that they all saw themselves as part of a pan-Iraqi resistance movement on the one hand, or an Iranian-sponsored breakaway group on the

Camp Abu Naji from the east

A Chinook takes off from Abu Naji

other, though there were some who fitted comfortably into either camp.

Lieutenant Colonel Matt Maer, commanding 1st Battalion The Princess of Wales's Royal Regiment (1 PWRR), met me as I got off the helicopter. A few minutes later, in his office – one of those white-walled, grey-tiled rooms that seem standard issue in Iraqi army camps – he suggested that Maysan was 'an independent, insular, introspective, violent province' before, during and after Saddam's time.

Before I arrived there had been a grazing dispute between rival tribes, and in the shoot-out that followed ten tribesmen had been killed and forty wounded. Men routinely carried automatic rifles, with versions of the ubiquitous AK assault rifle as their weapon of choice, and the disbandment of the Iraqi army after the coalition's victory had flooded the country with a wide array of weapons, from AKs and rocket-propelled grenades (RPGs) to ZSU 23/4 mobile anti-aircraft guns and SAM-7 anti-aircraft missiles. Maysan province had not been liberated by the coalition: the Iraqi army withdrew in the face of British success in Basra and American thrusts to the west, and there was spontaneous de-Ba'athification as most of Saddam's supporters, well aware of their local unpopularity, fled to avoid reprisals. There was at least a forty-eight-hour gap between the disappearance of the Iraqi army and the arrival of the first British troops, and it was about a fortnight before sufficient troops arrived to secure the area. In the interim, as Matt Maer observed:

> The huge depots that had covered swaths of Maysan were now abandoned and unguarded. Troops left their barracks in many cases carrying their weaponry with them . . . Widespread looting which affected the whole country now affected the barracks as well. The population had always been armed and now there was a release of even more weapons systems. The locals became a major supplier of weaponry to other parts of the country and mortars and rockets entered the arsenal of almost every group – if indeed they didn't already have them.

In the gap between the departure of the Iraqi army and the arrival of significant numbers of British troops, the tribal militias (fawjs) had held the ring, taking over policing and security. It was hard for coalition troops to ascertain who the real leaders actually were. In part this was because of language difficulties. But to an even greater extent it was because society in Maysan was imploding after the departure of the Iraqi army and the Ba'ath party. Sheikhs, the traditional tribal leaders, wanted to occupy the positions their families had held generations before, but many of them, starved of political experience under Saddam, lacked the dynamism required, and some clerics also sought political authority. All this sat uneasily beside the coalition's declared aim of creating a democratic state. 'Leadership in Iraq,' wrote Matt Maer,

> is often a very confused affair, with separate chains of command running simultaneously along religious, tribal and organizational lines. Therefore an Iraqi National Guard captain might defer to a lieutenant who has religious training, who might defer to a sergeant with tribal connections,

7

who defers to the captain because of his rank. This is further confused as some individuals have split loyalties between organizations, for example the Chief of Police is also the former commanding officer of one of the Badr Corps fawjs.

Iraqi military collapse had also flooded the region with unemployed sixteen- to twenty-five-years-olds, many of them angry and humiliated as well as jobless. In Maysan there was 70 per cent unemployment. The old regime had deliberately denied the province industry, and there was no base to build on. Although there had been a widespread popular assumption that the fall of Saddam would be followed by a rapid improvement in living standards, this had simply not materialized, and many people blamed the coalition – which had, after all, shattered Saddam's state in a mere six weeks – for its failure, after six months, to enable them to live like Kuwaitis.

Not only did things not improve, but they actually got worse. A good deal of the war damage had not been repaired, and by the time I arrived insurgents – whatever their political and/or religious allegiance – had realized that attacks on public utilities (notably the electricity system) not only demonstrated that the coalition could not rule effectively, but increased popular frustration. Moreover, if coalition troops were hard targets, contractors were much easier ones. Ironically, the means of repression so easily available to Saddam could not be used by the coalition. One 'community leader' in Basra helpfully suggested that the public connection of saboteurs to the national grid would be an effective way of indicating disapproval of their deeds. Fellow Iraqis, he was sure, would take the point perfectly. And the disbandment of the Iraqi army had not simply thrown soldiers back into civilian life: it had deprived many of the inhabitants of Maysan province of the jobs that rippled out from the huge army camps of the old regime. Although some had become locally employed civilians (LECs) on coalition bases, this was but a drop in the ocean when compared with the employment offered by what had been the fifth-largest army in the world.

A busy slide in a PowerPoint briefing – thrown from the ubiquitous laptop computer on to a fly-blown wall – showed local groups strewn across a wide spectrum. On one side, members of the Shi'ite,

Iranian-sponsored Badr Corps had come out of hiding or returned from exile. This group had originally been the paramilitary wing of the Supreme Council for Islamic Revolution in Iraq, and although the two had split the breach was not acrimonious. The Badr was increasingly active in the interim provincial government, and extended their control of the province through their influence on the police. On the other there were Sunni groupings, and a few former-regime loyalists. However, the Ba'ath Party had never been well entrenched in the area, and neither it nor Al Qa'eda-linked organizations had much impact in Maysan at this time. If, on the one hand, there were multiple groups of insurgents and terrorists with no common command-and-control structure, on the other the groups were rarely self-contained, and the slide showed them intermingled in cigar-shaped balloons that brought tribal, economic, religious and political motives together.

As I look at the notes I took that morning, I see that my briefer spoke of 'a complex insurgent environment with many disparate elements working on parallel tracks without being truly united at the top. It is a polyglot mix of bad actors . . .' Iraq had by then become the destination for Muslim men drawn to the fight for ethnic brotherhood and faith. They had a wide variety of skills and experience, and were of widely differing value to the insurgents. Some provided technical expertise as bombers or weapons experts, while others were simply expendable footsoldiers for suicide bombs or hopeless ambushes. As foreigners their local knowledge was limited, and they needed local contacts to operate successfully. Islam provided an important motivational and rallying element, although here too there was little consistency: some were wholly sincere, others were more manipulative and yet others were nationalists enfolded by Islam. And, as was so often the case in a bright and irreverent British army, there was a spoof version of the same slide which included 'spurious experts', 'wannabe ninjas' and, of course, brigade headquarters, away in Basra, in this broad and complex archipelago of smouldering tension.

At the centre of both slides – serious and spoof – was OMS, the Office of the Martyr Sadr. This organization stood in the same sort of relationship to the Mahdi army, chief arm of insurgency in the south, that Sinn Fein does to the IRA, although it is perhaps even harder to say where one ends and the other begins. Its leader was Muqtada al-Sadr, son of Ayatollah Mohammed Sadiq al-Sadr and nephew of Ayatollah Mohammed Baqir al-Sadr. Both had been outspoken leaders of the Shi'a opposition to Saddam: the uncle had been executed in 1980, and the father, as we have seen, murdered, with two of Muqtada's brothers, in 1999. Muqtada had inherited the network of schools and charities constructed by his father, as well as the allegiance of many of his older followers.

There was a palpable reticence on the part of some older, devout Shi'a when it came to the subject of Muqtada al-Sadr. He might not, they said in that opaque Arab way, actually be a properly qualified imam. He was not, er, notably bright. He did not display that profound understanding of the Holy Q'ran which would have enabled him to weave together sermons embodying the finest rhetoric and the most earnest religious sentiment. It might well be true that he was endangering the holy places for his own ends. But his father and uncle had been martyrs, he had the guts to stand up to the Americans, and, above all, the young believed in him. His main power base was in the teeming Baghdad slum of Sadr City (once Saddam City) where there were about two million Shi'a, so many of them young and frustrated. He also enjoyed a substantial following in the holy city of Najaf, where the Prophet's cousin and son-in-law, Ali ibn Abi Talib, is buried, and in Nasiriya, Karbalah, Kufa and Al Amarah. The two major upsurges of violence that feature in this book were the result of the Mahdi army's uprisings, and thus, in that sense, the 'enemy' were his footsoldiers. But even that is an oversimplification, for within the ranks of the Mahdi army were genuine religious zealots, men with a blood-feud caused by the death of family or tribe members to avenge, and youngsters eager for the cash payments available to those prepared to take on the Brits. Sometimes they were all the same person.

A REGIMENT OF THE LINE

On that first breathless morning it was hard to remind myself that I was not in Al Amarah in my academic capacity, to ponder the complexities of counter-insurgency in a collapsed state, but to visit my regiment. I have long blurred the line between academic theory and military practice, and when, in 2000, as a Territorial brigadier, I was offered the opportunity to become Colonel of The Princess of Wales's Royal Regiment, I seized it with both hands. The post of regimental colonel dates from the very beginnings of the British regular army in the 1660s, when an individual received a royal commission to raise a regiment. A 'beating warrant' authorized him to seek recruits by beat of drum, and parties of officers, sergeants and drummers scoured the chosen area seeking the enthusiastic, the unlucky or the easily deluded. In his 1706 play *The Recruiting Officer*, George Farquhar, himself a former infantry officer, put these words into the mouth of one of his sergeants:

> If any gentleman soldiers, or others, have a mind to serve
> Her Majesty, and pull down the French king; if any prentices
> have severe masters, any children have unnatural parents;
> if any servants have too little wages, or any husband too
> much wife; let them repair to the noble Sergeant Kite, at
> the Sign of the Raven in this good town of Shrewsbury,
> where they shall presently receive relief and entertainment.

Colonels were not simply responsible for raising their regiments, but for equipping them too, and by spending less on uniforms and accoutrements than the sum allowed them by the government, they were often able to make a tidy profit. They kept a watchful eye on the careers of their officers, and their 'interest' in matters of first appointment and subsequent promotion was crucial. They were generally too busy or too grand to command their regiments in person – colonels of regiments were usually generals or local magnates – and the day-to-day exercise of command was left in the hands of their lieutenant colonel as the regiment's commanding officer.

Over the succeeding centuries the system has evolved. Colonels of regiments have, quite properly, lost most of their former powers. They exercise no operational control over their regiments, and what was once a powerful voice in the appointment of commanding officers is now simply consultation. But they still control a full-time regimental headquarters (RHQ), usually in the regiment's recruiting heartland. RHQ is the day-to-day responsibility of the regimental secretary, generally a retired colonel or lieutenant colonel. Mine, in Canterbury, has seven officer-grade staff working in it, has a major interest in soldier-recruiting which it shares with the Army Training and Recruiting Agency, and uses regimental non-public funds to supplement money from official sources. There will, typically, be one regular officer and two or three warrant officers and senior NCOs involved in recruiting at any RHQ, and most regiments maintain a 'black economy' – regular NCOs who are held on the strength of the regiment's battalions but who actually work in recruiting offices. This practice is regularly condemned but as regularly reprieved, for the truth is simple. Potential recruits with the best educational qualifications are usually persuaded away from the infantry into more technical corps, and the only real way of ensuring that likely infantry recruits finish up wearing the local regiment's cap-badge is to have a regimental NCO at hand when they first appear in the recruiting office. Sergeant Kite was right all those years ago.

RHQ is constantly on the lookout for potential officers, and strives, with varying degrees of success, to identify likely candidates even before they attend the Regular Commissions Board, and, through the regiment's representative on the instructional staff at the Royal Military Academy Sandhurst, keeps track of them while they are being trained. Officer cadets, near the end of their year at Sandhurst, attend a regimental acceptance board for the regiments or corps of their choice and, in a process not unlike a marriage market, vacancies and candidates slide together. There are inevitably upsets: some officer cadets set their sights too high (for instance, the Parachute Regiment generally has far more applicants than vacancies) and others simply gauge their own interests and aptitudes wrongly (easily done in any relationship which is as much about affection as about logic), perhaps opting for a combat arm like the infantry, artillery or armoured corps when a logistic corps would be more suitable, or, indeed, vice versa.

A regiment's headquarters is also responsible for managing its funds and looking after its chattels such as silver and pictures. Most regimental money originates in bequests, many dating back decades or longer, and the profit on investments, and its use, is monitored by trustees. Benevolence accounts for substantial annual expenditure. Many previous members of regiments, or of former regiments which were amalgamated to constitute their modern successors, fall on hard times for one reason or another, and RHQs both receive requests for financial support and, through their network of local associations, hear of deserving cases where no formal application has yet been made. No regiment can be expected to bear full financial responsibility for the many thousands of men who have passed through its ranks, but there is usually a grant available to help with a stair-lift here or a new fridge there. And there is always advice and comradeship.

RHQ fosters links between the regiment's recruiting area and its regular battalions. The days when each infantry regiment maintained a depot in its heartland have long gone, and it is left to RHQs and part-time Territorial companies to help keep the regional connection alive. This connection is vital, all the more so as regimental titles with a clear regional identity are often replaced by others in which the link is harder to discern. RHQ acts as the focal point for contact with all units of the Combined Cadet Force and Army Cadet Force that wear the regiment's cap-badge. Many regular soldiers or Territorials first wear uniform as cadets, and, although the pace of operational deployments often makes it difficult, we try to ensure that there are regular or TA NCOs available to help train cadets at their annual summer camps. Lastly, my RHQ also produces an annual regimental journal and supervises the management of the regimental museum in Dover Castle.

The colonel of a modern regiment may not wield the power of yesteryear. But, not unlike a constitutional monarch, he has the ability to advise and to warn the chain of command. Moreover he is (I hope) a useful sounding-board for commanding officers putting their short-term battles into a broader context, and goes a long way towards establishing and maintaining his regiment's distinctive ethos.

For example, I am not in the least concerned whether potential officers in the PWRR went to Eton or the local comprehensive, or whether they are interested in backgammon or ferreting. However, I do expect them to pass out of Sandhurst towards the top of their respective platoons, and to be absolutely certain that they want to join the infantry. Our recruiting area runs from North Foreland to the New Forest, and from the south coast to Middlesex, and I particularly welcome young officers who hail from this area because it helps put them on the same wavelength as the soldiers they will command. I am at least as much influenced by the reports I receive on the visits they make to one of the regiment's battalions while they are still at Sandhurst as I am by academic qualifications. Glad though I am to see good graduates, there is no room for intellectual elitism in a Warrior armoured vehicle or in a trench, and character is every bit as important as intellect.

The Princess of Wales's Royal Regiment was formed on 9 September 1992 by the amalgamation of The Queen's Regiment and The Royal Hampshire Regiment. The former was itself an amalgamation encompassing all the old county infantry regiments of south-east England – The Queen's Royal Regiment, the Buffs, The East Surreys, The Royal Sussex, The Royal West Kent and The Middlesex Regiment. Welding together the three regular battalions of The Queen's Regiment and the single battalion of The Royal Hampshires into a regiment with two regular battalions and one TA battalion was no easy task, and the Army Board's decision to amalgamate was, as I now know, particularly heartbreaking for the two regimental colonels, Major General Mike Reynolds of the Queen's and Brigadier Bob Long of the Hampshires.

At least part of the reason for the grief in 1992 was that there had been long-running tension within the army between 'large' regiments and 'small' ones. To understand how this came about we must dig deep into the past, for this past, as is so often the case with the British army, helps illuminate the present. No regiment is allowed to formally take its history back beyond the founding of the regular army by the restored monarchy of Charles II in 1660. Were earlier claims allowed, then the Buffs would trace their origin to 1572, when members of the London Trained Bands volunteered to aid the Dutch in their revolt against Spain. But as far as infantry regiments of the line are concerned, the most senior, The Royal Scots (which, like the Buffs, claims a longer lineage in foreign service), starts its history in 1660, while The Queen's Royal Regiment, next in seniority and thus the senior regiment of English line infantry, was raised in 1661 to garrison Tangier, recently brought to the English Crown as the dowry of Charles II's wife, Catherine of Braganza.

Until the middle of the eighteenth century regiments were known by the names of their colonels, and thereafter they were numbered, taking seniority from the date of their founding: 1st Royal Scots, 2nd Queen's, 3rd Buffs, and so on. From 1782 regional titles were added in brackets, as in 37th (North Hampshire), but there was little real alignment between titles and recruiting areas, and it is striking to see just how much of the army of the early nineteenth century was recruited from amongst Irishmen desperate for a job. Some regiments had two or more battalions, each of them separate lieutenant colonel's commands, but which rarely served together, while others had only one.

In an effort to link regiments firmly to recruiting areas and improve the status of the army more generally, a series of reforms between 1870 and 1881, associated with the name of Edward Cardwell, Secretary of State for War, created the 'linked battalion system'. Numbered battalions, with, wherever possible, similar regional affiliations, were brought together to form county regiments. For instance the 37th (North Hampshire) and 67th (South Hampshire) became The Hampshire Regiment, which gained the title 'Royal' in 1946. Most had two regular battalions, one at home and the other abroad; a depot in the regiment's recruiting area that trained recruits; and, from 1906, they had Territorial battalions too, cap-badged the same as regular battalions of the regiment and drawing their permanent staff from the regulars. The system could be expanded to meet the needs of war, with wartime-raised 'service' battalions being added after the outbreak of war (the Hampshires had a total of thirty-two battalions in 1914–18) and then disbanded with the advent of peace.

The regimental system created by Cardwell had many advantages.

There was a strong sense of regional identity, although in practice many recruits often came from outside the regimental area. Past achievements were linked, through the iconography of cap-badges and battle-honours on regimental colours, to current structures and thus to future performance. To take but two examples, on Minden Day (1 August) each year every officer and man of the Hampshires (and the five other regiments involved) wore a rose in his headdress to commemorate the fact that the 37th Foot was one of the six regiments that attacked a superior force of French cavalry at the Battle of Minden in 1759 and 'tumbled them to ruin' with disciplined volley-firing. The Middlesex Regiment bore 'Albuhera' on its cap-badge, remembering its heroic conduct on 16 May 1811 when the regiment earned its nickname 'the Die-Hards', losing 89 men killed and 339 wounded and 6 missing from a total of 647 who had gone into battle.

There was a direct connection between the depot, which trained the soldiers, and the regular battalions, which employed them. Officers and men posted from one battalion to another could expect to find themselves amongst friends. The county's gentry often held regular or Territorial commissions in its regiment, and the policy of giving regiments royal colonels-in-chief linked the monarchy to the system. Although the turnover amongst private soldiers was often relatively high, officers and NCOs remained in the same regiment, and even in the same battalion, for much of their service, and it was not unusual for the lieutenant colonel commanding a battalion to find that his regimental sergeant major, the battalion's senior non-commissioned member, had been a private soldier in his platoon when he was first commissioned.

It must be said, though, that the regimental system creaked under the burden of two world wars. In the first, regional recruiting effectively broke down after the summer of 1916, and reinforcements who arrived in France with a cap-badge they had been taught to admire were often re-badged as they passed through the sprawling base area round Étaples on their way to the front. In the second, the growing demand for technical specialists, aircrew and elite forces like parachutists and commandos left the infantry with a recruiting pool that grew increasingly shallow, and as the war went on it became ever harder to match recruitment to cap-badge.

After 1945, as the army's strength declined, second battalions disappeared, and the repeated laceration of the Territorial infantry made it ever harder for the TA's local 'footprint' to make up for the lack of regular military presence. In the 1960s the Army Board tried to restore a measure of the old flexibility by grouping regiments into regional organizations such as the Home Counties Brigade, and then suggesting that these brigades might wish to become large regiments, adding that those who chose to do so would be looked upon favourably in future reorganizations. Some agreed to merge: the Home Counties Brigade duly became The Queen's Regiment, with four regular battalions. Others, like the Scottish infantry regiments, preferred to remain single-battalion structures.

With the next round of reductions, the Army Board of the day did not consider itself bound by the promises made by its predecessors. A slice off a cut loaf is rarely missed, and it was easier to trim a battalion from a large regiment than to grasp the nettle of amalgamation elsewhere. Large regiments first lost their 4th battalions, and then their 3rd battalions too. The amalgamation of The Queen's and The Royal Hampshires (the latter, as a single-battalion regiment, no less pained than The Queen's) was part of this process. The Queen's lost not simply their cap-badge, but a regular battalion as well, and it was hard for former members of the regiment (and not a few serving officers and NCOs too) not to feel that they had been shabbily treated, or to observe an eerie coincidence between the cap-badges worn by the generals on the Army Board and those of regiments that sailed through unscathed. Of course the process was anything but simple. No government was anxious to run the political risk of forced amalgamations in areas where local reaction might imperil parliamentary seats, but it was often the case that vocal support for an old and distinguished regiment, which made politicians reluctant to touch it, was simply not matched by the propensity of young men in that area to actually join the army. It was, therefore, not always the fittest that survived.

In truth, the 'system' that existed in early 2004 was no system at all. There were a number of 'large' regiments, each representing many former regiments, and in consequence recruiting across a huge geo-graphical area, with two regular battalions apiece. There were single-battalion regiments which were themselves amalgamations (The Devon and Dorsets, for instance, of two, and The Royal Regiment of Gloucestershire, Berkshire and Wiltshire of three former regiments). And lastly, there were single-battalion regiments which, like The Black Watch, had never been amalgamated.

The relationship between structure and recruiting potential was blurred, and it was evident that some regiments, despite ancient lineage, glittering history and emotional local links, would never be able to recruit to fill their establishments. It was also argued that as the army strove to reduce peacetime turbulence by giving up what was termed 'arms-plotting' – moving whole battalions from place to place, in favour of a more stable system which would leave regiments in garrisons far longer – and to rotate individuals between them by what is known as 'trickle posting', regiments with two or more bat-talions would have a flexibility which single-battalion regiments must necessarily lack. This was not a view that commended itself to all, especially members of single-battalion regiments.

In the late summer of 2004, when I first visited Iraq, the whole structure of the infantry was formally under review. General Sir Mike Jackson, Chief of the General Staff, had produced a list of criteria that should be embodied in any future structure, and it was evident that he inclined to the view that large regiments would best meet the needs of the future. When the army's adjutant-general, Lieutenant General Sir Alistair Irwin, assessed the virtues and vices of the regi-mental system in May that year he reckoned: 'The first and probably the most important example of the best of the current regimental system is a sense of belonging to an entity which has an existence, a past, present and future of its own . . . all our officers and soldiers acquire a sense of belonging when they join.' Continuity, the next of his virtues, meant 'the ability of individuals to keep returning to the regiment or corps in which they began, to their individual benefit and the benefit of their units'. Regional connections helped provide a focus for recruiting. Here he acknowledged that the evidence was equivocal, but believed 'that those examples of where regional connections are strong represent part of what is best in the current regimental system'. Lastly, he emphasized the importance of famous names and traditions, and of esprit de corps.

Although he was himself, by both career and distinguished family tradition, a product of The Black Watch, General Irwin was too honest and too astute not to observe that the existing system had failings. He feared that it could create inflexibility. 'The talents and skills of the best officers and NCOs are often ignored,' he wrote, and 'their ambitions thwarted, by keeping them with their own regiments, regardless of where those regiments may be stationed.' He suspected that 'the main, perhaps the only, reason that we continue to arms plot is to ensure that the current regimental system is preserved'. And 'by tying individuals to particular units (as opposed to regiments or corps) we ensure that when the unit moves they move too, regardless of whether it is convenient or desired'. Lastly, he feared a 'lack of critical mass'. As establishments (the strength to which battalions are authorized to recruit) had grown tighter, simply recruiting to establishment was no use because 'that established strength gives no room for manoeuvre; it has excluded the human dimension from the numbers equation'. The result of all this, he wrote, 'is that today's single-unit regiments struggle on a daily basis to make ends meet in manpower terms, regardless of their role or readiness state'.

Both head and heart drew me towards large regiments. I had spent two years as a private soldier before being commissioned, and thereafter I had served in 5th (Volunteer) Battalion, The Queen's Regiment, commanding a rifle platoon, the mortar platoon and latterly a rifle company, and felt conscious of being a member of a large regimental family. As Colonel of the PWRR I had seen the practical benefits of being able to slip officers and men from one battalion to another, and to ring the changes in experience and career development by moving them from, say, the 1st Battalion with its armoured infantry role to the 2nd Battalion with its light role. We were able to replace both battle casualties and victims of sickness and accidental injuries from within the regiment. It also seemed to me that mobilized Territorials – and the large-scale mobilization of the TA, over eleven thousand in the past three years, has not received the attention it surely deserves – fitted more comfortably into full-term service if they were deployed with the grain of the regimental system, not against it, and having a TA battalion which was also part of the regiment gave us an important advantage. Two of 1 PWRR's company seconds-in-command, Captains Marcus Butlin and Nick Thasarathar, came from the Territorial 3rd Battalion, and their presence in these posts raised no eyebrows; both did very well indeed.

What happened in 1992 was that a new regiment was formed from the forced amalgamation of two others. However, most of the real unhappiness was at the very top, and the two regular battalions of the new regiment quickly meshed together well. At the very beginning, because they represented the merging of four battalions into just two, the battalions were comfortably over-establishment, and this absence of an immediate crisis encouraged the regiment to ease its foot off the recruiting throttle. A combination of lack of sustained regimental effort, and a change of name which had weakened community links within the recruiting area, meant that three years after amalgamation both battalions were badly under strength. When I took over as Colonel five years ago I suspected that this would leave us dangerously exposed in the event of further restructuring, and I made recruiting the regiment's main non-operational focus.

I had the easy job: the fact that we clawed our way back up the graph in terms of both recruiting and, no less important, the retention of trained soldiers speaks volumes for the application of one of my deputy colonels, Brigadier Paul Newton, and his team. Also, the fact that we were one of the few fully recruited line regiments in the army, with both regular battalions a little over full strength in early 2004, was enormously encouraging. So too was the fact that even if a snapshot of recent success was widened to constitute a ten-year panorama, we did not feature amongst the ten worst-recruited battalions over the period. Interestingly, four of the ten were Scots, and all were from single-battalion regiments. Moreover a busy multi-coloured 'regression line analysis' produced by headquarters director of infantry in an effort to aid an informed decision suggested that the long-term trends for both of our regular battalions were moving in the right direction.

Success in recruiting terms, therefore, gave me considerable confidence that we would be more than unlucky to be compelled to amalgamate yet again. However, during the autumn of 2005, as the

Army Board grew closer to finalizing the recommendation it would make to the Secretary of State for Defence, it became clear that all the bets were off. None of my counterparts in other regiments had any intention of going to the scaffold quietly, however persuasive the verdict might originally have seemed. Men who would not have betrayed their country's secrets if you tore out their fingernails leaked like sieves to the press, and political supporters were mobilized to put pressure on the government. The standard of debate, commendably high during the early stages of the study, fell off markedly as the dispute became acrimonious and often personal.

There was briefly a suggestion that no regiment should be able to include Foreign and Commonwealth recruits amongst its numbers for the purposes of the study. Happily, wiser counsels prevailed, not least, I suspect, because although we have more Foreign and Commonwealth recruits than many regiments, there are those with greater long-term recruiting difficulties who actually have more. Moreover, there was a widespread feeling that it was little short of racist to encourage Foreign and Commonwealth soldiers to serve and then to imply that they counted for less than their British-born comrades.

On the morning that the Secretary of State's decision was announced Mike Jackson rang me to say that we were safe. When, later that day, I was able to look at the full details I was encouraged to see that the new structure had edged the line infantry decisively towards the large-regiment solution. Of course there are still rearguard actions to be fought, and it will probably take some time for the new five-battalion Royal Scottish Regiment of Scotland to behave like a single regiment rather than five distinct battalions. But although the process of amalgamation will, I am sure, cause soul-searching and grief, the infantry that emerges will be organized to meet the demands of the early-twenty-first century, and will not represent Cardwell's system patched and trimmed almost beyond recognition. I am no less certain that, even if the new structure infuriates some (and how can it not? – for these are issues of deep pride and emotion), it will be recognized by most serving infantrymen as meeting the requirements identified when a large group of infantry officers attending the Joint Service Command and Staff College wrote to General Jackson in July 2004, telling him of their desire to see a system that fits the demands of the present day and future so that we deliver the most effective possible level of fighting capability. We anticipate that the initiative proposed achieves this, and trust that the implementation will be sensitive to all, swift in execution and bold in scope. We respect the legacy of our forebears which will always be enshrined in any Regimental System, but hope that they will support us in making these changes that we believe are crucial to the infantry's ability to fight and win in the conflicts of today and tomorrow.

This does not mean that I applaud all of the 2004 decisions. Overall there will be four fewer regular infantry battalions, and one less Territorial infantry battalion. The former reduction is justified by the argument that 'Network-Enabled Capability' – smarter communications, in short – the end of 'arms-plotting' and substantial reductions to long-standing commitments in Northern Ireland enable the smaller number of battalions to operate more effectively. Yet it remains to be seen how it will actually increase the brief interval between operational tours. One of the reasons why The Black Watch's 2004 tour in Iraq was so emotive was that the regiment had served there the year before. Since I have been Colonel I have visited each regular battalion on three separate operational tours, and by the time I relinquish the post at the end of 2006 I will have added one more. If the pace of life is hectic for the infantry it is even more so for some other arms. Captain Liz Sandry commanded the Royal Electrical and Mechanical Engineers (REME) detachment with 1 PWRR in Iraq last year; she is now back in Iraq commanding the REME with another armoured infantry battalion. Let it never be forgotten that most soldiers join the army with the intention of going on operational tours. But there are times when the sheer repitive turmoil of operations wears out officers, soldiers and, by no means least, their families. What is exciting and rewarding for an unmarried lance corporal in his early twenties is too often a growing strain for a married major in his mid-thirties. There is a limit to how much more one can do with even the most efficient less.

*

This survey of the army's internal politics will help to put 1 PWRR's deployment to Iraq into a necessary perspective. Its officers and men were glad to be going, not least because it promised to be 'a tour like no other' with the prospect of doing what they had been trained to do. There has long been pronounced tension between the line infantry on the one hand and the Parachute Regiment and Royal Marine Commandos on the other, with real fears that there was a two-tier army, with one tier doing the more routine and prosaic deployments and the other taking on the more difficult and publicity-earning tasks. Men wearing red or green berets too often seemed the military instrument of choice. However compelling the argument in terms of the composition of rapid-intervention forces, the logic of sending an amphibious unit to landlocked Afghanistan was less than persuasive to hard-bitten corporals in the infantry. 1 PWRR was aware that its performance would not simply reflect the quality of British soldiers in general, or, in a smaller sense, put one battalion on the map: it would show that line infantry, the descendants of the old county regiments that bore the brunt of a hundred battles from Blenheim to Waterloo and from the Somme to Normandy, could still do the business. The battalion I flew in to visit had a point to make.

SIX HUNDRED FIGHTING ENGLISHMEN

One of the consequences of the end of National Service and the steady reduction of the army, regular and Territorial, since the 1960s, to the point where it is now smaller than at any time since the late eighteenth century, is that a decreasing proportion of the population has any real idea of what the army is actually like. Ask a friend the difference between a brigadier and a bombardier and I doubt if he or she will be able to tell you. Sometimes television dramas and observational documentaries begin to bridge the growing gap between the army and the society it serves, but the process is erratic and incomplete. The press is prone to flash-floods of reportage, with the very good (Private Johnson Beharry's VC) and the very bad (the excesses of Camp Breadbasket) alike attracting attention.

There is a persistent feeling within the army that its interests are not well served by the Ministry of Defence's publicity system. Previously, each service had an upwardly mobile one-star officer (brigadier or its equivalent) responsible for its corporate communications. The abolition of these posts has led to a blander relationship between the army and the media, often more focused on short-term damage limitation than on gaining and maintaining a relationship of mutual trust and confidence in which the media report not simply the good and the bad but the broader ground between them. In consequence, comments embodying breathtaking ignorance pass for fact. In March 2005 a correspondent assured readers of the *Independent* that officers in Iraq were rarely about because they were,

> as anyone who has served in the army will know, of course, in the officers' mess, a combination of sixth-form public school common room and London club. The officer chaps, junior ranks of course, will on occasion emerge from the mess, nod vaguely to the NCO who will be told to 'carry on', and will then disappear, as quickly as possible, to their very comfortable and sheltered world.

He based this on personal experience: he had been a National Serviceman over forty years ago, long before most officers and soldiers serving in Iraq were even born, and often before their parents were born. The post of Director of Public Relations (Army) was temporarily reinstituted as I worked on this book, but much important ground has been lost in its absence.

On two trips to Iraq I did not manage to find an officers' mess, and somehow this 'comfortable and sheltered world' eluded me. I did eat with two British generals – in the same cookhouse and from the same menu as everyone else, regardless of rank, in their headquarters. When soldiers make mistakes the question of officer supervision must indeed be raised; but superannuated assertions that on operations there is a boss class insulated from reality are an insult to the hundreds of officers who are separated from their soldiers only by the responsibility they exercise. Many of the *Independent*'s readers, themselves ignorant of army life, will probably take such rubbish seriously, and there is, it seems, nobody to disabuse them. On the one hand, serving members of the armed forces cannot write to the press without either getting permission to do so or, alternatively, risking their careers. On the other, the army is less good than it ought to be at explaining to a demilitarized society just why it preserves structures and practices that may seem at odds with twenty-first-century Britain.

And so to one particular set of structures and practices. Even the most resolutely civilian reader who has followed me so far will, I hope, understand what The Princess of Wales's Royal Regiment is. Its 1st Battalion, with which this book is concerned, is an armoured infantry battalion of around six hundred men, with a headquarters company, three rifle companies (A, B and C Companies) and a fire support company (perversely designated Y Company). When it deployed to Iraq in 2004 it was based at Tidworth, on the Hampshire/Wiltshire border, and soon after its return it moved to Paderborn in Germany, where it will remain for the foreseeable future. A battalion is commanded by a lieutenant colonel, in the case of 1 PWRR by Matt Maer, a police officer's son and agricultural economics graduate who had his fortieth birthday in Iraq. Like all other mainstream regular officers in the battalion he had spent a year at the Royal Military Academy Sandhurst before being commissioned into The Queen's Regiment in 1986.

Matt Maer did a number of junior officer's jobs within the regiment before becoming a captain instructor on the famously tough Platoon Sergeants' Battle Course at Brecon, where he found: 'I had fallen in love with Brecon. Subsequently I had also fallen in love with and married a lady whose maiden name was Jenkins and [who], not unrelatedly, had a cottage in Brecon. It was here that I always liked to go when I was tired and in need of true rest.' He attended the Army Staff College at Camberley, and afterwards served as chief of staff of 19th Mechanized Brigade, earning an MBE in Bosnia, and had held one staff appointment in the MOD as a lieutenant colonel

Lieutenant Colonel Maer (*left*) and the commander of a
Danish Life Guards company which temporarily
reinforced the battleground at Al Amarah

before taking command of 1 PWRR not long before it deployed.

Matt is six feet three inches tall and solidly built, a fact that
perturbed Captain Nick Thasarathar on 18 April 2004, flag day,
when 1 PWRR formally took over from the outgoing battalion,
1st Light Infantry (1 LI). Thasarathar set out for downtown Al
Amarah from Camp Abu Naji with the CO and his rover group – a

small mobile command team and protection party – in three stripped-down Land Rovers.

Weapons were loaded, crews mounted up, radios checked, goggles fitted, engines started and those of us on top cover assumed our positions. I rode top cover in the rear vehicle, facing backwards. This involved standing up in the rear of the Wolf [Land Rover], through the gaps in the roll cage, and covering potential enemy firing points with my weapon while we were on the move. A strange position for a commander you might think, but this was my first trip out with the rover group and I needed to learn the ropes. The rover group had spent months together prior to the tour practising their 'actions on' [various specified events] and SOPs [standard operating procedures]. I had not joined them until the start of the tour so it was necessary to see how they operated first before leaping in.

A Company 1 RWF on border patrol

Alongside me was Private Mackenzie, an amicable Rasta-farian from Jamaica serving under the Commonwealth soldier programme, he was our vehicle's radio operator and also helped with rear top cover. Facing forward on top cover was Lance Corporal Kev Phillips. He was a short, stocky PTI [physical training instructor] who took great pride in his job but was forever getting injured. He was armed with a Minimi light machine gun, the bulk of our vehicle's fire-power. The CO emerged and mounted up in the middle vehicle, he too preferred to ride in a top cover position. This caused all of us a little concern because being well over six feet tall he stuck out above the roll cage a lot more than the rest of us. This made him an easier target and as we were there primarily to protect him, naturally it worried us. However, the CO throughout the tour shared the same dangers as his men, and that is what is expected of a leader, so no one was going to object.

Like almost everyone else in the battalion, Matt Maer habitually carried an SA80 rifle, and that day found himself using it in earnest, cut off in Al Amarah in a low-walled garden with the wall gradually disintegrating under the impact of machine-gun fire. Although the battalion's chief PTI, Quartermaster Sergeant Instructor Sibthorpe, was responsible for his personal security, commanding an infantry battalion in a place like Al Amarah does not exonerate a man from being a soldier first.

Matt Maer commanded his battalion with the assistance of a small headquarters. His second-in-command (2ic), Major Toby Walch, is a year younger and came from the Royal Hampshire side of the regi-mental family. Normally the 2ic's operational task is to run the battle while the CO plans the next move, but he must also be prepared to take command at short notice if the CO is killed or wounded, or when he goes on leave. The particular circumstances of Al Amarah meant that Matt Maer was often operating at the political level, negotiating with local leaders, and so Toby Walch dealt with many of the issues that would normally have fallen within the CO's remit. His appetite for hard work and his easy, confident manner inspired one young officer to suggest to me that 'it was obvious that the only person on earth who scared him was his wife'.

The Operations Officer, Captain Charlie Curry until July, and then Captain Dom Sweny, turned the plans conceived at the CO's planning group into actionable orders and then fought the battle either from the 2ic's vehicle or from an operations room, a large room with maps and radios. In Northern Ireland, say, a major incident would be run by the CO, 2ic or ops officer, but at Al Amarah there were often so many incidents going on at the same time that some of them were run by relatively junior personnel. The Ops Warrant Officer, WO2 Andy Wiseman, universally known as the Wise Man, who had once joined the French Foreign Legion before it was pointed out to him that the fact that he was already in the British army was a significant disadvantage, helped the Ops Officer. At Camp Abu Naji the Regimental Communications Officer, Captain Ross Noott, a keen *Archers* fan and, as the tour wore on, a no less keen tobacco-chewer, who commanded the signal platoon (the battalion's trained radio operators), also generally worked in the ops room. The Intelligence Officer, Captain James Rands, with his tiny staff, was busily engaged in tracking hostile activity and predicting future enemy action.

Lastly, the adjutant, first Captain Duncan Allen and then Captain Simon Doyle, was the CO's chief of staff, responsible for a whole host of matters to do with personnel and discipline that went far beyond the next week's operations. There was a general feeling that discipline was not a significant problem on operations, as 'soldiers don't have the time, freedom or alcohol to mess up'. But confidential reports still needed attention, and the CO's diary was remarkably full: 'There is a tendency for every lurker from the UK to come and poke around and they all expect a full tour.' It is good to be put in one's place. The entrance to the CO's office – occupied, in the recent past, by a senior Iraqi officer – lay through the adjutant's, which says much for the relationship.

The regimental sergeant major (RSM) occupies a unique position in the structure of a British battalion. As a warrant officer class 1 he is its senior non-commissioned member, with a formal responsibility for maintaining standards and discipline but with a deep and pervasive influence on almost everything that happens in the battalion. He is unfailingly 'sir' to his juniors, even to the company sergeant majors, warrant officers class 2, and only a step behind him in rank. WO1 Shaun Whyte had joined the Royal Hampshires almost twenty-three years before and had retained the accent of his native Dorset, in which he subjected the unwary to a barrage of Frank Carsonesque jokes. On 16 April RSM Whyte, part of the CO's rover group that had headed into Al Amarah, characteristically seized a quiet moment to get his hair trimmed by the barber, a local man who was visiting Y Company in CIMIC House* at the time. 'Halfway through the shearing,' he recalled,

> I noticed that there was a sudden increase in activity all around me, culminating, to my horror, in the QMSI telling me 'We're off.' With half a hair cut I gestured to the barber to hurry up and then thrust $5 into his hand as I left to rush back to the vehicles, hoping that I didn't look like the lead singer of the 80s pop group The Human League. This would not be good for the RSM!

A few minutes later he was involved in a firefight:

> An RPG had been fired and exploded above our vehicles in the trees, knocking out one driver [Private 'Corky' Cawkwell – whose unruffled and deliberate approach to driving, even under fire, led the RSM to nickname him 'Driving Miss Daisy'] and hitting another with shrapnel [Private Jacobs] ... I saw two terrorists firing their weapons Beirut style towards us, as I raised my rifle to return fire I saw Lance Corporal Phillips to my forward left on the floor face down with arms and legs going ten to the dozen obviously in trouble. I returned fire and then rushed towards Lance Corporal Phillips. As I closed in on him I saw the wound on his neck and without thinking I put my hand straight on it to try and stop the bleeding telling him he is going to be all right. I don't know why but while I was struggling with things to say to Lance Corporal Phillips,

---

* A palace in the northern part of Al Amarah on a great bend of the Tigris, which had initially been used as a base for the Civil-Military Cooperation teams that were striving to rebuild the local economy.

looking at him it suddenly occurred to me that his side-
burns were too long and so I told him . . . It made him
laugh for a short moment anyway, some relief from the
pain.

Although I never got to know him well, I admired RSM Whyte
enormously. While I was waiting to be flown out of Al Amarah from
a desert airstrip codenamed 'Sparrowhawk' we chatted about what
he called 'the values and qualities that make us a professional army',
and he repeatedly raised his rifle to use its individual weapon sight
(IWS) to scan sandy crest-lines in the middle distance, muttering
approvingly that the boys in the company securing the airstrip were
working well, getting on with their jobs without the need for orders.
It was a warm extraction in more ways than one, for the RAF C-130
Hercules eventually arrived kicking out flares to decoy heat-seeking
missiles, an early warning of a coming take-off accompanied by cork-
screwing so as to put hostile marksmen off their aim. I shall remember WO1 Whyte that hot Iraqi morning, calm, unhurried and
somehow omnicompetent, as long as I remember anything. Offered
a commission at the end of his time as RSM, he turned it down,
preferring to see out his time to pension in a recruiting job in the
south-east of England, with his last major military appointment as
RSM of an excellent battalion at the height of its powers. I lament
his loss, but somehow I do not blame him.

Headquarter Company comprised the various departments needed
to administer the battalion. The clerks, members of the Adjutant-
General's Corps, abbreviated to AGC – and unkindly, though not
wholly inaccurately, known as the All Girls' Corps – came under
the control of the Regimental Administrative Officer, Captain Alf
Garnett, his real first name a matter of deep and unresolved speculation. They were responsible for the battalion's pay and records,
and most were housed in an office next door to the CO's, its roof
holed by an incoming 107mm rocket which, happily, had not burst
properly – had it done so, all the occupants would have been killed.
Each company had its own clerk, a cap-badged AGC, to link it – it

might be deployed well away from base – to the admin office, generally on one of the laptops which were so common in offices across Iraq. In case this sounds perversely bureaucratic, it is important to remember that it is part of the army's obligation to ensure that soldiers receive the correct pay and allowances, get promoted when they are eligible and are sent on career courses at the right time. These requirements do not stop simply because they are temporarily living alongside an open sewer in the middle of an inhospitable desert.

Most of the clerks in the admin office were female, and one of them, Private Nikki Oliver, often went out to provide vehicle checkpoints (VCPs) with a female searcher, once arriving to help a company with its records shortly before it came under concerted attack. 'Since I've been out here I reckon I've been in more contacts than most of the British army,' she observed,

> which in a way I'm proud of. The first time I was in a contact I had to pull bodies from a burning vehicle. Whilst giving cover I never felt nervous or worried about getting injured – all I wanted to do was to help the casualties. I suppose in a way you could say all the training I've ever done had kicked in and made me do some real soldiering instead of sitting behind a desk, and to be totally true this is what I joined for.
>
> When I look back at all the things I've done and analyse it, I can't believe I've had RPGs and small arms fired at me and it scares me a little bit knowing that one of them could have been the end of me. But if anything it has made me a more confident person and I could honestly say that now if we were to go out on patrols or a search op, I feel I could perform just as well as any of the blokes ... I remember one time going out on a VCP and I had to get a grip of one of the blokes because he didn't have a clue about what he was doing. That to me says a lot. No matter what trade you are in I feel it is your own professionalism which makes you a good soldier. Overall I feel this tour so far has been a great experience and I feel I've proved the worth of a

Lance Corporal Rides, Lance Corporal Butler
and Private Oliver

clerk working with infantrymen and gained the respect to
do my job ... Within myself I feel capable of doing the
same job as the men to a certain respect.

In case you imagine Private Oliver to be a martial lady of Ama-
zonian stamp, she is in fact pretty and slightly built. She was very well
regarded by her male comrades, and when I visited the battalion she
was far more interested in showing off her newly acquired engagement ring (she had become engaged to Lance Corporal Pearce of the
recce platoon) than in drawing sweeping deductions about women in
combat, about which she now knew a good deal. She was a soldier
doing her job, and that was that. She has now married her fiancé
and, as I was completing this book, picked up her first stripe, so the
battalion now has two Lance Corporals Pearce.

Another notable woman was Captain Liz Sandry, who, as mentioned earlier, commanded the Light Aid Detachment, two dozen

mechanics, armourers and electricians who wore the cap-badge of the Royal Electrical and Mechanical Engineers. Liz, married to a major in the Parachute Regiment, 'did not seem to sweat for the whole tour and was known as the Princess Royal because she was always immaculately turned out and spoke impeccably'. Her soldiers provided a fitter section for each company, giving it a degree of independence for the repair and servicing of its vehicles, and maintained a small workshop in Al Amarah. I should have had the wit to realize just how much an armoured infantry battalion relied on its LAD – one of my lasting memories of Iraq is of mechanics hard at work deep inside Warrior armoured vehicles in what I considered to be the insupportable heat of an Iraqi late summer.

Not only were they busy servicing vehicles and repairing the damage done to gearboxes and running gear by the gruelling conditions, but as new threats from improvised explosive devices (IEDs) developed, so various types of specialist armour were added to enable Warriors to keep pace with the threat. Nor was life much easier for the company armourers, responsible for the upkeep of weapons. The Minimi light machine gun, unusually for a weapon in British service, was an off-the-shelf buy, procured at the start of the second Gulf War. It was popular with the boys, because it provided the infantry section with firepower midway between that of the SA80 and the heavier GPMG. Several armourers pointed out, however, that keeping these weapons 'on the road' in view of the large amounts of ammunition that they were devouring at the height of the fighting was anything but easy.

The Motor Transport (MT) Platoon managed the battalion's fleet of Land Rovers and lorries. The MT is often regarded, as one young officer put it, as 'a reserve of the podgy and the lazy', but there was no sign of that in 1 PWRR, partly because the platoon commander, Captain Lou Gale, attached to the battalion from The Worcesters and Sherwood Foresters, was an impressive-looking customer, more than six feet tall, heavily set and with a shaven head. He was what is known as a late-entry officer, commissioned after passing through the ranks, and had been RSM of the 1st Battalion of his regiment. Life in the MT was no easy ride.

Two other significant late-entry officers were Captain Mike

McDonald, the Quartermaster (QM), with overall responsibility for all the accommodation and equipment entrusted to the battalion, and Captain Taddy MacAuley, the Quartermaster Technical (QMTech), who had charge of specified military hardware such as weapons and ammunition. Mike McDonald had been attached, as a colour sergeant, to The Royal Regiment of Fusiliers in the 1991 Gulf War, and had been commissioned after serving as RSM of a PWRR Territorial battalion. He was an avid Manchester United fan, but unhappily for him the tour took place against a background of Arsenal ascendancy.

Taddy MacAuley was a supremely fit man whose accent still bore the unmistakable twang of Northern Ireland, although he has not really lived there for half a lifetime. He had served as an instructor at Sandhurst as both colour sergeant and sergeant major, and there was at least one officer in the battalion who still quaked when he heard that distinctive voice. The two quartermasters were assisted by the Regimental Quartermaster Sergeant, WO2 Ashton, and the Regimental Quartermaster Sergeant (Technical), WO2 Elsey. Individual stores' accounts were maintained by hardworking corporals, often reviled as 'base-rats' by the free spirits of the rifle companies, but responsible for ensuring that the battalion's holdings of everything from bayonets to blankets and magazine springs to mortar bipods were up to date, and that lost or damaged items were swiftly replaced. The delights of doing this in a steel container under a grinning sun can well be imagined.

Bodies and souls were the business of doctor and padre. The former, Captain Angus Forbes, Royal Army Medical Corps, was a doctor who had attended the short course for professionally qualified officers at Sandhurst, impolitely known as the 'vicars and tarts' course. He had already worked hard to reduce the number of medically downgraded soldiers in the battalion. Any unit will have a small proportion of its strength unfit for duty at any given time. These soldiers are on the battalion's strength and thus cannot be replaced, and, given the fact that establishments are themselves shaved to the bare minimum, even a small proportion of unfit soldiers creates a real difficulty. Given time, trouble and physiotherapy many of the unfit can be brought back on to the deployable strength, and Angus

Forbes had been very successful in helping the battalion depart at full strength. He was also a talented guitarist, but I had to judge that from hearsay, not from evidence.

Angus had a small staff of trained medical assistants, headed by Corporal Caz Carrol who, they told me, had been at the medical centre since Florence Nightingale's time. Each company had its own medic, usually a corporal. I watched some soldiers refreshing their medical training: they took it very seriously indeed, for by then everyone knew that it was a matter of life and death. WO1 Whyte put 'the need for realistic medical training and lots of it to make the basics instinctive' at the top of his list of lessons learned from the tour.

The padre, who wore the three pips of a chaplain to the forces class 4, was Fran Myatt. He was a Scouser who had worked the doors of Liverpool clubs in his younger days. Like so many soldiers in the battalion he spent a good deal of time in the gym, and a typical comment of his would be to point at himself and say 'Body of a Greek god', and then point at someone who took fitness less seriously and observe 'Body of a Greek restaurant'. Fran was on leave when I visited Al Amarah, but I heard him preach at the battalion's open day at Tidworth in December 2004 when we were striving to put the tour into perspective before everyone went on Christmas leave, and can confirm the assessment that 'every sermon he gave was blunt, direct and very funny'.

But there was a good deal more to him than humour. Some soldiers can look death in the face without the need for spiritual solace, but others – even if they are not normally religious – feel better for the presence of a man who believes in a God who may not turn away a bullet but will never turn away a soul in need. When soldiers were killed, it was important that their bodies were treated reverently and with respect. Young men, who might not previously have encountered the rituals of death, saw off their fallen comrades on the journey that would take them to RAF Brize Norton and then on to burial or cremation at home, with pride and dignity.

Y (Support) Company was commanded throughout the tour by Major Justin Featherstone, and was to become particularly associated

Corporal Carroll in the Regimental Aid Post (*above*) and Lance Corporal Muir, C Company's medic (*above right*)

Padres pray as Private O'Callahan's body is repatriated from Basra airport

with the defence of CIMIC House. There were two sieges of CIMIC House, and in the first, the place was hit by 525 mortar rounds in ten days. The mortar platoon had six 81 mm mortars, which provided the battalion with its own intimate indirect fire support. Their rounds, fired at a high angle so that mortars could be tucked in behind buildings or other cover, were directed on to the target by fire controllers (MFCs) attached to the rifle companies. In Iraq mortarmen were often used in the infantry role, although in the course of the tour the mortars fired 1,180 illuminating rounds, projectiles which burst in the air and descended by parachute to light up the landscape beneath, as well as a much smaller quantity of high explosive.

The anti-tank platoon had six firing posts for the MILAN anti-tank missile, and this was the only one of the battalion's weapons not to be used in anger. Yet taking MILAN to Iraq made good sense, for three reasons. First, it was entirely possible that the insurgents could have procured armoured vehicles from the Iraqi army's abandoned arsenals. Second, the sheer pace of life turned out to be a surprise, and it had been hoped that both mortarmen and anti-tank gunners would have some slack time when they could keep their skills up to date. Third, MILAN could be used as a bunker-busting weapon, and if the insurgents stood firm in a fortified building (as indeed they did in Basra), then MILAN could blast a hole in the wall and either destroy them or shock them into surrender. Even if they were denied the opportunity to use their principal weapon, the members of the anti-tank platoon were, as we shall see, kept very busy.

Y Company also included the reconnaissance platoon. For Northern Ireland duties recce platoons receive specialist training for dismounted work, but they deployed to Iraq with their combat vehicles reconnaissance (tracked) (CVRTs). Many male readers in their thirties will remember the Action Man Scorpion light tank, a version of the CVRT, as a much sought-after Christmas present. This gives a clue as to its age: one of its original design requirements had been the need to fit between the rows of rubber trees in Malaysian plantations. Although CVRT are now decidedly venerable, they are fast and offer small targets.

Sometimes a battalion's snipers are concentrated in the recce platoon, but in Iraq they formed a platoon in their own right under Colour Sergeant Dennis, a short and purposeful man with a broad grin. True snipers are not simply excellent shots, but are also well trained in fieldcraft, the art of moving and operating in the field. In addition to killing selected members of the enemy from long range, and so eroding his cohesion and morale, snipers are also an invaluable surveillance asset. They operate in pairs, and in Iraq each pair consisted of one full-trained sniper and one slightly less skilled sharpshooter. They fired over 300 rounds from their specialist 7.62mm sniper rifles and, although I take no particular pleasure in 'the woeful crimson of men slain', they did not miss much, and the damage they did to the insurgents attacking CIMIC House was enormous.

The British infantry fields three different types of battalion. There are those in the light role, which fight on foot and march to their objective, or are delivered there by parachute, helicopter or soft-skinned transport; mechanized infantry battalions, equipped with the Saxon wheeled armoured personnel carrier; and armoured infantry battalions equipped with the Warrior. A light role battalion plays a part in our story. A company of 1st Battalion The Argyll and Sutherland Highlanders was operating in Maysan province for part of 1 PWRR's tour, and happened to have with it, to bring it up to strength, a composite platoon drawn from both regular battalions of the PWRR. A company of 1st Royal Welch Fusiliers (RWF), under Major Charlie Vere-Whiting, was attached to 1 PWRR for its tour. It had the Saxon, essentially a four-tonne truck with armour bolted to its frame, designed, in the days of the Cold War, to move infantry about the excellent German road system. Saxon was not designed to take troops into battle where it might be engaged by direct-fire weapons, and it is less well protected (if a good deal more comfortable) than Warrior.

The essence of an armoured infantry battalion like 1 PWRR is Warrior, a tracked armoured infantry combat vehicle weighing in at 26 tonnes and powered by a chunky Perkins V12 diesel engine. Like

The front entrance and sangar, CIMIC House

Warriors at CIMIC House: note mortar damage to the
screens on the left

so much of the army's equipment it too is a child of the Cold War,
originally designed for the mercifully unfought armoured battle
on the North German Plain. It has an aluminium hull and what is
evasively termed 'special' armour, which keeps out all small-arms fire
and most RPG rounds. Indeed, although Warriors were frequently
engaged in Iraq by RPG gunners who sometimes pressed in to point-
blank range at the risk (and often the cost) of their lives, no Warrior
was lost to a sudden catastrophic explosion. Warrior has a two-man
turret which houses the commander, usually standing on his seat on
the right, and the gunner, sitting down on the left. The latter mans
a 30mm Rarden cannon which can fire either high explosive or
armour-piercing rounds, and a 7.62mm Hughes chain gun. The
Rarden is accurate and hard-hitting, if slow to reload; during the
tour 401 rounds of HE and 14 armour-piercing were fired.

Private Somers sniping from the roof of CIMIC House

An A Company Warrior disembarking from a low-loader

A B Company gunner loading the chain gun

The chain gun was originally designed for a helicopter, where the ammunition was stored above the gun and fed downwards in the chain links of the ammunition belt. In Warrior, however, the ammunition is held in a storage space below the turret crew and dragged upwards by electrical power, which makes the gun prone to stoppages. Most of the gunners I spoke to had learned to live with the chain gun; there were frequent comparisons between the weapon's idiosyncrasies and the darker labyrinths of the female psyche. Getting the first couple of rounds and their connecting links placed just right made all the difference, and it was possible for a skilled gunner to calculate roughly how many rounds his gun would fire before jamming, and to judge matters accordingly. In all well over 30,000 rounds of 7.62mm ammunition were fired in action, some of it from chain guns and some from GPMGs.

A company is commanded by a major, known as the officer commanding, universally abbreviated to OC. He will normally have around ten years' military experience. In 1 PWRR some company commanders (like James Coote of C Company) were relatively junior, and had not yet attended the Joint Services Command and Staff College at Watchfield near Swindon, whose year-long course is essential for those hoping to get on in the army. Others, like David Bradley of B Company, were commanding companies after their graduation from Staff College, and after doing two major's jobs might find themselves appearing on the annual Pink List naming those fortunates 'provisionally selected for promotion to the substantive rank of lieutenant colonel' in the coming year.

Getting promoted to lieutenant colonel is one thing, but securing the much coveted command at battalion level is quite another. The annual Command Board grades lieutenant colonels and promotable majors, and only those clearing a specific hurdle can expect to command. An officer's pattern of confidential reports, recently rechristened Officers' Joint Appraisal Reports (OJARs), are fundamental to onward progression. These reports embody comments by his immediate commander as well as by a second, and sometimes third, reporting officer too. The process is inevitably taut, for those hoping to rise to the highest ranks in the army, whose number has shrunk markedly over the last decade, need a flawless pattern of reports; simply being very good is not generally good enough.

There is a perceptible annual frisson amongst senior majors as the Pink List is imminent, for missing it by a year or two will put an officer just on the wrong side of the power curve, still capable of enjoying a satisfactory career but unlikely to get beyond the rank of colonel. Almost any officer will tell you of comrades gut-shot by a less than glowing confidential. Successful command at company level is fundamental, then, in career progression, but an officer who dwells too much on the career implications of his job will probably neither enjoy it himself nor relax enough for his subordinates to enjoy it either. Company seconds-in-command are captains, with anything between four and seven years' military experience. In practice a shortage of officers – for there is an abundance of courses to be done at this stage in an individual's career – often means that this post is vacant.

The company sergeant major, warrant officer class 2 by rank, is responsible for discipline and administration in peacetime, and on operations also deals with casualty evacuation and ammunition supply. He is unlikely to have less than twelve years' military service and may have as much as twenty. Although, on the one hand, a company sergeant major will doubtless be 'a hard man with a great deal of experience', there is a good deal more to him than the barking and braying of popular portrayal. He is the vital link between the non-commissioned members of the company and their OC, a barometer of their feelings and an astute judge of their mood. I was unprepared to find just how much most soldiers in 1 PWRR respected their sergeant majors. Several soldiers in C Company (who would have died rather than have their names put to a quote) spoke with affection of Sergeant Major Dave Falconer. His vehicle, predictably named 'the Millennium Falconer', would clatter into sight immediately a soldier was hit, with the great man dispensing death and destruction from its turret; many of C Company attributed the fact that all their wounded ultimately survived to his courage and skill. And as the consummately professional Sergeant Major Barnett of B Company, hard hit in a severe day's fighting in Basra, was stretchered off, he forcefully observed to a platoon commander, briefly shocked by seeing such a figure felled, that his hair needed cutting without delay. That, at least, was what B Company gleefully told me, for that is how they liked to remember this iron man.

If the company sergeant major stands in much the same relationship to the OC that the regimental sergeant major does to the CO, then the company quartermaster sergeant (staff sergeant by formal army rank, but colour sergeant in the infantry) is the company's equivalent of the quartermaster. He is responsible for all the company's equipment, from night vision devices to stew. The Myrmidons to his Achilles are the storemen, usually soldiers possessing a mystical combination of sin and experience, who rarely feature in song or story but make all the difference to the successful running of a company.

There are three platoons to a company, and each of them has four Warriors. One carries the platoon headquarters, commanded by a subaltern, a lieutenant or second lieutenant. He will have passed the Regular Commissions Board at Westbury in Wiltshire, and then completed the year's course at the Royal Military Academy Sandhurst. The overwhelming majority of platoon commanders are university graduates, and in a regiment like mine perhaps a bare majority will have been to public school. One young officer described his comrades with pride as 'a mixed bunch', and so they were; what mattered was not family background or accent but the ability to command soldiers who often hail from tough urban backgrounds and have the keenest of noses for bullshit.

Robbie Hicks, who leaves the army the very day that I write this, to marry his Amy and pursue a career in recruitment, is mixed race (his father is South African) and slightly built. He was widely known as 'the little Arab boy', and used to joke about how scared he was of running into an American patrol who would take him at face value and shoot him. He had been very badly hurt in an accident two years before, but, against the doctors' advice, managed to complete his combat fitness test and returned to A Company to command a platoon. I went out with him on what I am sure was the gentlest of patrols, and could not have been in more competent hands. We spent part of the day putting in snap vehicle checkpoints on Route 6 just south of Al Amarah. It was a pleasure to see how easily everyone slotted into the job, and a lanky Grenadian lance corporal with a flair for languages bypassed the interpreter by chatting comfortably to drivers and their passengers in self-taught Arabic. It was a platoon at the height of its powers, easy with itself and with its commander.

The platoon commander's right-hand man is his platoon sergeant, an NCO with some eight to twelve years' service, who will have risen from the rank of private, having attended two crucial courses at Brecon, the Section Commanders' Battle Course and the Platoon Sergeants' Battle Course. Both are tough courses, the latter designed to instruct him in platoon-level tactics, range management, leadership and command as well as to identify those who are weak or unsuitable. The division of labour between the platoon commander and the platoon sergeant is typical of the divide between officers and senior NCOs across the army. The platoon commander is responsible for developing a plan in the context of his company's operation, and commanding in combat. In peacetime he spends a good deal of his time on the morale and personal welfare of his men. The platoon sergeant is responsible for discipline and administration, and works closely with the CSM (company sergeant major) and the company quartermaster sergeant (CQMS). Yet he is anything but a bloodless administrator, for he stands ready to take over if the platoon commander is sick, wounded or on leave. In addition, as a result of its experience in Northern Ireland the army developed the use of the multiple, essentially a half-platoon, one multiple commanded by the platoon commander and the other by the platoon sergeant.

The other three Warriors in the platoon carry a rifle section apiece. The section is in theory commanded by a corporal with a lance corporal as his second-in-command, but in Iraq it was common to find lance corporals in command of sections. They would, typically, have joined the army at seventeen or eighteen, and at the time – things have changed recently – would have carried out basic training at one of the army training regiments before finishing off infantry training at Catterick in Yorkshire. Most lance corporals will not yet have attended the first of their Brecon courses, but will have been promoted after completing a battalion-run junior NCO cadre, fitting them for the first step on the long ladder of promotion. The real burden of operations like those in Iraq is shouldered by junior NCOs in their twenties, commanding soldiers whose average age will be no more than nineteen.

I spoke to one corporal in Basra, whose section had played a leading part in storming the old Ba'ath Party headquarters in the city. By the time he reached it his Warrior, which had pressed on through a blizzard of RPGs, was hard hit, its turret jammed and the electrics shorting out and shocking anyone who touched bare metal. He was a man who commanded respect: cropped hair, a frank and unyielding glance and abundantly tattooed arms. There was a powerful chemistry, recognizable even to an outsider, binding his section together. He admitted that he thought they were going to die in the assault, but would do it again with the same boys in the back. And one of them, as much accomplice and younger brother as subordinate, said that they would all do it again with him in the turret. 'He was like the angel of fucking death,' he mused.

Corporal Green in the back of a Warrior

There is room in the back of a Warrior for only seven men, and even then it is a tight squeeze, though life can be more comfortable if the mortar hatch – double armoured doors in the vehicle's roof – is open. The driver sits at the front left in a small cockpit with the engine on his right. Visibility is limited even if his hatch is open, and with it closed it is severely restricted. Both drivers and gunners are required to complete specific courses and vehicle commanders must also be trained gunners. This applies regardless of rank – the CO is a trained Warrior gunner – and when 1 PWRR converted to armoured infantry I remember a dinner night in the officers' mess when everyone seemed to have skinned knuckles or mangled fingers ('Rarden rash') from the weapon's unforgiving breech.

If the infantry in the rear dismount from their Warrior, through the large door at the back, the empty Warrior is commanded by the platoon's Warrior sergeant, an expert in the vehicle's maintenance and tactics. His role is mirrored at company headquarters, where there is a Warrior sergeant major who can fight the company commander's vehicle as required if the company is away on foot. Armoured infantry battalions are larger than light or mechanized battalions, and until now have been brought up to strength by the addition of the AIMI – the armoured infantry manning increment – which includes key personnel like Warrior sergeants and sergeant majors. In 1 PWRR's case many of the Warrior specialists came to it from the Worcesters and Foresters, who were losing the armoured infantry role, and many of them were very experienced indeed. They had moved to the battalion to help it convert to Warrior, but had then chosen to change their cap-badges and stay on. Colour Sergeant Owen, once a Welsh Guardsman, had moved from battalion to battalion to stay with Warrior. The end of arms-plotting will mean that battalions will no longer need to change role with such frequency, and there will be less squandering of hard-won expertise in the process.

The platoon commander and his platoon sergeant normally travelled in the same vehicle, so that the sergeant could take over the platoon if the commander was hit, or could command the Warrior if the platoon commander left it. Exiting the turret by the recognized route required elaborate choreography. The turret had to be rotated so that the turret cage could be opened; the platoon signaller would hand his officer his bulky kit, including his radio, as he slid out breathlessly, through the rear compartment. This was such a frolic that it became the accepted practice that for short bouts of dismounted work the platoon sergeant would dismount to command the troops on foot, leaving his boss with the vehicle, but for longer operations the commander himself would climb out of the vehicle.

There are sixteen Warriors in an armoured infantry company, twelve of them the 510 variant within the rifle platoons, and two 511 command variants for the company commander and his second-in-command which, instead of having parallel benches in the back for their troops to sit on, have two small tables and map boards, and are fitted with additional radios. The company's REME fitters had two Warriors of their own which could be used to assist with the recovery or repair of bogged or broken-down vehicles. There were also three very elderly armoured personnel carriers of the FV 432 series, which have no turrets, although a GPMG can be fitted to the commander's hatch. One was used by the REME, one was the company sergeant major's vehicle, and the other was the ambulance. The company quartermaster sergeant stands in the same relationship to the company commander as the battalion's QM stands to the CO. He had a four-tonne truck for his logistic duties, while the Warrior sergeant major had a Land Rover. Neither trucks nor Land Rovers enjoyed the protection or cross-country capability of a Warrior, and the 432s, designed in the 1950s, were not up to the job, so Warriors were used for a wider variety of tasks than had been planned.

Few battalions, whatever their role, go on operations configured as they are in peacetime. At one extreme, infantry need tanks to support them, and vice versa. The addition of elements that are not organic to a battalion makes it into a battle group, and for its tour in Iraq 1 PWRR became the PWRR battle group. The most notable additions were Major Charlie Vere-Whiting's A Company 1 RWF, and Major James Coward's A Squadron The Queen's Royal Lancers. We have already seen that the former were equipped with the Saxon wheeled armoured personnel carrier. The RWF company's soldiers were described by my own in a variety of ways, but expressions like 'short-arsed', 'traditional' and 'tough and aggressive' generally featured. Despite this creative friction, there was no doubt that the Welch Fusilier company would do well: it came from a battalion with abundant Northern Ireland experience, and a terrific, albeit little-publicized, performance in the defence of Gorazde in Bosnia nine years before; furthermore, internal bonding and external community links in Wales were alike very strong. Soldiers from Wales and the south coast would bicker, but there was a deep and abiding recognition that both came from the hard end of the infantry market.

It has to be said that there was initially less confidence as far as the Lancers were concerned. They were a cavalry regiment normally equipped with the Challenger 2 main battle tank, and had worked alongside the PWRR the previous training year, demonstrating that they were fine armoured soldiers. But they were due to deploy to Iraq without their tanks, and would patrol on foot or by Land Rover. 'Without Northern Ireland experience there were concerns as to how quickly the squadron could pick up the drills which were basic to most infantry commanders,' thought one PWRR officer. In the event these concerns could not have been more misplaced. Although it had been assumed that the scaling-down of the British commitment to Iraq after the 'war proper' had been won would result in the removal of all the Challengers, sufficient in fact remained to equip A Squadron after its arrival in Iraq so that it went, at a stroke, from taking on a role for which it was not ideally suited to playing one that brought it confidently centre stage. The Lancers were a well regarded part of the battle group, not least because the appearance of their 'fat tanks' on the battlefield induced the insurgents to concentrate their fire on precisely those vehicles to which they could do least damage.

There was to be a platoon of Royal Military Police (RMP) attached to the battle group, intended to assist with the monitoring of the embryonic Iraqi Police Service (IPS), together with an RMP liaison officer at battle group headquarters to advise on police matters. But while the liaison officer was part of the battle group, the RMP platoon actually reported direct to Multinational Division South-East in Basra. This did not always make for a happy relationship. One PWRR officer suggested:

> Divisional troops can exercise a belief in their own importance totally out of proportion to their rank, status or role, and sometimes felt that they did not have to toe the battle group's line. The logic of the situation (we were all in a small camp getting mortared together) and a genuine terror of Toby Walch tended to cure people of this attitude quite quickly.

Neither was the RAF detachment at Camp Abu Naji under the direct command of the battle group, and its personnel, working to a different system, rotated every few days. The RAF provided an immediate reaction team (IRT), consisting of medical personnel and an RAF fire service cutting crew. There were generally one, or sometimes two, helicopters at Abu Naji, depending on the situation. Although Angus Forbes's medics had been reinforced for the tour, there were no surgical facilities in camp, which meant that serious cases would have to be flown back to Shaiba Logistic Base, just south-west of Basra, a short flight away. Although the departing helicopter would be replaced by another, flying up from Basra, this would take some time. But, as Matt Maer observed:

> The chances were if we needed to move casualties, so did others, and there would be a scarcity of helicopters. Therefore, the casevac helicopter could be a one-shot weapon. Once it was released south there was no guarantee when it would be back. Therefore if a soldier had minor shrapnel wounds but needed fragments removed it was always a decision as to whether to release the helicopter for him, but fifteen minutes later have a casualty with life-threatening injuries requiring a flight.

Y Company was to retain the ability to man its mortars and provide the recce platoon, but would otherwise serve in the infantry role, and so was given an extra platoon's worth of reservists, Scots Territorials from the Lowland Regiment. Although this went firmly against the grain of the regimental system, it worked well, and if the Scots recognized that they were being thrown in at the deep end they did not let it daunt them. A Squadron was also beefed up, in its case by the addition of Territorials from The Royal Yeomanry. Arguably the most significant use of reservists was in what the army calls CIMIC – Civil-Military Cooperation. If reservists sometimes (though, as we shall see, by no means always) find themselves at a disadvantage when compared with regulars if called up to do jobs at the cutting edge of combat, there was widespread recognition that they often added great value where CIMIC was concerned, as one regular PWRR officer acknowledged:

> The TA with their somewhat different background are capable of deploying some very capable G5 personnel and we were to be very well served by some excellent personnel. These men and women were often able to bring their experience from civilian life into the battle group. This fact was recognized by the battalion 2ic when he visited their

training at Lydd [a training area in Kent]. He made the point that we needed accountants as we were taking over public funds, and engineers who could help to rebuild the state and its infrastructure.

Major Walch pointed to one reservist and asked him: 'What do you do in civvy street?' 'I'm a record producer,' was the reply. 'Then you're fuck all use to us,' affirmed Toby Walch. He was wrong, for the reservist was in fact Nick Thasarathar, who had been a platoon commander in 1st Battalion The Royal Regiment of Fusiliers in 1991. Mike McDonald, now the QM, had been colour sergeant in the same company: Nick 'was to serve with absolute distinction from the first firefight on our first day . . . to the final siege of CIMIC House'.

There were also officers and soldiers added to the battle group from several regiments of the regular army. The radars of K Battery Royal Artillery provided early warning of incoming mortar bombs and rockets, and accurate information as to how many had actually been launched; this was important because unexploded rounds ('blinds') had to be located and made safe to avoid accidents. Dealing with blinds and with the improvised explosive devices (IEDs) which were, increasingly, hidden by the roadside to be triggered when convoys or patrols passed was the task of ammunition technical officers (ATOs) of the Royal Logistic Corps. At the time of my visit the insurgents had taken to using necklaces of three 155mm shells taped together, laid out in groups of five. This amount of high explosive would give even the mighty Warrior pause for thought, and it was IEDs of various types that killed and wounded soldiers of The Black Watch at the end of 1 PWRR's time in Iraq.

Lastly, Captain Chris Conroy of The Royal Gurkha Rifles came across to head the battle group's psychological operations and information operations departments, though there was a general view that the natural wit that inspired some of his work did not quite have the local impact it deserved.

If the RWF and QRL, with an assortment of other officers and soldiers, were to join the battle group, two of 1 PWRR's organic companies, Major Simon Thomsett's A and Major David Bradley's B, would leave it. The former would become brigade reserve, reinforcing battle groups within the brigade as the need arose, and mounting surge operations when there was a requirement to flood a particular area with troops. The latter would stay in Basra as part of the Cheshire battle group, which was built around the nucleus of 1st Battalion The Cheshire Regiment just as the PWRR battle group was based on 1 PWRR. The Cheshires were a Saxon battalion, and the addition of B Company would give them some much needed punch in case things became ugly in Iraq's second city, as, indeed, they did.

A small rear part was left behind at Tidworth, under the command of Major Ian Townsend of HQ Company. Captain Bob Wells, WO1 Whyte's predecessor as RSM and now Regimental Careers Management Officer, had done the first part of the tour with the battalion and then returned to the UK. It was hard to keep him away, and after delivering me safely to Camp Abu Naji he stayed on. The rear party's jobs were unglamorous, but we could not have survived without it. It contained all the soldiers who were medically unfit for Iraq, including those who had been wounded and were recovering. It also looked after the few under-eighteen-year-olds who had completed their training but were not yet old enough to be sent on active service.

The welfare office was the responsibility of Captain Chris Wright, assisted by WO2 Ken Furie and Sergeant Richard Kendall Tobias, with Christine Waugh manning the front desk. Ken Furie was 'an experienced sergeant major known as cuddly Ken to most because of his manner with the families, but known to the others as Colour-coded Ken due to his dress code of scarlet corduroys, double cuffs and blazers. The officers of the battalion never looked as officer-like.' The welfare team helped maintain contact with wives and families and with the more seriously wounded, all of whom were sent to Selly Oak Hospital in Birmingham, where the MOD maintained some military staff after the closure of dedicated military hospitals. And although we had not actually rehearsed the reception back into the UK of the bodies of soldiers killed in action, when the time came the rear party furnished a bearer party and a bugler. It was a source of real pride that the Welsh Guards warrant officer responsible for such ceremonial at RAF Brize Norton told me he had not seen things done with greater dignity.

The PWRR battle group was responsible to 1 Mechanized Brigade, whose headquarters was initially in Basra Palace. An officer wrote:

> This was a typical Ba'athist complex with ornate fascias and appalling plumbing and wiring. Some of the buildings were structurally unsound by the time we arrived ... A huge pond, almost big enough to be a lake, had been built in the shape of Palestine. It was overgrown and neglected. Brigade headquarters operated from what they called the dance floor, a huge wide room around which various desks were arranged in an open-plan office. The decor was over-wrought arabesque with an impressive wooden ceiling.

During the tour brigade headquarters moved to the same airport hotel occupied by Multinational Division South-East. It was a more modern and functional building, but the amenities worked.

In addition to the PWRR battle group, 1 Mechanized Brigade comprised the Cheshire battle group in Basra, The Royal Welch Fusiliers battle group in the south, and a battle group based on 1st Regiment Royal Horse Artillery (1 RHA) which was known as the Deep Operations Group, responsible for security-sector reform across the whole of the British sector. The Argyll and Sutherland Highlanders were already in Iraq mentoring the Iraqi National Guard, and The Black Watch would arrive later.

If most of the tension within the battle group was helpful, much of the friction between the battle group and the denizens of the airport hotel was not. Staff officers at brigade and division have titles which reflect both their rank and their speciality. SO1s are lieutenant colonels, SO2s are majors and SO3s are captains. The SO2 Visits at division, for instance, was a charming gunner major without whom I would probably still be in Iraq. The proliferation of tasks with which the army was involved meant that in addition to more familiar titles there were some not instantly redolent of military glory, like the SO3 Sewerage. Friction between front and rear is one of the best-polished facets of military history, and there is no doubt that it existed in Iraq in 2004. Take one disgruntled infantry officer:

> It was a typical ploy of those working at higher headquarters to demand something with the implied threat that the Brigade Commander or General Officer Commanding would be very upset if it wasn't done immediately and the implied suggestion that any other work we were doing was peripheral. There was often an assumption amongst divisional troops that they were working direct to the senior officer. This caused some amusement at battle group level when petty bureaucrats tried to invoke the wrath of senior officers who probably knew us by name but had probably never even spoken to the SO3 Solid Waste or whoever it happened to be.
>
> Brilliantly we received one email stating that we were required to return a laptop forthwith to divisional headquarters. The author of this message emailed it to everyone in Abu Naji complaining that no one would be allowed to leave theatre until it was retrieved and that its retrieval had become the main effort for brigade and division. In military terms the main effort is that activity which the commander deems essential to the success of his mission. It seems unlikely that a five-or six-hundred-pound computer clogged with dust was vital to the success of implementing free and fair elections, restoring law and order and other essential services. It does show something of the mindset of some of the people that a relatively junior officer felt he was qualified to decide for the Brigade Commander and GOC what their main efforts should be.
>
> There were men and women at all levels at headquarters who would work all day and night to ensure that we had all the support we needed, but one thoughtless idiot could easily leave us with the impression that no one cared and no one understood.

The point is not that brigade and divisional staffs were callous or pompous. But it was all too easy for someone in the (relative) comfort and safety of Basra to forget that a lost computer was not the first thought of a man who had already risked his life several times on the day that the querulous email arrived. We can begin to see why the denizens of Basra Palace and the airport hotel were indeed known as REMFs.

CHAPTER 2

A Tour Like No Other

GOOD TO GO

I T WAS 5 NOVEMBER 2003, and the officers and men of 1 PWRR were seated in a large gymnasium at Tidworth to be addressed by their newly arrived CO. 'My name is Lieutenant Colonel Matt Maer,' he announced. 'I am your new Commanding Officer and in twenty weeks' time we deploy on operations in southern Iraq – it will be a tour like no other. You will all be in a contact. You may remove your berets and sit easy.' The speaker later admitted that 'awfully dramatic though those words were, they did stick firmly in the minds of most of those under my command and were to be quoted back to me a number of times during the tour . . . I sense my Edward Fox impression had the desired effect.' He recognized that the army offered 'a number of opportunities for crass amateur dramatics, and I have never been, as many will attest, one to turn my back on such opportunities'. Captain Charlie Curry, then the ops officer, thought that the announcement was 'setting a standard of showmanship that we came to know and love'.

Major David Bradley, who after a year at Staff College had arrived in the battalion that August to command B Company, was relieved to get the news, for there had been constant rumours since the summer that the battalion would in fact be going.

The waiting was over, and we had our confirmation. There was practically a cheer from the floor and you could feel the excitement buzzing around the room. Many of us had served in Northern Ireland or Kosovo, but there was an expectation that this theatre of operations would be different. It was still fairly new, and we would have the opportunity to take part in a fast-moving and exciting situation. The CO went on to say that this wasn't Northern Ireland, it wasn't Bosnia or Kosovo; those of us sitting there could expect to fire our weapons on the tour. As we left the building the prescience of those words was not fully understood. I walked back with the company officers and we discussed this possibility. Really, how likely was it that we would come under fire? How many of us would be in contact? There would no doubt be some action but, as in other theatres, it would probably only affect a few. No doubt many people shared my thoughts – 'Well, if it is going to affect anybody I am going to bloody well make sure it affects me.' As a soldier and in particular an infantryman it is an unspoken desire to be in contact, to fire your weapon in anger and test yourself in combat. There was never the expectation that we would encounter the level of violence that we did.

Private Bobu Cham of C Company also thought that the announcement had marked an important point of departure: 'Our new incoming CO stood before the whole battalion and cleared the air for everyone by saying, "My name is Lt Col Maer, I am your new CO and in twenty weeks' time we are going to southern Iraq."' Private Nikki Oliver admitted that she felt a lump in her throat. 'The news that we were going to Iraq was the best news the battalion had in 2003,' thought Charlie Curry, adding, with genial self-deprecation:

I thought that it sounded the almost perfect tour: hot (I am definitely a fair-weather soldier), good patrolling with a decent level of excitement, and at the end of the day a relatively comfortable base complete with showers and decent food to return to. Not that I would be doing any of these things, of course. As the Operations Officer, my job was to fill in the detail that would make the CO's plan work, and then to sit in the air-conditioned operations room listening to the radio while the real soldiers of the battalion went out into the heat to be shot at.

By the time Matt Maer arrived to take command, the battalion was in fact close to the end of its annual training cycle. It had only just returned from a three-month spell in Canada, at the British Army Training Unit Suffield (BATUS). This was the culmination of a training cycle that had been compacted by the firemen's strike in the winter of 2002–3 when the army took over firemen's duties, and this had itself followed close on the heels of a tour of duty in Kosovo. There most of the operations had been in the light role, and although the battalion had its Warriors, there was little enough chance to use them. In consequence, everyone went back to basics, starting with classroom lessons with Airfix Warriors so that the theory of minor tactics could be hammered home. 'The next phase,' as James Rands, then a Warrior platoon commander, recalled,

> was to take the Warriors out on to Salisbury Plain in platoons. Four vehicles tearing around can move in a variety of ways: line abreast, T formation, box or single file, and they can do so under three different tactical states. Green is no enemy suspected, and in this state we just bimble along all watching our own arcs but not taking any special measures. Amber is where there is a perceived possibility of enemy and so we caterpillar with two vehicles moving and two vehicles static. Vehicles 1 and 3 stay put whilst 2 and 4 move up level with them and then go static. Once they are static, 1 and 3 move off again. Red is when we expect to see enemy and so we leapfrog – or pepper-pot, as it is also called. In this situation 1 and 3 will go static while 2 and 4 move past them a tactical bound [a distance which varies with the ground, but might be to the next cover or crest] and then stop.
>
> These drills had to be learned again almost from scratch, but after about a week of day-long exercises, movement and the rapid advance into the assault were skills that we had reacquired. The assault consists of the Warriors

bearing down on the enemy position as fast as we can possibly go, firing the chain gun all the way. All four vehicles go as fast as they can, which provides our greatest protection. The armour in the vehicle will stop a lot, but actually not getting shot in the first place is better. It is actually extremely difficult to hit a fast-moving vehicle with anti-tank weaponry. Fire support on the way in could come from tanks or Warriors to a flank or mortars firing over the attackers' heads. Either just in front of, on top of or immediately behind the first row of enemy trenches, the vehicle comes to a sharp halt and the troops dismount to carry out an attack and clear the positions.

A sharp stop is exactly that. The Warrior has a top speed of between 60 and 70 mph and can go almost as fast cross country. When it stops quickly, the vehicle stands up on its nose, and the sensation in the back is, let me tell you, shattering. As platoon training swelled into company training, whole companies of Warriors would hurtle across the Plain, streaming on in an apparently amorphous mass as they barrelled up hill and down dale, but taking station from the company commander's vehicle in the centre of the pack, capitalizing on the ground and jockeying into formation as they neared the objective. James Rands continues:

This was hard going as commanders were thrown hard around inside the turret, bouncing off the aluminium shell and bruising ribs. It also shook up the insides so that on occasion people had to leap out of the turret at the first stop to retch. The effects were worse on those in the back who could not see what lay ahead and usually had a poor understanding of the tactical situation. The passengers in the back are supposed to have a headset wired to the vehicle intercom, but we were lucky if we had one working headset per vehicle. In the back seasickness was quite common. We called this manoeuvre 118, after the 118 runners in the Directory Enquiries adverts, and Major Coote could usually be heard shouting 'Straight through 118' over the net as the company tore across the Plain.

From Salisbury Plain the battalion moved to Castlemartin ranges in Wales for live firing. During the Cold War this had been a training base for German tank units: the signs are in German and many of the range wardens who work on the training area are Germans who have settled in the UK. The live firing package was organized to build skill and confidence. It began with single Warriors firing from static positions, progressed through pairs of Warriors moving and firing, and culminated in a whole company of Warriors advancing down the range, firing as they went, eventually unleashing the troops in the back ('dismounts', in the jargon) on to a series of enemy positions represented by dummies and plywood bunkers. 'Firing a Warrior is awesome fun,' recalled James Rands:

> There is a really loud bang (though nothing like a tank's) and the weapon is surprisingly accurate. Targets disintegrate and as the anti-tank rounds strike the hulls of ancient tanks you can see . . . sparks appear across the surface. We had a few of these to show the men, but most of the rounds we fired were practice shells which don't explode or pierce armour. The most fun, however, was always to be found rushing headlong on to an enemy position firing the chain gun on the move. The weapon would spray rounds around which would be thrown into the air as the vehicles hit bumps, or into the mud as they hit ruts. When we examined the targets we found that few of the rounds struck the targets, but you couldn't imagine sticking your head up if you were on the other end.

From Castlemartin the battalion moved on to the virtual world of the Combined Arms Tactical Trainer. This is effectively a huge hangar, subdivided into a number of vast rooms and cinemas. Armoured vehicles are represented by large cream and beige boxes, whose interiors are a good approximation to those of Warriors or Challenger tanks. Turret crews have to operate battened down, as they might in combat, using the seven periscopes dotted around the turret, or the sight systems for the Rarden cannon and the chain gun, to see a landscape peopled with computer-generated images. 'Vehicles are quite well presented,' recalled one officer, 'but people

A Company dismounts going into action on TESEX

are rather blocky and tend to move awkwardly, becoming little more than cannon fodder whichever side they were on.'

The next step was to combine previous training by moving on to battle group exercises on Salisbury Plain. These were what is termed TESEX: every man and vehicle was equipped with a laser on each weapon; men wore receivers fitted to vests, and vehicles had them attached to their turrets. When a weapon was fired receivers recorded hits, setting off a beeper and incapacitating the laser on an individual's weapon or a vehicle's gun. The exercises were great fun, although there was some concern that casualties tended to be high. There was also a mountain of administration to be dealt with, as James Rand remembered.

> The Warriors needed cleaning, refuelling and lots of minor repairs every time they entered the gates of camp. This takes time and manpower and inevitably happens on a cold, damp Friday when people haven't slept properly for a week. These were the worst parts of the exercise and always included a long, tedious check of all the equipment on the vehicle. The Complete Equipment Schedule (CES) is

several pages of tightly printed text detailing every spanner, spade, wheel or bungee rope carried on the vehicle. To check all this would take a minimum of an hour if everything could be found, but usually it would take longer – as much through sheer tiredness as anything else.

The culmination of the training cycle was a trip to Suffield, a vast area of prairie near the Canadian town of Medicine Hat. 'We had been consistently told that BATUS was the closest thing to going to war short of actually going to war,' recalled James Rands.

This was all terribly exciting, but we were also eagerly anticipating the delights of Medicine Hat, the nearest town of any consequence some forty minutes' drive away. The British army abounds with tales of the strippers of Medicine Hat and their shockingly debauched behaviour. On arrival in the flat arid wastes of Suffield the first thing most of us wanted to do was to get into town and visit the Sin Bin – the most notorious bar in the town.

One thing we hadn't realized is that a new female mayor had taken charge and banned strippers. A hundred squaddies descended upon what was effectively a large black-painted room with an empty stage with a lone pole and no female clientele at all. The bar served what they called 'paralysers', which are some hideous cocktail based on milk, and so inevitably the soldiers were drunk in no time at all. Alternative nightlife was fairly bizarre. Bars often had arcade games which simulated duck-hunting and were decorated with red velvet and deer antlers. Huge cowboys in big hats would hang around at the bar being hugely protective of any Canadian women who we got within twenty feet of.

At BATUS the training started on small ranges by integrating vehicles and dismounts, both elements firing live ammunition. There was the opportunity to use weapons that were rarely encountered in Britain, like the new hand grenade, as Captain Rands describes:

It is small and round with a fuse assembly that fits into the top. From this there is an arming lever which fits into the

An A Company Warrior on TESEX

web of the hand when one prepares to throw it. When this is depressed the grenade is safe, but as soon as the pressure is released the arm flies off and the fuse starts to burn down. Before use a safety-pin retains the arming lever in place . . . In addition there is also a metal clip which fits around the arming lever as a second safety-catch. This was a welcome addition as occasionally in the past safety-pins have worked loose in people's pouches and become unsafe . . . There are some excellent grenade ranges in Suffield which consist of a series of corridors built out of heavy wooden beams. These absorb shrapnel so that we can move down them in section strength firing rifles on full automatic and hurling grenades round the corners. This represented clearing a trench network . . .

There was also the chance to fire the light anti-tank weapon (LAW), a 10kg anti-armour rocket which comes in a huge two-part composite plastic tube that slides open, extending to a length of about a metre. The warhead has a shaped charge which 'works in the same way as the enemy's RPGs but is rather larger and more effective'. When the weapon is opened the sight, consisting of a small crystal, pops out on the firer's left; when he looks into it a gridded sight pattern appears, its lines enabling him to allow for both the range and crossing speed of his target. There is an integral 9mm rifle that fires spotting rounds, designed to flash when they hit metal, which helps ensure a hit when the main weapon is fired. 'It is quite exceptional when fired,' observed one platoon commander, 'as it feels like being punched from every direction at the same time. The noise is incredible and you find yourself surrounded by smoke.' All weapons were gradually integrated into live firing exercises involving several different sorts, as a platoon commander recalled:

> There was one particular exercise where two sections were deployed in trenches overwatching a field in which various targets would appear. The men put down quite exceptional amounts of fire with GPMGs, rifles, LAW and 51mm mortar. It was noisy and exciting and each man fired a LAW apiece. I think that was the best part of the entire exercise for most of us.

The scale of training increased so that individual platoons and companies were being exercised with TESEX as a combined battle group fighting a resident opposing force, an 'enemy' with vehicles based on the CVRT but tricked out with false turrets and other additions to make them look like Soviet vehicles. Matt Maer, who had visited Suffield earlier in his career, described the directing staff as 'the fascists of armoured warfare, assisted by an opposing force whose sole aim is to beat up and humiliate those who are not quick enough, sharp enough or well drilled enough in the ways and means of armoured warfare'. Another officer noted:

> Canada vindicated some things we had been doing and proved others wrong. Our 118 manoeuvre was a very effec-

tive way of covering ground quickly, but we found ourselves moving back into a more rigid formation as it didn't provide enough cover to the flanks, and we found ourselves becoming the victims of lone tanks sat on hills overwatching valleys where we stopped. We had adopted a cruciform formation for when we rested, which consisted of all vehicles backing on to each other. The cam nets would then be arranged over the top to create a covered area. This worked well and we were told by some of our soldiers who had returned from the Gulf that this is what they had done.

Suffield also revealed individual strengths and weaknesses. Private Stuart Taylor turned out to be a truly exceptional shot with his LAW, knocking out most of an enemy tank company on the TESEX phase, while 'at the same time those who were inclined to shirk when they were tired were quickly found out'. The business of working the battle group up to the army's highest collective performance standard (CP5 in military jargon) inevitably involved activities like the crossing of major obstacles (with rivers marked out by shallow trenches running across the prairie) that exercised the chain of command but left most individuals seized with corrosive boredom as battle procedure ground methodically on. The fact that it all became a little tiresome for most of those concerned could be deduced from the fact that the report lines – superimposed on maps to show how far subunits had got, or the stage an operation had reached – were named Flog, Dead and Horse.

There were also rumblings of discontent from those who could not see the point in it all anyway. The battalion was slated to go to Northern Ireland the following year, 'so what was the point of training for conventional war in Warrior?' But, as David Bradley remembered, there were growing rumours that the battalion was actually bound for Iraq, although it was still two months before Matt Maer's dramatic announcement:

> The hectic training and intense schedule initially put back any thoughts of Iraq, but as the exercise progressed rumours of our involvement, or not, kept circulating. Unofficially it became clear that we were going, but there was

no confirmation from the chain of command. The CO [then Lieutenant Colonel James Cameron] took the OCs [company commanders] aside and said that he believed strongly that we were going but that he did not want any concerns raised by the families while we were still in Canada. He felt it would be better to wait until our return in order to allow everyone to deal with one issue of separation at a time. Every phone call home involved trying to explain to my wife Lara why I did not know what was happening. She seemed better informed than me and . . . was positive that we were going.

Once the training had finished, officers and men got away on rest and recreation (R and R) to a variety of locations in North America. Most of the soldiers went to Calgary, which had retained many of the delights that had vanished from Medicine Hat, while many officers and senior NCOs headed for Vancouver where there was not only a film fair and art galleries – but also some entertainments of the Medicine Hat variety too. There was plenty of adventurous training, with white-water canoeing, hiking in the mountains and survival exercises on the glacier at Banff. Major Justin Featherstone, the spare and rangy commander of Y Company – and probably the only member of the battalion to hold the Fellowship of the Royal Geographical Society – was a notable mountaineer whose exploits on the ice at Banff gave even the local guides pause for thought. He was next to distinguish himself in a wholly different environment.

It was soon after the battalion's return to Tidworth that James Cameron departed on promotion and handed over command to Matt Maer, whose memorable announcement in the gym at Tidworth told the battalion that it was indeed Iraq-bound. Ironically, he found himself something of a stranger:

> I was not of the 1st Battalion of the regiment, having served my entire career hitherto in its sister 2nd Battalion. Both battalions are essentially the same and where one serves is as much a matter of happenstance as planning. But the battalions in a regiment are best described as branch offices in a company. It was as if I had worked up the ladder at the

Canterbury branch and was now coming to take over the running of the Tidworth branch. As a result I knew only one person, Toby Walch the second-in-command, on my first day in command of 630-plus men and women of 1 PWRR.

Once Matt Maer had known that he was to get command of the battalion, he had visited it on its tour of duty in Kosovo. 'The tubbier members of the battalion were looking forward to his arrival,' observed a platoon commander, 'as . . . it had been noted that he was more rotund than the previous commanding officer and they thought he might not be so keen on PT. That was clearly just ill-conceived wishful thinking.' On the credit side, 'he had a very detailed knowledge of the situation, having previously worked at JTAC – the Joint Terrorism Analysis Centre'. His style was quiet and consultative rather than flamboyant and extrovert, though there could be a good deal of studied irony in his pronouncements. Many of his subordinates were to recall him as the man of the match, an ideal blend of coach and team captain.

Colonel Matt occasionally lost his temper, but not often and rarely for long. He could be cold when needed, when dealing with the insurgents, but he cared deeply about his men. In every planning session where we were looking at dangerous options he would finish by saying: 'Would I be prepared to do this with this equipment?' If the answer was no the plan needed to be rethought.

Training went on, although the news of the imminent deployment lent it a fresh intensity. First, the battalion had to be battle-grouped, reconfigured for its task. David Bradley's B Company departed to provide the Cheshires, who would be based in Basra, with a Warrior company to beef up their Saxons. Charlie Vere-Whiting's company of Royal Welch Fusiliers was bussed up regularly from Aldershot to take part in collective training, while the Catterick-based A Squadron of The Queen's Royal Lancers made several trips southwards to stay in one of the smaller camps on Salisbury Plain, for there was no room for them in Tidworth. Toby Walch had organized a package on Salisbury Plain, designed to see how training standards compared across the battle group and to physically and mentally test all concerned. It consisted of

> a Marathon-length tab [march] in a circuit around Salisbury Plain. There were about a dozen stands which multiples would visit on their way round the Plain. These included cultural awareness, Arabic, vehicle recovery, first aid, media-handling, minor aggro and two two-mile runs. The test was arduous and demanding and did identify some areas where we needed to improve. What made it somewhat bizarre was that there was a thin dusting of snow on the ground throughout the entire exercise.

Private G. Cooper of C Company's 8 Platoon was also struck by the weather:

> This was . . . the usual round robin of 36km, carrying full kit, performing a number of different tasks at twelve different stands whilst being placed under pressure with a cut-off time of twenty-four hours. The final straw being that we carried this out in snow on one of the coldest days we had this year. What, I hear you cry, has this got to do with Iraq, that hot, hot, hot country I've heard so much about? Well, I will tell you!
>
> All the stands that were in place were relevant, starting with the language, vehicle recovery, first aid, NBC [nuclear, biological and chemical], foot contact drills, vehicle contact drills, crowd control, media ops, electronic countermeasures (ECM), route clearance, VCP drills and weapon-handling. And just to keep the QMSI employed, a quick two-miler in between! . . . Even though as Toms we all moaned about this SAS selection day, it had its purpose. Each man was placed under pressure with the amount of kit he was carrying, and for the first time most soldiers had a go at leading as commander. That meant he had to navigate cross country from one stand to another, plus go through as commander at each stand. This was aiming off

in case the commander became a casualty and one of us had to step up. The distance played a big part as well as carrying the kit, as this added to the mental and physical barriers, especially coming towards the last few stands not knowing how far you had to go, plus remaining switched on for tasks ahead. This would prove to be our most valuable training day for this tour, as when the first contact went in, it didn't stop for two months.

In broader terms, though, these were Matt Maer's thoughts on the predeployment package:

> The training . . . prepared us very little for the subtleties . . . We were taught about the Islamic faith (to a greater extent than most of the soldiers had ever been taught about Christianity), what motivated Muslims, the five pillars of Islam, what offended Muslims (showing the soles of one's feet, speaking directly to their womenfolk, smoking and eating during Ramadan etc.), and a smattering of Arabic to get by . . .
>
> The training was useful . . . but there was no critical analysis of the Iraqi people we would meet – for example, how violent they would be – nor a substantive explanation of the difference between the Sunni and Shi'a sides of the religion. This was akin to sending troops to Northern Ireland and teaching them about Christianity and not the differences between the creeds, needs, desires and agendas of the Catholic and Protestant communities. Nor did we see a single person from the Foreign and Commonwealth Office [FCO] during our training, who might have explained both the cultural situation we were entering and what HM government wished us to do there. This was the first sign of a disconnect between the civilian and the military strands of the campaign which was to become increasingly apparent as time passed.

One of the major weaknesses detected was in medical training, abruptly summed up by one officer as 'crap'. The army's individual training directives for this are themselves set at a low level, and in any event 'we pay lip service to them'. It was clear that soldiers had to be trained in life support so that their comrades did not die needlessly while awaiting the arrival of a trained medic, and that to accomplish this 'there was a necessity therefore to increase the amount of medical training soldiers received well beyond what we were supposed to teach'.

Battle casualties tend to fall into three broad categories. At the dark end of the spectrum, a relatively small proportion of those injured by enemy action are so badly hurt by gunshot wounds, explosion or fragments that they are bound to die instantly or very quickly indeed, and the most expert medical aid, even delivered swiftly, could not save them. This is why the large IEDs which have become so common in Iraq are so dangerous. At the other end of the spectrum, many wounds – like the less serious splinter injuries caused by shells or mortar bombs – are not now life-threatening although they might well have been so in an age when infection was a major killer and antibiotics did not exist. The middle group constitutes wounds that are life-threatening but not necessarily fatal: everything hinges on the quality of first aid, the speed with which the wounded soldier can be evacuated to a medical facility and the accuracy of the primary surgery he receives on his arrival.

The very effective Kevlar helmets and body armour always worn outside camp (and routinely worn in it, whenever there was a threat) prevented many hits which once would have put their recipients into the first, bleakest category from being even moderately serious. Some men received hits from high-velocity weapons directly on the ceramic plates inserted into the pouches of their body armour and had no physical ill-effects whatever. Others (David Bradley is perhaps the most striking example) had what would have been instantly lethal hits even ten years ago converted into serious but ultimately survivable wounds by the quality of helmet and armour.

The combination of enhanced training – taken very seriously once it was clear that Iraq was imminent – and emphasis on prompt casualty evacuation within platoons and companies in action, meant that the regiment had not a single soldier killed who was not dead within seconds of being hit. Here 1 PWRR was lucky in that most of its battle injuries were caused by small-arms fire, the ubiquitous RPGs, rockets or mortar bombs.

From its training on the Plain the battalion moved down to the Hythe–Lydd complex on the Kent coast for its specific pre-deployment training (OPTAG). Private Tom Ferguson of 7 Platoon C Company, one of those 'senior Toms' – experienced private soldiers – who form the backbone of most platoons, writing from Abu Naji in the summer of 2004, was initially unimpressed:

> As we pulled up into the car park at Lydd, we soon realized that this was going to be another boring training package full of the usual: NCOs screaming at us, area cleaning, bad weather, just the norm for a training package. However, two months down the line, you wish you had taken notes. As the OPTAG instructors were shouting at us to 'get low' and 'keep your heads down' as part of another blank-firing attack, we always thought that if they were that close, there's something seriously wrong. When a bullet comes whizzing past you your instinct alone makes you take cover. You don't realize until that moment that maybe, just maybe, your instructors were talking sense.
>
> Don't get me wrong. I'm not a fan of everything we do during training. I'd like to see a lot less of the menial tasks such as area cleaning. But I used to think of sangar bashing [guard duty] in the same way. We all know the usual proced-ure for taking over guard; the 'actions on' and 'in case of'. But at the end of the day, you stand there for two hours looking into the same boring places that the previous guard have been looking at, knowing full well that Lydd is not about to be attacked by some extremist force. However, in Iraq you take things on board and the importance of what you are doing is quite evident. You properly start switching on, knowing that a couple of mortars have gone over your head a couple of minutes previous. Your training really matters out here, knowing that your buddy won't just have a continuous beep on his TES vest, but just a continuous

silence. That is where you can separate the boys from the men.

Second Lieutenant Adam Styler had completed his platoon commanders' course at Warminster in time to join the battalion

at the start of the Lydd and Hythe training package, sadly after the Battalion 2ic's death march across Salisbury Plain. I was still lamenting this missed opportunity when I met my platoon at the end of their first day in Lydd.

If I had to choose one defining moment from my two years in uniform to date, it would be that encounter with what I was later to find out was the finest body of men in the battalion . . . 7 Platoon. It's a bit of a cliché, I know, to say that meeting my platoon was a really big moment, but it was, and not just because Private Ferguson [who was to be mentioned in dispatches for his bravery] had shown me something the likes of which I had never seen before and hope never to see again. It was an important moment because it's the one occasion that really signals to you that your training is over. For those of us who entered Sandhurst intent on joining an infantry battalion, our main effort was to become a platoon commander. To be in command of, and to lead, men. It was only on that February evening in Lydd that I became a platoon commander.

Now, having talked it up to have been some great union on a par with when 'Kelly' met his 'Heroes' or when the 'Dozen' came together and got 'Dirty', it was actually a bit of a non-event. Sgt Page spent the first fifteen minutes laying down the law and briefing the lads, while I sat there being inspected by twenty-eight pairs of eyes (for at least thirty seconds, before they lost interest) whilst trying to maintain the illusion of being cool ('Adam, you've got to stop sweating'), authoritative ('Is the Sgt going to grip me for having dirty boots') and in control ('How does this work then? When do I get to talk? What am I even going to say? What's that? What did he say? What are we doing tomorrow?

Oh bugger!' In short – they met me, I met them. Bust! But the main effort had been achieved.

After Lydd came a final battle group exercise on Salisbury Plain, and then a last trip to Castlemartin to hone live firing skills. In Private Ferguson's opinion, the package bore little resemblance to his own experience of combat:

> If the truth be told, Wales is not the ideal place to train. It seems to me that Wales is the focal point of rain and cloud and generally miserable weather. But they say that if you can train in the harshest conditions you'll be ready for anything. Did they not take into account that Iraq rarely sees rain and the average temperature is over forty degrees centigrade? Maybe some foreign training in a similar climate might have been more use. The only thing I found useful was the Warrior firing package, which freshened up my skills, and maybe how to send a decent contact report rather than just ignore the radio and pretend nothing is happening. You have the usual gunnery gods who actually think they were put on this earth to be right and always reminding you to wait ten mins for a top stoppage [on the Rarden cannon] and raise your barrel. In Iraq, if you wait ten mins to carry out the 'proper' drills your wagon would be destroyed or overrun . . . Even now, I'm still expecting a member of the DS [directing staff] to have a word with me or for someone to tell me I should make ready. But that's the way it goes over here. You have to be continuously flexible and able to overcome certain situations you thought would never pop up.

For Adam Styler, though, the process brought him closer to his platoon:

> I felt I'd got to know the Mighty 7 quite well by this stage. Being thrown straight into it and living at close quarters with the lads for the duration of an intense period of training like OPTAG is certainly the best and quickest way of getting to know them, and a million other things that you

never knew you wanted to know. Why anyone would want to squeeze someone else's zits is beyond me, but it illustrates a lesson I learnt early on and have seen exemplified time and again in Iraq: soldiers never cease to amaze. Whether it's the actions they choose to do or actions they are forced into by circumstance, they will always surprise you when you least expect it.

However, it was at Castlemartin that I noticed a division within the platoon, and so presumably also within the battalion. I don't think it is unique to this battalion, but likely applicable to all armoured infantry battalions: the division between crew and 'dirty dismounts'. Crew spent the week live-firing on the ranges while dismounts ran all sorts of low-level tactical lessons and exercises. As well as the strong sense of loyalty and uniqueness within the platoon, there is also a sub-loyalty between dismounts and crew. Although 'division' implies all sorts of negative connotations, I think it is actually quite positive. It's a lower level of camaraderie within two groups rather than a division between two groups.

Military historians and commentators alike are often inclined to downplay the impact of training on battlefield performance, and to focus instead on the more softly focused aspects of morale. In the case of 1 PWRR there was widespread recognition that training made an incalculable contribution to the battalion's success. Toby Walch summed it up with characteristic perspicacity:

> The basics have not changed and still remain for the infantry and, dare I say it, for anyone else entering the combat zone. They are shooting, fundamental fieldcraft, navigation and fitness. Digitize what you like, but without these you have nothing in the military context. And so it proved on our tour to Al Amarah. We as a battalion were fortunate enough to have partially completed a conventional training year under the British Army's Formation Readiness Cycle. The distraction of supporting the government's industrial fight against the firemen in 2003 had prevented

much of this basic training taking place, but this did not deter our deployment to Canada for collective training on the plains of Suffield with our brigade in the autumn of 2003.

This trip proved invaluable on a number of counts. Firstly, it allowed us to spend fifty nights actually soldiering in the field as an armoured infantry organization with our supporting elements. With the continuous drive to push down the military budget this has become an increasingly rare event, but the physical and psychological weathering it provided was vital. You can't replicate in a simulator (though some would suggest you can) the friction, weather and human frailties which make manoeuvring a large number of soldiers difficult and at times frustrating. This experience at BATUS bonded us, forcing us to synergize not only at unit level but equally with our brigade, its headquarters staff and our commander. This along with our theatre-specific pre-deployment training worked, and resulted in an intimate team spirit based on the pillars of a common ethos and mutual understanding at all levels.

During the pre-deployment training much emphasis was placed on the basics, which we demanded from all, no matter what their background or role. It is perhaps not surprising, but still remains interesting, to witness the sharp difference in soldiers' attitudes and performance within an organization that is going to war against one on routine training. Motivated by the reality, soldiers need less motivation and contribute far more in terms of feedback and contribution to getting it right. Their constructive feedback shaped our preparation and at times markedly reorganized our preparation training. The fact that we as a battle group insisted on these basics across the unit proved an absolute life-saver once we had deployed, as statistically the supporting elements (chefs, clerks, vehicle mechanics or the Quartermaster's storemen) were just as much if not more likely to be engaged by the Mahdi army.

The value of training was clearly perceived at the other end of the chain of command. Private Alipate Korovou:

> A gruelling eight weeks' training culminated with a variety of ranges. The ranges were seen by many soldiers as exciting. It was a totally different training altogether from any other operational tours. Our success on the tour was mainly due to the training we undertook on Salisbury Plain and Lydd–Hythe. As a young soldier, I really benefited from the training as it was carried out in a very realistic way . . .
>
> The tour was one of the most memorable ones. It would be difficult for me to personally describe it in detail. Sometimes things are better to be kept to yourself because it brings some bitter memories.

Another Fijian, Private Maciu Tatawaqa, who started the tour in the MILAN Platoon of Y Company and was then attached to 8 Platoon in C Company, wrote: 'all that we learnt in training and OPTAG was useful. For a change we actually did fire and manoeuvre with live rounds and a real enemy . . . The most important thing I learnt was team work and trusting your comrades.' Private Cooper reckoned: 'We have been put in many difficult situations and being this successful could only have been achieved by the relentless bouts and hard work prior to the deployment. All the training carried out at Salisbury, Lydd and Hythe and Castlemartin now seems worth it . . . The events that have taken place here have left us in no doubt why we train one level up.'

An anonymous private soldier, who went to Al Amarah up the dangerous Route 6 in a convoy of soft-skinned vehicles at the very beginning of the tour, testified to the importance of ensuring that everyone in the battle group was ready for the unexpected:

> We were driving up there without armour. It was a convoy of about fifteen vehicles, three lorries and the rest were civvie cars. We also had a low-loader with us. The journey was long and the heat was almost unbearable. Coalition patrols up Route 6 had stopped five days before and we were one of the first to go up it. We were given a hundred

per cent chance of ambush. Just before we hit [illegible] our convoy commander got every top cover up and told us to be alert in the area. There was a sure battle indicator: kids ran from the streets, I knew something was about to happen. Then it did. Two RPGs were fired at us but luckily flew over the top of us. We took some small-arms fire but pushed through the ambush. One of the RPG men was shot dead and others injured. Our convoy continued with no injuries or damage. I couldn't believe how ally [cool, tough] it was and the adrenaline was still going when we reached Abu Naji.

'It's mad, but when you're training for an attack and you hear the usual pop of a gun going off it means nothing,' thought Private Ferguson.

It's only when you hear the clap and bang of a live round landing around you that your body suddenly responds auto-matically by getting your head down. 'What do I do next?' It's at that point, and only at that point, that training kicks in. It's like a little voice within you helping you throughout, saying 'Come on! Pull yourself together! That's right, weapon up, sights on, let's start pulling that trigger, Tom!' You freeze. Anyone who's shared in that first initial moment will know that for a split second your body is in shock, not realizing you're inches away from being a statistic. You think of everything at once yet, in a sense, you think of nothing. Just a numbness fills your body. You get over it, as all men do. But after that contact you look into other people's eyes seeing if they had the same feelings running through them as you did. After a few well deserved fags and some boiling-hot water, you soon realize that you are human after all and you are not one of those weird individuals who thought you were the only one. You weren't; that panic-stricken sense was shared by all. There are some who deny it but it just makes me think that they're afraid to admit it like the rest of us. It's during the contact phase when your brain alters from basic training where your Sgt has always been called

Sgt to the point where he is now being called by his first name. Because during contact, he isn't the bloke who was shouting at you this morning for not doing areas [area cleaning]. Both of you are making sure you return together, safe and sound, from people who don't even believe in areas and are armed with fossilized machine guns trying to take you down.

If someone asked me if my training was good enough for combat, my reply would be this. If I hadn't had this training, irrespective of area cleaning, then I would just be a civvie in uniform. And would a civvie still be here to write this?

THE LAST DETAIL

Over the past twenty years the clothing and equipment issued to British soldiers have improved immeasurably. There was a time when most soldiers supplemented their issue kit by lavish purchases of civilian items, but although most men buy a few extra bits and pieces and the occasional kit fetishist (there is one in every platoon) makes more substantial investments, most men are content with what the quartermaster produces. This is not to say that everything is perfect: there is a strong case for saying that the army needs an everyday dress somewhere between its current combat kit and the smarter (but generally unpopular) khaki jacket and trousers of No. 2 Dress.

For much of his life the soldier wears Soldier 95, a layered cloth-ing system based on a camouflaged shirt, trousers and jacket, with other items like fleeces or waterproof jackets available as required. This has two versions. Uniform issued to individuals serving in tem-perate climates – and, in this instance, to a few unfortunates, mainly individual reinforcements, who had not managed to obtain desert kit before deploying – is made of heavy material with a green/brown camouflage pattern. Desert uniform, worn by almost all soldiers in Iraq, is far lighter, and is coloured pale sand and light brown. According to Major James Driscoll, the issued trousers were 'fine. Lots of guys did not wear underpants in an effort to keep cooler.' Below the shirt soldiers could wear a T shirt: those issued in Iraq were a surprisingly dark brown. They were cooler to wear around camp than shirts

> but did look scruffier and unprofessional . . . so we required guys to wear shirts while moving around camp. I was guilty of making my guys wear shirts, but in my judgement, as we were meeting a lot of the local Iraqis, we had to look professional, even if slightly hot and professional. On patrol you would of course wear a shirt for both appearance and [the fact that] the pockets were useful.

The jacket, rarely worn for much of the year, is hip length with abundant pockets and double stitching to prevent rips from spreading. Slip-on rank badges, worn by all from lance corporal upwards, have now migrated from the shoulder to the centre of the chest, although some of the jackets issued to the advance party had retained epaulettes. They also had buttons which turned a vivid pink when the garments were washed, leading to ribald comments from those with more conventional buttons.

A cloth hat with a floppy broad brim completed the ensemble. It was considered cool and tough (the distinctive army word is 'ally') to trim the edge off the hat, or to wear the brim turned up at the back. The RSM was engaged in a long and earnest guerrilla war against such violators: when I visited the battalion he seemed to have the edge, but there were doubtless parts of the field where allydom ruled unchecked. Indeed, James Driscoll believed: 'It's well known that you can spot a senior officer or a signaller from a distance by their embarrassingly unshaped floppy hats.'

Since its first inception, camouflaged uniform has grown more colourful. In Iraq a Union Jack was worn at the top of one sleeve and a tactical recognition flash (TRF) in the regimental colours – blue/gold/blue – on the other, as well as on the hat. There was a time when the regiment also wore a gold-on-blue tiger arm-badge in combat kit, but despite an attempt to persuade an unsmiling officialdom that this was indeed a TRF – that is, a tiger rearwards facing – the practice has been proscribed. In relatively safe areas, like the vast logistic base at Shaiba, near Basra, soldiers wore stable belts in regimental colours and berets. Our berets are khaki, with a bronze badge which is dull in theory but grows brighter with repeated wearing – or with the zealous but covert rubbing practised by those who wish to give the impression that they have, as it were, been out since Mons.

Desert kit is as comfortable as any uniform can be, but in the heat of Iraq a man's shirt can be black with sweat within minutes. Discomfort is inevitably increased by the fact that a waist-length sleeveless armoured vest is usually worn. It offers a good degree of all-round protection, and the heart area is covered, back and front, by ceramic plates which slide into pockets. I cannot have been alone in reflecting on the fact that there were some parts of me where I would also have welcomed a bit of extra armour. The armoured vest also has facilities for slip-on badges of rank, and there is a widespread tendency for people to write their name and blood group across the top of the front plate pouch. The helmet, made of tough Kevlar, sits widely on the head so that earphones can be worn beneath it, and is kept in place by thick rubber lining bands and a webbing strap. It has a cloth cover of the same material as the desert uniform, which offers opportunities for self-expression – very sharply circumscribed, in 1 PWRR's case, by the zeal of the RSM and his acolytes.

Just as the army has at last managed to issue its soldiers with a durable and practical uniform, so too it is coming closer to solving the problem of boots. There were various sorts of calf-length desert boots about. The best seemed to be all-leather, with a tough fawn suede finish and cleated soles. These belonged to a fortunate minority from which I was certainly excluded. The rest of us had hi-tech boots with thick, heavily cleated soles, uppers made of synthetic material and with metal clips for the laces. There were several different types of this boot on issue.

Most people got on well enough with their boots, but some had real problems with what can most mildly be termed foot-rot. 'By halfway through the tour,' observed James Driscoll, 'everyone I knew had athlete's foot.' Even the best soles found it hard to take the unrelenting assault of hot rock, sand and scorching vehicle decks,

Reservoir Dogs: A Company soldiers returning from patrol

The recce platoon at ease: (*left to right*) Private Scheepers, Private Ratatakoka, Corporal O'Carol, Private Martin, Captain Doyle, Lance Corporal Pearce, Private Libra, Corporal Horme and Private Knott

and 'boots would be in tatters after three months'. The issue socks were incongruously thick and white, probably designed to wick sweat

Accommodation at the Al Tib border post,
with issue desert boots to the fore

away from the skin but also, if I am any judge, thermal. After my first visit to Iraq mine deserved to be towed out to sea and sunk by naval gunfire: I made private arrangements for the next trip.

Over the body armour the soldier carried his essential equipment either in webbing or in a vest. Webbing consists of a waist-belt with a yoke that fits over the body and pouches at front and rear to carry things like loaded rifle magazines and water bottles. The vests were sleeveless waistcoats that had the pouches sewn directly to them. Conventional webbing offered the best displacement of weight but made it hard to manoeuvre in and out of a Warrior or armoured Land Rover (known as a 'Snatch'), while the vest was best for vehicle-mounted soldiers but harder to march in.

There is an evergreen debate about the items that soldiers really need to carry with them. In a place like Iraq men needed water, ammunition and field dressings. Things like extra rations, waterproof sheets that could be converted by the use of hooked rubber cables ('bungees') into shelters (called 'bashas'), and all manner of extra items so useful in exercises in north-west Europe, were a diversion –

and all the more so, as BATUS had shown, because of the limited space in the back of a Warrior. When a man did need to carry more, he had a Bergen, a large backpack with a capacity of about sixty litres. This could be enhanced by the addition of two small side pouches (known as rocket packs because of their resemblance to some kind of sci-fi kit). These can be detached to wear as a smaller pack, but they tend to bounce around and feel uncomfortable, so commercially bought day sacks were often carried instead. Bizarrely, although almost everyone wore uniform of desert hues, most of the webbing was in the green and black of temperate camouflage.

James Driscoll, who was to be bottled up in CIMIC House for much of the tour, had tried carrying his kit in a vest but 'found during pre-deployment training that I couldn't change magazines very quickly with it. So, despite it looking rather "ali", I left it behind in favour of the issued chest rig which, now having had to use it in contacts, was certainly the right decision.'

His webbing contained, he recalled:

> pistol and 2 spare 9mm magazines
> mine-marking kit and mine-prodder (metal tent
>   peg)
> 3 × Cyclum (illuminating) sticks
> several tens of metres of cord
> 6 × SA80 magazines and a bandolier of an extra
>   120 rounds of 5.56mm
> mapping and air photos
> 3 × field dressings
> GPS (global positioning system) and spare batteries
> personal role radio (PRR) and spare batteries
> whistle
> notebook and pens
> small first aid kit
> plasticuffs (plastic handcuffs)
> telescopic baton
> monocular night-vision device
> toothbrush
> some elements of the weapon-cleaning kit

I would also carry a camel-bak of water and an extra bottle of water. If I was going to Abu Naji I would stuff a book in somewhere, as I have often gone to Abu Naji for what should have been a few hours but, because of the security situation in Al Amarah, I could be stuck there for days.

Immediately before departure everyone received a goody bag. This was a huge black holdall containing goggles, a mosquito net (parts of Iraq are malarial), rifle-cleaning kit, long off-white cotton sweat rags (worn in a variety of styles from the gentlemanly cravat, through the utilitarian greasy knot to the frankly Ramboesque head-band), a lightweight sleeping bag and a camel-bak water carrier. The latter was a large water bladder that could be attached to the belt kit, with a hose so that the wearer could drink without the fuss of getting his water bottle out of the pouch. Water discipline was strictly enforced, although few needed reminding of the importance of maintaining their fluid intake. Bottled water was available in huge quantities in Camp Abu Naji, and men swigged it all the time.

If much military kit has had a bad press, the rifle (properly termed the individual weapon, or IW in current jargon) has fared even worse. Its latest iteration is the SA80 A2, a vastly improved version of the original SA80 that generated such adverse comment, and the result of a substantial and expensive re-engineering programme launched in 2002. I encountered nothing but praise for the rifle in its current form: it is widely regarded as 'an excellent weapon', and achieves an overall reliability performance of 94 per cent, compared with the 42 per cent of the US army's M16A2 under similar con-ditions. It is what is called a bull-pup design, with its mechanism located behind the pistol grip which the firer grasps with his right hand. This means that the stock is much shorter than on a conven-tional rifle, but the barrel can still be long enough to maintain accuracy without projecting too far beyond the weapon's green plas-tic handguard, gripped by the firer's left hand.

A magazine holding 30 rounds of 5.56mm ammunition slots in behind the pistol grip. Fitted with a loaded magazine and an optical

Privates Tamani and Kacunisawana of C Company check
the Rarden and chain gun ammunition for their Warrior
at Abu Naji

sight, the weapon weighs just under 5kg, and can be fired either with
single shots or with bursts. Its effective range is some 400 metres,
statistically speaking somewhat less for an individual rifleman and
rather more for an infantry section all firing together. The rifle has
integral iron sights but can be fitted with the common weapon sight,
an image-intensifying night-sight, or – as a matter of routine in the
infantry – the SUSAT, a 4 × magnification optical sight which auto-
matically focuses on whatever is in the centre of its picture. This
occasionally produces difficulties if, say, there is long grass between
the firer and the target, but in general it is an admirable sight.

Also popular was the rifle's sling system. Instead of the familiar
strap that supports the rifle from one shoulder, the SA80 A2 has a
sling that goes across the body. When this is clipped together the
rifle is held firmly against back or chest. With the clip undone the
rifle can be held at arm's length, but is still attached to its owner so
that it will not be lost if he drops it. Unclipping the sling allows the

rifle to be fired, and also enables the bayonet to be fixed and used. The bayonet has a large hollow circular grip which slides over the rifle's muzzle and then clicks into place. It is housed in a plastic sheath with a sharpening stone and saw, and clips to the sheath to make a handy pair of wire cutters. In Iraq, bayonets were carried routinely, and were used at least once in the final stages of an assault on a staunchly defended position.

When 1 PWRR deployed to Iraq there was one light support weapon (LSW) in each four-man fire team. This is based on the SA80 but has a longer barrel with a folding bipod attached to stabilize it during firing, and was designed as a compromise between the rifle and a conventional machine gun. Although it is not without its uses, for its bipod and long barrel give it extra range and accuracy which a good shot can turn to his advantage, it is actually too awkward to use as an assault rifle and it lacks the firepower of a real machine gun (it uses the SA80 A2's thirty-round magazine).

Another member of the fire team carried an underslung grenade-launcher (UGL) mounted beneath the barrel of his rifle. This was one of the major discoveries of my visit, for the weapon is so dead simple that, as one soldier unflatteringly put it, 'even you could use it'. The graphite-coloured UGL is clipped on to replace the rifle's handguard, and its pistol grip and trigger are then seized by the firer's left hand. It fires a 40 mm round, a satisfyingly fat and stumpy explosive projectile with a maximum range of 350 metres but an effective range of perhaps 300. A simple sight, with different apertures for various ranges, flicks up on the left of the UGL, but many soldiers got to know the weapon so well that they fired it by dead-reckoning, lobbing its rounds as one might toss a ball of paper into a waste-paper basket. During the height of the fighting in August, Captain Steve Brooks, on the roof of CIMIC House, spotted an insurgent mortar team bringing their weapon into action about five hundred metres away. An officer told me:

> He had a rifleman's weapon which was fitted with a UGL. However, the sighting system had been broken clean off so the weapon had to be aimed by dead-reckoning. Steve may have fired a round or two through the weapon before,

but as CIMIC House ops officer it wasn't his bread and butter. He pointed the rifle in the direction of the enemy and elevated the barrel to what he believed to be an appropriate degree. One of his men looked on with a smile. Steve fired and the round went wide. It was flying through the air and was never going to hit and he'd clearly got the angle wrong. Then a gust of wind caught the projectile. The grenade arced slowly, dropping in the centre of the mortar team. The soldier beside Brooksie just looked at him and said: 'We're not going to hear much about that, are we?'

The limitations of the LSW had encouraged the off-the-shelf purchase of the Minimi light machine gun, also in 5.56mm but fed by a 100-round disintegrating belt and thus able to provide more sustained fire. The Minimi has a retractable butt which makes it easier to manipulate in confined spaces, but feels a little awkward in the shoulder. It is replacing the LSW as the fire team's suppressive weapon, although the LSW will survive to give the rifle section more accuracy and reach. The Minimi was a popular weapon in Iraq, widely used by soldiers providing top cover from the open roofs of armoured Land Rovers or fired from the back hatch of a Warrior, supplementing the firepower available in its turret.

The 7.62mm belt-fed general-purpose machine gun (inevitably known as the 'gimpy') used to be the section's machine gun, but its weight (nearly 14kg) saw it replaced by the LSW and then by the Minimi. It is equipped with a bipod, but can also be fitted to a tripod to fire out to 1,800 metres, though its tracer round, which enables the detachment to see where their fire is going, burns out at 1,100. Its range and hitting power make it the weapon of choice for the defence of static locations; when I clambered up to the top of the old control tower on the airstrip behind the Shatt al Arab Hotel in Basra, home of the Cheshires, I was heartened to see GPMGs, tripods sandbagged down for added stability, grinning out across the townscape.

Anyone who considered they had the least prospect of being involved in serious combat carried the rifle. Some vehicle crewmen, working in confined spaces, toted the 9mm automatic pistol, but there was a feeling that it was always better to have a rifle at hand. The pistol was popular as a back-up weapon with commanders and gunners, who also had their rifles with them in the turret, for there were moments when there might simply not be enough time to change magazines in a close-range assault by determined enemies who sought to storm a vehicle. Knowing that the probable outcome of capture was decapitation, recorded on a grainy video, most men felt happier with the thought that they had a last argument to hand. Knowing warriors, however, wore their pistols concealed in a webbing vest, as James Rands warns:

> Some people wore theirs as a kind of status symbol, which always raised a smile among the infantry. The naffest thing anyone could do was to wear an elaborate leg holster. Special Forces did this but all manner of visiting REMFs did it as well. Personally, I only ever carried one for a meeting for which we were supposed to be unarmed. However, I was not happy about having a pistol concealed inside my vest as I had often heard of pistols concealed in the front of soldiers' trousers going off and neutering them.

'A lot of soldiers carried an extra pistol,' commented Major James Driscoll.

> I noticed all American troops had a rifle and a pistol. I believe we should all have been issued with two weapons. I heard about one of our soldiers who was caught in a contact with a stoppage he couldn't clear, he was apparently terrified. I made sure I always took two weapons out with me after that.

Lastly, the baton gun, a veteran of Northern Ireland, proved its value in Iraq. This single-shot weapon fires a heavy plastic slug with low velocity, which generally knocks the target off his feet with severe bruising. It was thought 'much preferable to a 5.56mm round when dealing with children throwing petrol bombs'.

*

Perhaps the most striking difference between 1 PWRR in 2004 and a similar battalion ten years before lay in its communications. The British army is currently converting from its existing communication system, known as Clansman, to a new one known as Bowman and, as is so often the case with such things, the conversion process had proved taxing. 1 PWRR had not converted to Bowman before it went, and was using the Clansman series of HF and VHF radios, invaluably reinforced by UHF personal role radios, which enabled soldiers to talk to one another without the need for the bellowed orders of yesteryear. In addition, all vehicles and dismounted commanders were equipped with Clansman radios. For many types of operation it would be usual for individual companies to have their radios on the same frequency on a company net, with company headquarters connected to battalion headquarters (and the headquarters of attached artillery batteries or tank squadrons) on a separate battle group net.

In Al Amarah, however, company nets were discarded in favour of a battle group all-informed net, with all vehicles and commanders able to converse on the same frequency. Forcing company headquarters to man both company and battle group nets would have increased the burden on their signallers. But, more significantly, companies did not operate discreetly, and an all-informed net contributed greatly to the passage of information and thus to the reaction speed across the whole battle group. The use of this sort of net required crisp voice procedure, for there was always the danger of inessential messages getting in the way of more urgent matters. Captain Chris Yates of the QRL commanded a multiple fighting as infantry near CIMIC House in early August, and was being levered out of a tight corner, in heavy contact in the dark, by Warriors:

> The snipers crawled off the rooftop first, and the troop
> followed one by one . . . I left the roof last, a quick scan
> about showing it to be awash with 5.56mm cases, empty
> clips and bandoliers. After a confusing discussion with the
> Warriors about exactly which gate we wanted picking up
> from (the net had become jammed with all sorts of chat,
> including – frustratingly – callsigns unaware of the contact,

radio-checking), we finally piled through the vehicle back doors. Sgt Alsop was luckily close enough to scoop Tpr Barker up, as he missed his footing running for the Warrior. Even as we embussed, the enemy sniper to the north was still putting down rounds in our direction.

Radios are allocated callsigns which are used as a prefix to all communications over the air. Indeed, the notion of a callsign is now so deeply entrenched in military English that the word does duty to designate individuals, subunits or vehicles. On the air, callsigns are spelt out in the army's phonetic alphabet, so A30A is Alpha Three Zero Alpha, W20B is Whisky Two Zero Bravo, and so on. Listen to Corporal Kris Stammers of the Anti-Tank Platoon describing a sharp action in the centre of Al Amarah in mid-May:

> The teams moved round to the back gate where callsign A30A consisting of twelve men commanded by Capt Hooker and Cpl Rob Raynsford and LCpl Dave Larkey would move out first. The route was pretty simple, out of the back gate down to Blue 11, which was a roundabout where A30A would secure for my multiple. A30B would then push through, hang a left and push over a rickety old bridge to Green 9, a second roundabout. This was all routine and both teams had always anticipated the other's next move and positions in which they would hold up. I can't recall what time we left, but up to the point of A30B reaching Green 9 everything went as planned and there was nothing to suspect anything was going to turn bad . . . How wrong could I have possibly been?

In action here are two multiples ('half-platoons', if you will) from the Anti-Tank Platoon, Captain Paul Hooker's A30A and Colour Sergeant Clifton Lea's A30B – over the air, Alpha Three Zero Alpha and Alpha Three Zero Bravo.*

---

* The first letter is the callsign indicator (in this case, A for Y Company), which defines the company; these changed from time to time, and did not necessarily correspond with the company's normal initial letter. At this period battle group headquarters was K, C Company was W, the local Danish battalion (coincidentally,

So much for the theory. In practice, as Captain Steve Brooks observed, it was a case of

> shocking comms throughout. Same old story. However, I hate nothing more than civvies taking the piss about the latest article in the *Mail* or the *Mirror* about *the* army where rifles don't fire and radios don't work. Yes comms are shit, but we are the calibre of soldier . . . to work hard for comms; using Warriors as relays, the full spectrum of HF 320, VHF 353, 352, 351 UHF PRR, sat phones and the most horrendous mobiles were used in concert to achieve the desired result. It is worthy of note that when [the battle at] Yellow 3 kicked off on 16 Apr we had no VHF, POLYGON was down, I achieved comms to battle group from CIMIC by using a PRR relay from the ops room to a bloke on the roof who had to lean over the roof with a mobile phone and relay the first contact report of the tour over Nokia – as the advert goes, '. . . connecting people' . . . like all

The Royal Danish Life Guards, to whom PWRR is affiliated) H, A Squadron of The Lancers D, A Company of The Royal Welch S, and A Company 1 PWRR (the brigade reserve) N. The next two numbers identified the platoon and section. Thus as C Company's callsign indicator was W, W22 (Whisky Two Two) was the second section of its second platoon. The figure 0 identified a headquarters, so that A30 in Corporal Stammers's narrative would apply to the command element of the third subunit of Y company, the Anti-Tank Platoon, and W20 would be the headquarters of C Company's second platoon.

The suffix brings a greater degree of granularity to the identification. A always means a commander, so the commanding officer is K0A and the commander of the second platoon of C Company is W20A. Thereafter things become more complex, with B usually meaning a vehicle: W22B is the second section Warrior of the second platoon of C Company. C is usually used for a subordinate commander: W20C is the platoon sergeant of the second platoon of C Company. Where appropriate, the suffixes C and D refer to the two fire teams in each section: W21C is a dismounted fire team from the second section of C Company. The two figures of callsigns were painted on the sides of vehicles to aid identification.

Lastly, references such as Blue 11 and Green 9 used by Kris Stammers were printed on to the British maps of Al Amarah: they made sense only to somebody using the current edition of any given map and prevented an enemy listening in to radio communications from working out what was happening, but obviated the need for encoding map references. The colours used to designate specified spots also became a general shorthand: 'the Purples' denoted the central area of Al Amarah west of the Tigris, with 'the Greens' on the other side of the river. These have, it goes without saying, been changed since 1 PWRR's tour, so my narrative will give no aid or comfort to an enemy.

aspects of soldiering we had to fight for comms to remain effective. Battalions who have gone to Iraq after converting to Bowman have found things much easier.

When 1 PWRR departed for Iraq it constituted in its ethnic origins a microcosm of British society. Approximately 80 per cent of its officers and men were British white, with 2 per cent British black, 2 per cent British Indian, 1 per cent British Asian and 2 per cent of mixed race. The remainder were what the army terms 'Foreign and Commonwealth', with a substantial slice of Fijians but also Africans, South Africans and soldiers from the Caribbean. About 75 per cent of the battalion's overall strength came from within the regimental recruiting area, with Hampshire providing a solid 25 per cent, Kent 20 per cent and Sussex 13 per cent. About 10 per cent of the battalion came from London, with 3 per cent apiece from Middlesex and Surrey. The Isle of Wight and the Channel Islands (the latter Royal Hampshire territory for many years, as a recurrence of names such as Le Galloudec and Le Patourel demonstrated) provided 1 per cent each.

James Rands describes how these dry percentages were reflected in C Company's 8 Platoon, which he commanded shortly before deployment:

> I myself come from Crowborough near Tunbridge Wells on the Kent–Sussex border. We had soldiers ... from Faversham and other parts of northern Kent, but the numbers were relatively small.
>
> Sgt Adkins comes from Portsmouth, but having been a naval brat he had grown up partly in the Maldives. There are a lot of soldiers and a few officers from either Southampton or Portsmouth, and there is a real rivalry between the two towns much of which comes down to the football teams. For those of us who are neither Hampshire nor adherents of football it all seemed a bit alien.
>
> Geordie Davison was the Warrior sergeant and an ex-WFR [Worcesters and Sherwood Foresters Regiment] soldier who had transferred into the PWRR. When the battalion had re-roled from a light role battalion to a Warrior battalion, about one hundred WFR soldiers had come

across to provide the armoured infantry expertise to help us to re-role . . . This left a cadre of northerners . . . within a southern battalion.

Cpl Adam Llewellyn who became Sgt Llewellyn and took over from Sgt Adkins comes from Richmond, Southwest London. There are a significant number of South Londoners within the battalion who are often mocked by the northerners and Hampshire residents for being cockneys.

Cpl Joe Tagica who was another section commander along with Cpl Llewellyn came from Fiji. The British army has always recruited from other countries and the Commonwealth have provided soldiers for years. Many of the Fijians in the battalion had fathers or uncles who had also served twenty years before . . .

The Fijian soldiers are deeply religious, love rugby and are either teetotal or love heavy drinking. Fijians look a bit like Maoris and the biggest, like Cpl Tagica, are genuinely huge. The Fijians tended to hang around together when off duty and would form a choir which was quite exceptional. Most platoons had three or four Fijian soldiers. One of the remarkable things about the Fijians was that in the UK they would often wander around in shorts and flip-flops in the midst of winter.

There were many Caribbean soldiers . . . The platoon commander's wagon in 8 Platoon was crewed by Privates Troy Samuels and Johnson Beharry. Beharry (the driver) came from Grenada and had witnessed the US invasion as a child. Samuels (the gunner) came from Jamaica, as did Campbell who was in another wagon. Many of the Jamaican soldiers had either been in street gangs or the police, and in many cases Iraq was not the first time they had seen combat. There was a divide within the Jamaicans between the rural and urban Jamaicans which occasionally led to problems, and there was also a problem in that because they came from an extremely macho culture some soldiers had difficulty in backing down in the face of authority – but that is also true of South London soldiers.

Sammy the gunner: Private Troy Samuels, gunner in Warrior W20.
He was to be awarded the Military Cross for his bravery.

In addition there were a few African soldiers like Mensa and Golley-Morgan from Ghana and Sierra Leone respectively, or LCpl Shah from Kenya who had been a TV director in Nairobi before he joined the British army. In about equal numbers to the black Africans were white South Africans, most of whom had British ancestry and were keen to earn a British passport . . . many of these already had technical qualifications or had already worked either at home or in the UK. One of the differences that the Caribbean and African soldiers had from the Fijians was that many of them had family and friends in the UK already and had in many cases lived in the UK for some time.

The rich ethnic mix helped ensure that racism was never an issue. There were, though, sometimes tensions. Initially some of the Fijians – soldiers of proverbial toughness whose predecessors had made a marked contribution to the SAS in the previous major wave of Fijian

A proud Ulsterman in a Southern English regiment in an
Iraqi town: Lieutenant Richard Deane MC

recruiting a generation ago – wondered how the white boys would
cope: they were delighted to tell me later that they had coped very
well.

When James Rands stepped up to be Intelligence Officer he handed
his platoon over to Second Lieutenant Richard Deane, who was to
have the uncomfortable distinction of being the most shot-at officer
in the battle group, with almost three hundred contacts (and two
wounds) to his credit. He was an officer in a Home Service battalion
of The Royal Irish Regiment (a descendent of the Ulster Defence
Regiment), and wore his own beret and cap-badge at appropriate
moments throughout the tour. He also wore them when he was
invested with his Military Cross at Buckingham Palace the following
year.

James Rands concluded his observations with this reflection:

The regiment had many Commonwealth and northern soldiers but it is an avowedly southern regiment and most soldiers and officers came from the south-east of England. There was a mix of the rural and the urban and a range of backgrounds, but there was a great deal of commonality in the soldiers' and officers' experiences. Whenever they sat down together soldiers and officers from broadly the same area would find that they knew some of the same people.

For Sergeant Major Falconer of C Company, it was this that made regimental pride a reality:

Regimental pride is a fact not just because we are the 1st Battalion The Princess of Wales's Royal Regiment, the Tigers, and we will not back down from the fight! That all sounds as if I have been reading the last copy of the regimental journal, which by the way I have not.

It has to do with the fact that we are formed from county regiments. This means that the man next to you could be from your home town and you know him well. Back home you work and socialize with the same people all the way through your career. The effect this has is that when on the radio 'Contact wait out' is heard, all heads turn. 'That's one of our mates who is in trouble. He needs our help!!!'

CHAPTER 3

Into the Crucible

BOOTS ON THE GROUND

MATT MAER WAS TO ADMIT that the circumstances surrounding his battalion's deployment to Iraq in April 2004 were wreathed in 'drama and guesswork'. It seemed clear that, as 2003 drew to its close, Iraq was coming to the end of its honeymoon period with the coalition forces. In the British sector in the south, 1st Battalion The Light Infantry (1 LI), which 1 PWRR would relieve in Al Amarah, had been having an increasingly difficult time. In one incident a company of The Argyll and Sutherland Highlanders, attached to 1 LI, was involved in a sharp little action while searching for weapons in the small town of Qat al Salih, on Route 6. Because of the regiment's favourable recruiting situation we had been able to send a platoon of PWRR soldiers to reinforce the Argylls. This was a popular move within the regiment because at that stage we did not know that the 1st Battalion would deploy to Iraq – attaching a platoon to the Argylls would at least ensure that we gained a smattering of experience from the campaign.

The platoon sergeant, Paul Kelly, distinguished himself in two separate clashes. In one of them his multiple defended a compound under repeated attack from assailants who pressed close enough – under unusually accurate covering fire, suggesting that there were ex-soldiers amongst them – to put satchel charges of explosives against the walls. Although he was wounded early on, he animated the defence by his sheer courage, using an AK dropped by one of the attackers when his own ammunition ran out. His little band were still holding their own when relief arrived two hours later.

For his bravery Sergeant Kelly was to be awarded the Military Cross. To my mind this is quite the most handsome of British gallantry awards, with its simple silver cross suspended from a purple and white ribbon. Instituted in late 1914 as a decoration available only to officers and warrant officers, under John Major's democratization of the awards system it became the 'third level' award for gallantry in action, ranking after the Victoria Cross and the Conspicuous Gallantry Cross, and accessible to all ranks. Although the distinguished regimental forebears of the PWRR could count many Military Crosses over the years, this was the first won by a member of the new regiment. When I wrote to Sergeant Kelly to congratulate him on his award, I confess to a certain frisson: we all felt that he had set the standard, and there was no doubt in anyone's mind that the 1st Battalion – just arriving in Iraq when Sergeant Kelly fought his battle – would live up to it. It was indeed our first MC, but I was confident that it would not be our last.

Matt Maer went out on his first reconnaissance in late November 2003, and began to assimilate the problems posed not just by Iraq in general, where there was already a feeling that the security situation was beginning to shift, but also by Maysan province, whose particular circumstances are explained in Chapter 1. A recce like this is an essential part of the British army's system of battle procedure, ensuring that concurrent activity, the army's term for simultaneous work at several levels, takes place as units prepare for action. It is a telling comment on the situation that he was met at Basra Airport by a white Land Rover which drove him, by night, up Route 6, to Al Amarah. Less than a year later 1 PWRR was only able ·to move up the same route in well armed convoys, and in one twelve-hour period found nine bombs beside the road while doing so. By the time of his second recce, in March 2004, there was a marked sense that a storm was gathering.

If this was beginning to be apparent on the ground, it was far less evident in Whitehall, where there was a hopeful expectation that things were actually improving, and that operations in Iraq would be characterized not by what the army terms 'war-fighting', which had

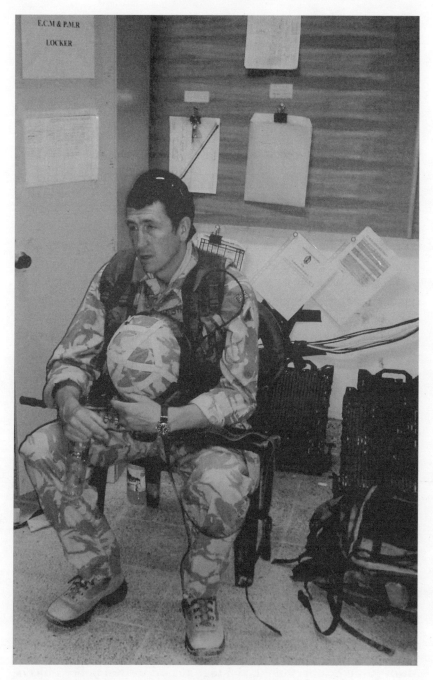

B Company's Sergeant Ben Kelly exhausted in Basra

typified the initial deployment of much of 1st Armoured Division to the Gulf, but by peace support. British forces in the theatre switched their emphasis. Tanks were to be withdrawn although there were, fortuitously, still enough left in theatre to mount A Squadron of The Queen's Royal Lancers in its brazen chariots. The focus was meant to shift from emergency assistance to the infrastructure to the building-up of the Iraqi security forces (ISF). This was to centre mainly on the Iraqi Police Service (IPS), but was also to include the Iraqi National Guard (ING) and smaller organizations such as the border force, the customs police and the highways police. The Iraqi army had been disbanded as a result of decisions made by the Americans soon after the war, and we have already seen the baneful consequences. The ING was an army in waiting: indeed, it has recently re-emerged as the Iraqi army.

The Iraqi law and order structures resembled the American rather than the British model, with towns, highways, traffic and serious crime having different policing structures answering to different chiefs, rather than the UK model of single police forces answering to one chief constable. Under Saddam the real authority had lain with the regime and the Ba'ath Party, and the police were struggling to come to terms with their new role and with the consequences of de-Ba'athification, which had deprived them of many personnel. Although some British soldiers had a poor opinion of the police, others recognized just how difficult their task was. Matt Maer admitted that he was not surprised at the reluctance of the police, wearing shirts and carrying pistols, to go to the same places where he might send a platoon of heavily armed infantrymen in Warriors. David Bradley observed that the police in Basra, headed by a brigadier and with four areas commanded by lieutenant colonels, 'were keen to learn and wanted to gain the trust of the population'. But whether in Basra or Al Amarah, the police, living in the community, were influenced by a variety of external factors and, as Major Bradley gently put it, often 'disappeared at important times'.

Major Justin Featherstone had a high regard for two police officers who worked closely with him at CIMIC House. One – let us call him

Warrant Officer Ayub – had 'bullish courage only matched by his loyalty', and when he heard that a previous battle group had lost one of its PRR he determined to recover it.

> When his father was murdered by Saddam's men, Ayub waged an independent war against the regime with his brother, personally killing fifty-two soldiers and policemen, one for every bone in his father's body. In character, he donned a dirty dish-dash and a shemagh and followed the enemy's patrols, with only a radio and a sidearm for protection. After a week, he identified the militiamen with the PRR as normally the enemy's 'tail end Charlie'. From a position in the souk, he jumped the fighter, wrestled the radio from him, and then ran back the kilometre and a half to CIMIC House. When presented with the recovered item, I was rendered simply speechless by this selfless action.

In one sense any campaign is unique, with characteristics that set it apart from any other, no matter how similar, and the complexities of Iraq mean that any attempt to impose upon it 'lessons' rigidly derived from another campaign is doomed to failure. But there are general truths that link what is going on in Iraq, even as I write, with many of the more complex, part-unconventional conflicts in history. There have been conventional wars in which the defeat of one side's armies in the field has, in and of itself, led to the victor being able to impose his terms upon the vanquished. The defeat of Napoleon at Waterloo in 1815, and of Germany in 1918 and 1945, are cases in point. Here, the losing side's social fabric usually remains largely intact, even if, for a time, the victor asserts his authority by imposing national and provincial governors.

But there have also been wars in which victory and defeat in the field have not necessarily decided the conflict, and in which the war's real centre of gravity has not so much been the regular armed forces of the adversaries as the population of the contested area. Here both the American War of Independence and the Vietnam War are useful examples. In the former the British won most (though by no means all) of the major battles, and even at the war's end retained a substantial military capability in North America and elsewhere. In the latter the Americans, as an exasperated US colonel observed to a North Vietnamese officer, had lost no major battle. 'That may be so,' replied the Vietnamese, 'but I fail to see the relevance of your point.' Winning and losing some sorts of war, in short, are far less a consequence of conventional military victories than of being able to command – by the use of the stick, the carrot, or, more usually, by a judicious mixture of both – the support of the majority of the population.

It is, then, popular support that represents the real objective of both sides. In this sense the British term 'hearts and minds', first coined by the then Lieutenant General Sir Gerald Templer in the Malayan emergency of 1948–60, has much to commend it. The conflict in Iraq was not a conventional one in which the defeat of the Iraqi army and the overthrow of Saddam Hussein would leave a decapitated but unified state readily amenable to the control first of an American administrator and then of its own democratically elected government. It was, and remains, a struggle to obtain at least the tacit support of the population. The ISF form the meat in the sandwich, neither wholly trusted by the coalition nor welcomed by all their countrymen, but both an inaccurate barometer of the state of Iraqi opinion and ultimately a key element in furnishing that 'soft security' without which there can never be a peaceful Iraq. It is no surprise that the insurgents devote so much of their time to attacking the ISF, just as in the North America of the 1770s and 1780s the 'Tory' militias and irregulars were the particular targets of 'patriot' vengeance.

None of this should have been a shock. Previous British military experience in Iraq both during and after the First World War demonstrated that even in an area where nationalism was far less well defined than it was in Europe, a combination of factors made the exploitation of conventional military victory extraordinarily difficult. There was then, as now, the unifying strength of Islam (despite the Sunni/Shi'a rift); tribal tensions and Kurdish separatism; and the fact, as an exasperated Turkish staff officer observed of the First World War, that 'the tribesmen of Lower Mesopotamia merely looked upon the war as a means of personal profit and were always ready to back the winning side'. The rapid internationalization of the 2003 war, so easily discernible across the whole of the Muslim world (an Egyptian friend, consciously plagiarizing that arch-cynic Talleyrand, described coalition policy to me as 'worse than a crime ... it is a mistake'), made it even less likely that the verdict of battle would be readily accepted. It is possible that had the coalition been ready to exploit the brief honeymoon period that followed its victory with the rapid rebuilding of the battered infrastructure and the nourishment of soft security, then the slide towards disorder might have been checked early on. But by the time the coalition bent its nerve towards these objectives the metronome had ticked on, and events on the ground were moving faster than the coalition's policy-makers reckoned.

When Lieutenant Colonel Maer conferred with Lieutenant Colonel Bill Pointing, CO of 1 LI, at Al Amarah in March 2004 their objective was to meet the policy requirement to support the ISF. 'As a result,' wrote Matt Maer,

> the Light Infantry, and ourselves in turn, were to organize so that virtually every man was to be engaged in either training or mentoring the ISF, with one company (C Company) the only reserve, in its Warriors. The Light Infantry had done a great deal of the staff work on how to achieve this situation, and I returned from the final reconnaissance having blatantly plagiarized their laydown, changed the company titles to reflect our own, and, the day before we were to leave on pre-tour leave, briefed the company commanders on their new roles. It was to be one of the most inappropriate sets of instructions I was to give.

And yet there were elements of this requirement that remained valid throughout 1 PWRR's time in Iraq. This was an instance of what US Marine General Charles Krulak called a 'three-block war'. As he saw it, in one city block, troops might be distributing food in a peace-support operation; in an adjoining block they might be patrolling, armed, in peace enforcement; and in a third block they might be at it hammer and tongs, war-fighting; all at the same time and all in the same city. Matt Maer fully agreed with the 'three-block war' concept, as he was to remark of other attempts at verbal simplicity:

The army often reduces the most complex concepts into pithy phrases or sayings; with mixed results. In Iraq at one time such a phrase was 'Smile, shoot, smile'. It conveyed the situation that many UK soldiers found themselves in: at one moment dispensing aid and assistance, training the police and carrying out the traditional tasks of 'winning hearts and minds'; next, engaged in a vicious firefight for their lives, before returning again to a softly, softly approach. It could also be argued that this was what the locals did to the UK forces. The phrase, used so often in our training, was to haunt me after a particularly nasty firefight when, having extracted from the ambush site to safety, one of my soldiers turned to me and said, 'Can we smile again now, sir?' A deft touch of irony, I felt.

There is rivalry amongst the armed forces. For much of the time it is good-natured (witness the annual Army v Navy rugby match at Twickenham). There are times when it hones a sharper edge. And there are times when it is downright hostile. In early April the battalion flew out from Royal Air Force Brize Norton, near Witney in Oxfordshire, in circumstances that exacerbated the tension between the army and the RAF, and even between the army and the movements staff of its own Royal Logistic Corps. This goes beyond simple rivalry, as one officer explains:

It borders on hatred and sits for the most part at loathing. It is their responsibility to move the men and materials required to carry out operations from their base, generally in the UK or Germany, to the theatre of operations. It is an unglamorous but necessary task and, on the surface, routine – a move from point A to point B. However, the 'movers' of both services combine to make it the most painful, drawn-out and seemingly badly run affair. They have done so consistently throughout my time in the army and our move to Iraq was to prove no exception. Despite our base at Tidworth being little more than an hour away from the airfield . . . we were to move there at least twelve hours prior to our flight. The reason for this was not explained to me or my staff. I still do not understand it to this day. Having taken our farewells of our families – in some cases tearfully – we sat at Brize Norton while nothing happened for hour upon hour. There was nobody above the rank of a junior NCO present and no evident reason necessitating our being there. It was annoying.

The journey began in the relative comfort of an elderly RAF Tri-Star, which took about four hours to reach the huge American-built base at Al Udeid in Qatar. Major James Coote of C Company was not impressed by what he called

a lesson in military excellence. It takes a civil airline two hours to check in five hundred strangers to fly abroad. Not so our armed forces who (at four hours' notice) demand the presence of two hundred carefully vetted soldiers twelve hours before the flight was due to take off, as they 'needed to sort our luggage out into three piles'. I would love to blame the RAF for this, but, sadly, there was some army input too. We passed the time sleeping on the floor until our plane was ready (somebody had forgotten to refuel it, so we had to go back to the terminal for more floor-lying) and then flew to Qatar. Here we slept on a tent floor for a bit before cramming into a C-130 Hercules (the only air-craft fitted with the anti-missile stuff) and landed at Basra International Airport. More floor-lying on Saddam's luxuri-ous marble, this time before being crammed into a coach to drive to the acclimatization centre. Fortunately, the coach curtains were drawn to provide some RPG protection.

Major Chris James, who flew out to replace Major Coote in command of C Company in August, was no more fortunate, and reported 'a quite dreadful thirty hours' (when I got here it turns out thirty hours was a good run – others had much longer) travelling nightmare, courtesy of the RAF'.

Sergeant Chris Adkins was part of the advance party that flew out on 3 April. He had recently handed over command of 8 Platoon to Second Lieutenant Deane and was now in the intelligence section, which was not his natural environment. But even he found the final section of the flight elating:

> The initial flight into Iraq from Al Udeid was a kick in the arse for me – I couldn't believe it, here we were low-level tactical flying into theatre in a C-130J with all defensive suites switched on, lights out. The hairs began to stand on end on the back of my neck, fuck me, I thought, this is it, we are going into a hostile area, about fucking time – let's show them what we are about. Then it dawned on me I had handed over the much coveted 8 Platoon C Company just two months earlier – fuck, I was pissed off with the Irish platoon commander 2Lt Deane who had needed operational experience. What did I have now – just a stint of sitting in the intelligence cell, deep joy!

From Basra Airport the troops travelled by coach to Shaiba Logistic Base (SLB), less than an hour's drive away. Shaiba, often known to combat troops as Shaibiza after its alleged resemblance to the popular resort, then had a very poor reputation. I stayed there in May 2005 and found it wholly transformed. In 2004, though, it was not an inspiring place for a combat soldier. 'I couldn't believe it,' thought Sergeant Adkins,

> after the euphoria of having such an operational flight in. I was astounded at the oasis that was SLB – there were girls in civvies looking and smelling great, bars, shops, even a live band . . . Over the next few days they gave us lots of bone lectures on health and hygiene, the threat, and loads of other shite which had no relevance, from fat REMFs who didn't know their arse from their elbow anyhow. They were just looking forward to tonight's entertainment in the all-inclusive resort that is Shaibiza.

James Coote was equally unimpressed.

> Those of you in the army will be familiar with the rear echelons and will be glad to know that this was no exception. Shops, cafés and bars, eerily cloned from those in Kosovo, were present in abundance to ensure that our logis-

ticians didn't feel too uncomfortable. The only danger facing them was D[iarrhoea] and V[omiting], notorious in the camp . . .

We were required to spend three days there to acclimatize and, needless to say, the army invented lots of nugatory stuff to keep us busy. We were welcomed on our first night by being mortared, but with no ammunition or body armour the immediate action drill was to roll over and go back to sleep.

The second day involved another nervous coach ride to 'the ranges' – a bit of desert (on an old Iraqi airfield) with some targets stuck in. As I tucked into my packed lunch which comprised exactly the same sausage roll and inedible fruitcake that we get in the UK, no doubt specially flown in on a 747, I was amazed to see that the army had managed to produce sausage rolls in the middle of the desert that were still frozen. How do they do it? The whole scene was made all the more surreal by my eavesdropping on the conversation of two cavalry officers behind me who were discussing the relative merits of the Harrods and Harvey Nicks food-halls.

The advance party had been busy assembling the body armour for the whole of the battle group. 'This was completed in just a day in two sittings,' wrote Sergeant Adkins, 'and those who could still feel their thumbs even managed to eat as well.' The 'range day', unpopular though it was, ensured that everyone in the battle group could check that their weapons were properly zeroed. 'After a day of solid firing,' exulted Chris Adkins, 'we had the tick in the box and could get out of this REMF paradise.'

Matt Maer had headed up to Al Amarah immediately he arrived in Iraq. While he waited at Brize Norton the continuously rolling Sky News, the only form of entertainment in the departure lounge, featured images of a quickly imploding situation in Iraq as Muqtada al-Sadr urged his followers to take direct and violent action against the coalition forces: there were scenes of rioting, bombing and shooting against British troops in the very area that the 1 PWRR battle group was to deploy to.

The deteriorating situation had so caught the media interest that I was interviewed whilst waiting by both Sky and ITN news crews about the situation and our forthcoming deployment. The angle the news teams were taking was very much one of the two events [the deteriorating security situation and the deployment] being linked. While I could not comment on the situation in theatre I could reassure them that our deployment was a routine one and offer some bland remarks along the lines that we would seek to assist in the stabilization of the situation through negotiation as much as action. Ironically we were to remain waiting for our plane so long that the crews had time to file their stories, for them to be edited and for us to see them on the very screens we were watching at the airport long before our departure. The broadcasts were met with much cheering and jeering.

He had no sooner arrived at Camp Abu Naji than the place was mortared, and he spent his first night there sitting outside with Molly Phee of the US State Department, smoking; he went from being a sporadic smoker to a forty-a-day man in the course of the tour. Sitting outside was, as he observed, not something that would be done so lightly subsequently.

American troops serve a year's tour of duty in Iraq, often for the whole time in the same place. I met four men of the Texas National Guard at the Safwan rebroadcasting site; they would share the same hilltop hut for a year, and were proud to be doing their patriotic chore. Most Americans I spoke to in Iraq linked their presence there to the events of 9/11, and few were amenable to my elegant academic arguments that Saddam was not directly involved in the planning of that outrage.

There is something of a received wisdom in Britain that the Americans in Iraq are uniformly hopeless and trigger-happy. 'All the gear – no idea', and 'All the kit – full of shit' are two of the most commonly heard putdowns, often uttered by those who have never served in Iraq. That the Americans have made mistakes is not in question: the decision to disband the Iraqi army may eventually emerge as the single biggest coalition error. Thomas White, formerly US Assistant Secretary of Defense, called it 'a terrible decision . . . [that] immediately made a bad situation a lot worse.'

At an individual level the average American soldier may not be as familiar as his average British counterpart with 'the small change of war', for years of experience in Northern Ireland and the Balkans have given the British valuable skills in what General Sir Rupert Smith calls 'war among the people'. Yet it is hard to resist the conclusion that this is the army of the world's only superpower engaged in what its leaders regard as a conflict of necessity, not one of choice. The British army goes on operations and its units serve in Iraq for six-month tours. But the US army is at war, and this conviction helps shape much of what it does, not least its preparedness to inflict and sustain casualties. The US assault on Fallujah received a uniformly bad press in Europe. What was drowned out in the torrent of abuse was the abundant evidence (credible to this potential critic) found of the presence of 'foreign fighters', the use of mosques for the storage of weapons, ammunition and explosive, the torture and murder of hostages (one was rescued alive, and there was uncut video footage of the beheading of Ken Bigley). Had Fallujah been in the British sector it is unlikely that it would have been allowed to remain in insurgent hands. While we may suspect that British methods may have differed from those employed by the Americans, wresting an urban area from a determined and well armed opponent has never been a pretty business.

The Americans do some things better than the British. They have put huge amounts of money and effort into the reconstruction of Iraq through CIMIC projects. They have available a weight and texture of airpower that dwarfs the RAF's contribution. Indeed, during 1 PWRR's time in Al Amarah almost all the offensive air support was American. Soldiers from C and Y Companies were eager to talk to me about the effectiveness of the AC-130 Spectre gunship, whose squadron motto was 'You can run, but you'll only die tired'. It provided not simply accurate all-weather surveillance, like the RAF's Nimrod, but it could do something about the targets it identified, quickly earning the confidence of the troops on the ground so that its fire could be called in to within 100 metres of their positions; there was no trigger-happiness there. Its effect on morale was palpable, not least because of its patter on the battle group net, with a rich Tennessee voice announcing, 'You got love from above . . . You got fire from the sky.' Spectre may indeed be old technology (like the Chinook helicopter, the aircraft was first used in Vietnam) and, as its RAF critics rightly point out, may be useless in many tactical circumstances, but some of 1 PWRR's soldiers undoubtedly owe their lives to the ability of Spectre crews to understand the ground battle, and weigh in with super-accurate fire at midnight in a burning town.

Matt Maer argued that there was indeed a special relationship between the British and Americans, although it was

> frequently criticized and often mocked both domestically in the UK and amongst some of my British military colleagues. But without their close air support many more of the battle group would have died or been injured due to enemy action. Both their close air support and Special Forces gun ships exemplified professionalism, restraint and bravery . . . It is this aspect of our tour which received the least publicity and continues to annoy me immensely. The ignorance and misunderstanding particularly by the British media and hence our public often beggars belief and represents a popular misconception. What impressed me most about this relationship was the speed with which our commanders and soldiers synchronized in understanding and developed a slick modus operandi with the US aircrew, despite to this day never physically having met. This was based on a common purpose and mutual respect. Every officer and soldier within the battle group, but particularly those who witnessed (through necessity) the US support at 'danger close', has nothing but praise and thanks for our coalition partners.

These comments on the Americans were triggered by my first mention of Molly Phee, the State Department's representative in Al Amarah. She spoke fluent Arabic, and had served in the region for fourteen years. When stateside she had worked in Washington on desks responsible for Arab nations. As Matt Maer wrote:

> She was able to get things done locally, with politicians and community leaders, because she spoke their language and understood their history, outlook and social structures. She could do the same with Baghdad and Washington for the same reasons. For the same reasons the commanding officer would only do his best with both: to limited success.

Captain Steve Brooks, Ops Officer of Y Company for the first half of the tour, caller her

> a tiger of a woman. Fearless and dedicated, and sympathetic to our plight. She would regularly visit the ops room to see if we were OK and pass the time as we cleared the camp after an attack. No matter how bad things got in those first few months she never once faltered or looked remotely interested in leaving for her own safety.

In Maysan province there was not a single official of the British Foreign and Commonwealth Office to provide political, cultural or any other form of advice. The commanding officer, an infantryman with a degree in agricultural economics, was left to get on with it. There were indeed two UK policy advisers (POLADs) who served with the battle group during its time in Al Amarah. Neither had a diplomatic background, spoke any Arabic, or had worked in or on the region; one came from a weapons procurement background. They were regarded as 'marvellous individuals who worked long and hard for the good of the battle group, [but] there was little that they could do to make a difference'.

Equally, there was little real help with reconstruction and aid projects. The Department for International Development (DfID) was not represented. The members of the CIMIC team, most of them officers and NCOs of the Territorial Army, initially ran their projects from CIMIC House in Al Amarah itself, despite the fact that it was under attack for part of the time. We shall see, later on, that the impact of these efforts was not inconsiderable. But what was lacking was a joined-up policy connecting Whitehall to Al Amarah. 'The fallout from this lack of support was twofold,' thought Matt Maer.

> Firstly, political and development issues did not progress as fast or as effectively as they could have. This in turn meant that the seeds of dissatisfaction, which led to a great deal of the violence, were able to germinate and grow in an environment of dissatisfaction, disillusionment and failed expectations. As a result the security situation would deteriorate and so the FCO and DfID would not be able to send personnel on to the ground. It was a vicious cycle of non-engagement.

Most of the four subunits of the 1 PWRR battle group, the battalion's own C and Y Companies, A Squadron of The Queen's Royal Lancers and A Company of The Royal Welch Fusiliers, arrived in Al Amarah in the second week of April, with vehicles moving up Route 6 and most personnel being flown in C-130s to a desert airstrip – concrete runways but no buildings – codenamed Sparrowhawk, just north of Camp Abu Naji. Relieved as he was to be leaving Shaiba, Major James Coote was not at his best:

> Our escorts arrived looking a bit flustered as they had just been in a gun battle on the way to pick us up, and we loaded on to another coach (curtains tightly drawn now!) for the airport. Our route was modified by an inconsiderate Iraqi who had left a car bomb at the front gate. Our driver was a master of coach off-roading. Cross country, driving at 70 the wrong way along the motorway or skipping the central reservation all provided no challenge for him ... I won't take any crap off Beeline coaches in Warminster in future; coaches can go anywhere! ... Eventually, we crammed into the middle seats of a Hercules again, shoulder to shoulder with all our kit on, to ensure that the maximum number of comfortable seats at the front was left for the loadmaster. As we took off as vertically as a Hercules can, the reassuring stench of chaff being fired filled the cabin. We levelled out briefly (all now crammed at the rear

of the centre) and then began a dive for the deck again, breathing more chaff fumes and now crammed at the front of the centre. We landed on yet another Iraqi airfield and were unceremoniously hoofed out by the now very nervous loadmaster – never a good sign. As the last Bergen came off the ramp the pilot put his foot down and was gone.

Sergeant Adkins, sworn enemy of all base-rats, was delighted by the change of scenery:

> We flew out of Basra by C-130 and landed after a thirty-minute flight in a deserted airfield with some red fire engines around us. Already this looked a hundred times better than the last dump and had the air of an old British outpost. Away from all the tossers in slipper city. We were bundled into an eight-tonner and driven for twenty mins to camp Abu Naji, soon to gain the name 'camp incoming'. As we jumped off the truck it was plain to see this place would be offering the basics in comfort – it was a real shit hole just as I like it . . . Once my bags were dropped off I quickly set about exploring the camp and finding my place of work. It was worse than I had first anticipated, just an office full of the sort of people I had always tried to distance myself from . . . I was back to miserable mode and set about trying to get a move anywhere out of there.

His chance would come soon enough.

By this time the Mahdi army uprising was in full swing. Further north, the towns of Al Kut and Nasiriya had been overrun, and in Al Amarah itself CIMIC House was surrounded and there were some three thousand demonstrators on the streets. On 6 April it was reported:

> Hostilities have continued between the Sadr/Mahdi army and coalition forces in Al Amarah. There have been sporadic periods of contacts involving small arms, RPGs, blast devices and 1 × IED which have generally been short-lived. Dialogue has been maintained with all key interest groups

in Al Amarah, including Abu Hatim [Maysan province interim governing council representative], Governor Riyadh [Maysan province and brother of Hatim], Abu Muslim [Da'wa party] and the Sadr leadership.

Both CIMIC House and Camp Abu Naji were mortared, and there were frequent attacks on mobile patrols in Al Amarah, with Warriors apparently the targets of choice, probably because the Mahdi army 'was anxious to mobilize public support for its cause by creating a perception of significant capability'. The Light Infantry, still in command pending the imminent transfer of authority to 1 PWRR, assessed that the Sadr was strengthening its demands in view of the impressive local support it had received, and that locally its aim was to achieve the withdrawal of coalition forces from Al Amarah or even from the whole of Maysan province.

FIRST BLOOD

As 1 PWRR's officers started to take over from their counterparts in 1 LI, they were subjected to a number of attacks: one pair of company commanders was engaged over a dozen times during the period of their handover. There were fierce little battles as companies of the two battle groups worked side by side in the last stages of the process. Private Sewell of C Company's 'Mighty Eight' remembered how it was for him:

Al Amarah is a very poor city with very little money and the people that live there have a very poor quality of life. The first thing you notice about the city is that it has a real bad smell about it. This is due to two main reasons, the first being that its sewage system is almost nonexistent meaning most of the human waste ends up on the streets. The second reason is that there is a small handful of brick factories situated next to each other and they burn certain materials that adds to the terrible smell. From my experiences the

Downtown Al Amarah

smell is so bad that when you are on top cover in a Land Rover, it really burns your eyes and nose.

... we were deploying on to what we believed to be a peace-keeping operation. That idea lasted approximately twenty-four hours. On arriving at the base location, C Company along with B Company 1 Light Infantry were deployed to the city to deal with an incident that turned from bad to worse in a short space of time ... For me, this was my first operational tour and I do not think anything could have prepared me for the next four months ... The contact was definitely a planned ambush on the coalition force callsigns as they moved through the location at that time. Unlucky for the enemy, I don't think that they were expecting such an aggressive response. If you talk to any-one involved in the contact, they would tell you that the rooftops were crawling with numerous gunmen equipped with a range of weaponry from AK-47s to RPGs.

Once everyone had returned to base, there was a differ-ent atmosphere amongst the men, especially C Company as we were in the thick of it. From my point of view, I think that B Company 1 Light Infantry had mixed feelings about everything that happened that day. For them, they were just about to return home and were probably feeling that this was not what they needed so close to the end of their tour. For me, I felt excited, scared and relieved.

In contrast, Lance Corporal Laird of 7 Platoon gained enormous confidence from the charisma of the Light Infantry platoon sergeant for whom he was acting as gunner.

He was a monster of a bloke who had really been hitting the weights big time and had the darkest tan I had ever seen. Just an aura of confidence beamed off him. He introduced himself as Oggie and immediately set about ragging and taking the piss out of me. I felt safe with him, as if he could get us out of any situation we would get ourselves into.

James Coote acted as gunner in his opposite number's Warrior during the handover so that, together in the turret, they could exchange information.

Fortunately for us the locals believe that their only role in the whole shooting thing is pulling the trigger . . . Unfortunately if you fire that many rounds eventually one or two will hit, and we sustained four casualties during Sunday's battle. All are OK, very lucky, at home now in UK. We don't know how many Iraqis died but several of my soldiers returned several chain gun rounds . . . I was gunning for the outgoing OC and fired 200 7.62mm at three very persistent RPG men who would not get the message. I can't confirm what happened to them, but they didn't come back after the last 100-round burst. It was just as well as we might have had to start using 30 mm and I might have had a harder task assuring the SIB [special investigations branch of the military police] that my actions were within the rules of engagement. It is impossible to describe the emotions I felt as the stupid bastards kept coming back to the same place to try and RPG us; I was left with no option but to shoot them before they killed one of us. Perhaps they are happily with their twenty virgins now. Perhaps (more likely, my sergeant major says) I missed them all.

These first contacts were an eye-opener to Sergeant Major Falconer:

Not until the return to camp when all callsigns were extracted off the ground did the effect on the soldiers come to light. They were keen to get back into the fight. I had thought that when small arms and RPG are all incoming to the Warrior, to send the dismounts out of the back of an armoured vehicle which offered some protection might require the use of a crowbar. Quite the opposite is true. From my own experience, the feeling of being sat in the back of a tiny box out of control of your own destiny sends you out into the incoming fire where at least you as an individual can return fire and so have a direct effect on the situation. Add to this the increased situational awareness by opening your fields of view; it is very disconcerting to watch RPGs fly past your 3-inch vision block and have no idea where they came from!

Private Kenny Hills of 7 Platoon agreed:

It wasn't until I arrived in Al Amarah that I realized that this is the real deal, this is the time I finally get to put my four and a half years of training into use . . .

I remember my first contact clearly, it was surreal – there were Iraqis riding around on bicycles whilst RPGs and rockets were flying everywhere. I recall the boys from the company when we got back to camp were so pumped up including myself, I'm sure every single man would have gone back out to take on an army with just sticks in our hands. It wasn't till later that day when it hit you and you thought, fuck me, that was madness, that was real. I will also remember the fear I have felt on this tour. I really did fear for my life and the lives of my friends.

His mate Private Bobu Cham commented:

> This was basically the first test for the troops on the ground.
> You could see fear and anger in everyone's face because
> it was the first time most of the troops in my regiment
> experienced being fired at with live rounds. It was hard for
> most of us to believe it but we had to face it and act accord-
> ingly because that was what we all joined the army for.

1 PWRR assumed command of the Maysan province area of operations from 1 LI at 0730 on Sunday 18 April. The situation was
deteriorating rapidly, with repeated violence in Al Amarah itself and
the rebuff of a joint PWRR/LI patrol in the town of Majar Al Kabir
to the south, where a party of Royal Military Police soldiers had been
murdered the previous year. Captain Marcus Butlin was a Territorial
in 3 PWRR who had been compulsorily mobilized:

> The brown envelope that arrived on the Saturday morning
> had been quite a surprise, but I had volunteered when I
> joined the TA and knew that compulsory mobilization was
> always a chance. Six weeks later I reported to the reserves
> Training and Mobilization Centre, Chilwell [Nottingham-
> shire], for two weeks of administration and training. Then
> I reported to 1 PWRR to join C Company as second-in-
> command and operations officer.

Marcus's father had been second-in-command of the rifle company I commanded, and I had known Marcus since he was in a
push-chair. Had I known that fate would put him in harm's way as
often as it did, I would have been even more worried about what I
might find myself saying to Mike and Mary if the worst happened.
His Land Rover patrol went down to Majar Al Kabir.

> The town didn't seem particularly welcoming, probably in
> response to the violence that was going on in the rest of
> the country. My first meeting with the locals was a little
> unnerving, as I kept thinking about what might go wrong.
> But in the end all seemed OK. It was when we were about

Lieutenant Colonel Bill Ponting, CO of ILI (*left*),
Lieutenant Matt Maer, CO of 1 PWRR, and RSM Shaun
Whyte (*right*) on flag day, Sunday 18 April 2004

300 metres out of town heading home that we came under
fire. I was top cover when I heard the first shots. It wasn't
till the second burst that I realized what it was. By then so
had everyone else. The Land Rover accelerated as I tried
to locate the enemy. A loud bang and a cloud of dust, 100
metres to our flank, told us that an RPG had missed. Once
out of the killing area we debussed and took cover. There
was still fire coming from the edge of town now aimed at
the last two Land Rovers, which were behind us. Two things
struck me, both of which I had heard before, from speaking
to World War Two veterans. First, why is someone who
doesn't even know me trying to kill me, and secondly, how
difficult it is to locate the enemy.

'Although we did not know it at the time,' admitted Matt Maer, 'this was to be the last time a coalition soldier was to enter Majar Al Kabir during our tour.'

Late on the morning of the handover Matt Maer left Camp Abu Naji with his rover group to drive up to CIMIC House. He intended to have lunch with Molly Phee and Ambassador Patrick Nixon, then the UK representative in Basra, and to meet Major Justin Feather-stone, whose Y Company was garrisoning CIMIC House, for the first time since the assumption of command. All was fine on the move up Purple Route into the city, although traffic was, as ever, heavy, and the bridges over the Tigris congested. The rover group crossed the Tigris over the bridge and on to the east bank of the river at Yellow 3, near the Office of the Martyr Sadr (OMS) building, but it was quiet, and there was no incident.

On arrival at CIMIC House, the vehicles were parked up while the CO went off for his meeting. Captain Nick Thasarathar, riding top cover that day to gain experience, went into CIMIC House to visit the G5 cell (responsible for civil-military cooperation), 'where most of my TA colleagues were working to help develop Al Amarah's woeful civilian infrastructure. The guys chilled out in the shade of a few palm trees, some catnapped, others talked football, girls, nights out on the town, the usual squaddy banter.' After lunch the rover group began to move back to Abu Naji, but it had scarcely set off when it received a radio message that communications had been lost across the area, so it followed the standard precaution of moving at once to the nearest base, CIMIC House. 'The reasons for this were sound,' argued Nick Thasarathar. 'If while transiting the city you came under contact, you would not be able to call for any support.'

As the group made its way in its Land Rovers through the back streets of one of the hardest areas of Al Amarah (something incon-ceivable shortly afterwards) it was shot at, first by a gunman whose fire was so inaccurate that it was not even certain that he was engaging the party, but then by a low-velocity weapon, probably a pistol, whose round popped past the rear of Thasarathar's vehicle. On its return to CIMIC House the party dismounted and sat down in the shade of some nearby trees, waiting for the radio problem to be fixed, while the RSM went to have his hair cut. 'The circuit must have taken no more than five minutes,' reckoned Thasarathar, 'but that was long enough to change most people's outlook on the day ahead. We felt like ducks on a fairground shooting range. We were pissed off and frustrated that we had not been able to hit back at the unseen gunmen.'

There was suddenly a burst of firing to the south: one of Y Company's patrols had been engaged near the OMS building, and Corporal Daz Williamson had been hit. 'For a moment I thought of my options,' wrote Matt Maer:

> I could move to the Y Company operations room to assist in the incident there; I could try to push back to Abu Naji via another route to my own operations room; or I could deploy on to the ground. All had merit. However, a second radio message stated that the patrol had sustained a casualty and were under heavy fire. It was evident that Lt Steve Brooks could run his own ops room in CIMIC and I would waste time getting to Abu Naji. It was equally evident that my team were closest and could get to the injured and pinned-down the fastest. We mounted up, leaving Agnes my interpreter at CIMIC, and moved down the road towards the contact location.

The RSM was summoned back, half shorn, from his haircut. Nick Thasarathar observed:

> LCpl Phillips and Pte Mackenzie went through some bizarre Jamaican hand-slapping ritual that was their way of saying 'Let's go for it.' I watched and smiled – that simple gesture reminded me so much of my own youth, waiting on the start line at Operation Granby, ready to commence our first full-scale battle against the then Iraqi army of Saddam Hussein. Nervous but united, firing our men up. I knew I was witnessing a rite of passage for these two young men, and bizarrely I was happy for them in some small way. Perhaps the years in between had made me forget the sheer chaos and horror that war can be. Whatever my feelings

were at that moment, I was about to get reacquained with
the beast in the next couple of minutes.

Sergeant Danny Mills's multiple (accompanied by Major Tait, a
TA Black Watch officer who worked in the operations support group
in CIMIC House) had left CIMIC House at about 1500 and patrolled
the neighbouring area, putting in a temporary vehicle checkpoint
near Blue 6, then calling in to the police station near the OMS
building. He spoke to three policemen at the gatehouse but, 'sensing
that they didn't really want to talk to me anyway, I turned and walked
away'. He noticed that his second-in-command, Corporal Williamson, was talking to two policemen on a motorcycle outside the Sadr
Mosque. Then, at least four unidentified men left the mosque; Sergeant Mills could tell, from their body language, that they were
agitated. A policeman told him in broken English that they didn't
want the British in their neighbourhood. As he and Corporal Williamson walked back to their respective vehicles there was a shout of
'Gunmen top window!' Using his PRR, Sergeant Mills told everyone
to mount, 'top cover first, so we could move under cover'. At this
juncture a grenade was thrown from the Sadr Mosque grounds:

> We all shouted 'Grenade!', instinctively crouched and took
> cover. The explosion happened and for a split second I
> thought we'd got away without casualties. The next second
> my 2ic shouted twice that he had been hit and ran limping
> to my Snatch, he had blood running from his left leg ...
> me and one other dragged him and put him in the rear of
> my vehicle. The remainder of us then came under small-
> arms fire from the mosque, we took cover behind a wall
> running down the length of an alley with courtyards and
> dwellings on each side ... The 2ic then sent the contact
> report. I deployed my callsign along the length of the wall
> to defend. I then noticed 1 × gunman, keeping low, climb
> over a wall trying to sneak up on us. He wasn't sure of our
> location. I put 3 × rounds into him ... and then two more
> rounds over the wall to suppress others. Major Tait said he
> saw his head come apart. Firefights then broke out all along
> our position as more gunmen appeared on the E side of

the mosque to engage us. The enemy appeared at roof-tops, windows and behind walls and many rounds were engaged. 2 × RPG were then fired at the Snatch – the first went into the house behind. Black smoke was billowing from the Snatch.

The three vehicles of the rover group moved down the road, parallel with the Tigris, towards Yellow 3, and soon their occupants could see Y Company's patrol. A Land Rover was in the centre of the carriageway under the bridge they had crossed earlier that day, with smoke pouring from it. Other vehicles were parked under the bridge, and soldiers were engaging enemy positions to the south-east. To screen them and permit the casualty to be extracted, the rover group would go under the bridge, and then push on to dismount and cover the adjacent roads and alleyways. As they did so they were engaged by gunmen firing AKs from the doorways of houses alongside the road.

Matt Maer at once noted the contrast with Northern Ireland. In his experience there, incidents were isolated and, having achieved their aim of causing a casualty, the gunmen disappeared. Here they stood their ground and fired repeatedly, but 'we were travelling at a fair speed at this time and I was not unduly concerned as I was working on the principle that if we could not hit them they could probably not hit us'. As they approached the area of the contact, RPGs were fired into the small column and a blast bomb rocked Maer's Land Rover. He told his driver, Private Corkie Cawkwell ('I still swear he carried out mirror–signal–manoeuvre at this time'), to 'floor it', and they roared back underneath the bridge.

'No sooner had we emerged from the cover of the bridge,' recalled Captain Thasarathar,

> than the boom of an RPG launch rang out and a warhead, identifiable by its vapour trail, sped towards my vehicle. It hit about a metre or two short of our left wheel and exploded. I had time enough to shout a warning and identify the firer. He was on the rooftop of a building close to the north flank of the bridge. I started to engage him with my rifle. It was not easy to do. Our vehicles were speeding

further south to push through the killing area and the distance between me and the RPG man was growing every second. I saw my first few rounds kick out dust as they hit the parapet of the building just below the firer. He started to hop around in an almost comical fashion as I adjusted my next rounds to land higher. They must have been zipping past his ears because he dropped the RPG and disappeared behind the cover of the parapet . . .

We were now about 200 metres south of the bridge and into a residential area as I fired my last rounds at the RPG man, when a long burst of automatic fire from our right whipped across the front of my nose. I literally felt the air parting and my neck shot into my CBA [combat body armour] instinctively, like a tortoise trying to hide in its shell. A gunman had stepped out into an alleyway, less than 50 metres away to the vehicle's left, and poured a magazine of AK-47 into us as we sped by. You could almost hear the brass [empty cases] hitting the pavement. Mackenzie was covering that side of the vehicle and managed to get off several shots as we sped further south to get out of the second killing area.

'We were saved by speed, covering fire from our own top cover and the pinned-down callsigns and a lot of good luck,' wrote RSM Whyte. 'However, still for the rest of my life I will wonder how all three vehicles and their occupants came through this part of the contact unscathed.' They had got perhaps 400 metres south of the bridge and were no longer under fire, but Matt Maer decided that they could not accomplish anything from there, so they swung round and headed back to the firefight. Deciding that driving through it again was not an option, they dismounted about 100 metres short of the bridge to move forward on foot. 'Now we could go no further,' said Nick Thasarathar,

we were pinned down under a hail of fire. Elements of the enemy, in platoon-plus strength, had manoeuvred away from the bridge and were attempting to flank round our team, using the myriad of small alleyways running off to the east to do so. If they succeeded, we would be cut off and unable to link up with the cut-off team at the bridge. We were definitely diverting a great deal of the enemy's efforts from them, but were in danger of becoming isolated and destroyed.

QMSI Sibthorpe, acting as the CO's bodyguard, now forced entry into a high-walled garden and threw the CO and his two radio operators into it. Using a variety of means they established contact with the pinned-down team, with another Y Company patrol that had been sent down to help and was also with the ops room in Abu Naji. While making a swift plan for their extraction he decided that a cigarette was in order. It seemed clear that the deadlock could only be broken with the use of C Company's Warriors. At that stage there were two of them at thirty minutes' notice to move, and it was a twenty-minute journey to camp: help might just arrive in fifty minutes.

Meanwhile, Nick Thasarathar and RSM Whyte went round the little perimeter

> positioning soldiers to cover the alleyways, buildings and rooftops surrounding us . . . it seemed that every man and his dog had brought out his rifle for the day and had decided to take out his frustration on us. Although not deadly accurate at this stage, the sheer volume of lead in the air meant that somebody was going to get hit eventually. Rounds were kicking up the tarmac around our stationary vehicles and ricocheting off the pavement . . .
>
> An old man gingerly stuck his head out from around a high garden gate and smiled at me. He stepped out into the alleyway. 'No trouble here, sir, this is a good neighbourhood, no trouble, no shooting,' he professed. 'Unbelievable,' I thought. I had seen people in an advanced state of denial about things in life but this old boy was really taking the biscuit.

There were other civilians about, as the RSM noted:

> While covering a minor road, I observed men stopping women and children and sending them down the road

towards our location, then with their human shield formed coming into the open to fire at us. I will never forgive or forget the mentality of the people that did this, or the mentality of the adults who blindly obeyed. Credit goes to all the rover group who like me gestured and shouted warnings in pigeon Arabic to them to get out of the way.

Captain Thasarathar saw two gunmen – 'both had Russian-style chest rigs and both were carrying AK-47s' – who profited from his conversation with the old man to emerge from an alleyway 100 metres away. One was wearing a black and white shemagh over his head, and the other wore a black T shirt and jeans. He at once engaged them, and they returned his fire, shooting from the hip, before making for the safety of the alley.

At the corner, Black T Shirt seemed to make a final act of bravado and stood . . . for a brief second spraying away at me, now looking over the top of his sights. I fired probably my fifth shot of the engagement and saw him hit. He looked as if someone had punched him in the shoulder. I saw him sharply expel breath as he wheeled round and fell with the violence of the impact . . . He was young, perhaps in his late teens/early twenties, and I can still see his face at the moment he was hit today. However, outnumbered and out-gunned and with rounds still zipping past us, this was no time to get moralistic.

No time indeed. Matt Maer got only snapshots of the ebb and flow of the firefight, because every time he looked up the QMSI, looking after him well ('like all mothers do,' noted the RSM, with professional approval), shoved him back down behind the engine block of a Land Rover. Nick Thasarathar saw that there were now small firefights at every one of the road junctions they covered, but thought that their only option was to stay spread out: falling back into a single building would have left them easy meat for RPGs and for a heavy machine gun that had already demolished part of the compound wall. He saw Lance Corporal Mark Ryder halt a deter-mined rush with his Minimi, killing at least one attacker and driving off the rest. Civilians were being propelled forward into the battle, and he heard soldiers yelling 'Kiff!' – which means 'stop' in Arabic. At this juncture he saw a stocky man in a white dish-dash pushing his car across the road, and glimpsed something moving behind it.

I shouted a warning to LCpl Phillips who was covering south with his Minimi. Instantly there was a boom and I saw the vapour trail of an RPG heading straight towards me. I had just enough time to instinctively get down and then there was a deafening explosion and a crushing blast all around me.

The next few seconds were a blur. I looked up and it appeared to be silently snowing. In fact, leaves and small branches were falling down on top of me from the tree I had been taking cover behind. The RPG had hit the tree a metre or so above my head. My ears were ringing and the right leg of my combat trousers had been torn open. I reached down and felt my leg, there was no blood on my hands and miraculously I was still in one piece. I looked towards LCpl Phillips and saw that he was lying flat on the floor, face down, and his right leg was convulsing. There was blood on the wall in front of him. The RSM was running over to him. I gave myself a mental kick up the arse and shouted across to the RSM 'How bad is he hit?' He shouted back he was 'hit bad' and it looked like he'd been shot in the neck . . . My moment of disorientation now turned to anger. I was not going to lose a soldier on this filthy street for anything. Kev had been hit with a round that had entered at his shoulder blade and exited through the side of his neck. We had to get him out of there as soon as possible.

While the RSM patched the wound with a field dressing, Privates Cawkwell and Gray (the former briefly concussed by the RPG) ran forward and helped drag the injured man under cover. Private Jacobs, another member of the little group, had also been hit: some fragments from the RPG had penetrated his CBA, not causing serious injury but burning him. 'He was still good to go, though,' noted Nick Thasarathar.

The battle group's communications were now back up with a vengeance, and Lance Corporal Laird of 7 Platoon was back in Abu Naji, half-listening out on the net and hearing the zap number – a quick and secure method of nominating casualties without using names – identifying the rover group's first casualty:

> It was unreal what I was hearing over the net. Pinned-down callsigns under contact ... Then K22A's [the CO] voice broke into life on taking control with a stern voice re-questing information from the callsigns on the ground. Information started to trickle back. During this I caught the back end of a CASREP [casualty report], then I was informed that it was the CO's rover group. I couldn't believe it – of all the callsigns how would the battalion cope if we lost the CO? Then it started: I was trying to think of the casualty ... Had the zap I had heard in the rover group ... been Kev my best mate, the man who had been best man at my wedding? ... If he didn't survive I was dreading telling my wife that the friend she had grown fond of who was going to be godfather to our eight-month-old baby ... I just wanted to get there and help ... It was probably one of the hardest things not being out there helping my best friend who was in trouble ...

Out at Yellow 3, the feel of the battle began to change. Sergeant Mills had quickly been reinforced by a party of Argyll and Sutherland Highlanders (A&SH). Lieutenant Colonel Grey, their commanding officer, with his own rover group, was travelling along the same route on an entirely different task; happily for all concerned, he was moving mob-handed, with tough Scots who were only too happy to help, as Danny Mills recorded:

> I got an A&SH NCO to get his men in all-round defence and protect our rear and asked that if they could spare any men to send them over. A welcome sight it was to see a big Jock with a GPMG come running over with his No. 2 carry-

ing ammo boxes. Also a WO2 and his team came over and
provided flank protection at the far end of the alley.
Coming under fire from two sides we now had to move
position – we did pairs fire and manoeuvre [one man firing
to cover the movement of another] across to a better position from which we could engage both threats. Firing was
still continuing all around by both sides, RPG rockets too
many to mention, with occasional lulls in battle.

The enemy to the south of the rover group dispersed, possibly
because they had heard that relief was on the way, opening up a
direct route to Abu Naji. Sergeant 'Solid' King, the provost sergeant,
who had been on the other side of the road, threw a smoke grenade
to enable him and some others to cross over to lend a hand. The
wounded Phillips was loaded on to a Land Rover commanded by
Sergeant King and driven safely back to camp. The battle went on,
with the RSM now busy with Lance Corporal Phillips's Minimi, which
had been retained to beef up the rover group's firepower.

Private McAllister of 7 Platoon had turned eighteen in February
and arrived in Al Amarah with 1 PWRR's advance party. That afternoon he was waiting by Sangar 2 in camp, expecting a demonstration
of snatch operations, when a Land Rover roared up with new orders:
'The CO's rover group has been ambushed and pinned down in
town. Get to the block and get your kit and get up to the Warrior
park.'

> Straightaway the CSM says to us: 'Get in two groups, one
> who's got ammo, one who hasn't.' The blokes who had,
> including me, gave our details to go on the flap sheet . . . I
> was in W10, in the back was Pagey my platoon sergeant,
> Cpl Byles, Kenny Bosch, myself, and the coy medic Phil.
> Moments later we were rolling towards the town . . .
>   We crossed the bridge to get to the main situation at
> Yellow 3. We could hear small-arms fire outside. The boss
> and Fongy the gunner were observing in the turret, we were
> under quite heavy contact by now when I heard the boss
> shout: 'Fongy, enemy behind the wall' followed by a burst
> of co-ax. I remember feeling very hot. I was sweating

uncontrollably but quite pumped up as well. We could hear RPGs and small arms whizzing past . . . Soon after Cpl Byles saw some enemy to the rear of our wagon. Without hesitating he shouted 'Open the door, open the door,' and as the door opened I remember everything becoming louder. For a split second I thought 'Fucking hell, this is real, we're getting out here.' Suddenly we heard a whoosh followed by the explosion that rocked the wagon. The RPG hit below the door. The blast blew off a road wheel, and pushed the whole door up . . . The next thing I knew Mensah was taking us back to Abu Naji, W10's back door still half open . . .

With W10 out of the battle, the rest of the relief force barrelled on to the ambush site.

'Finally, after what seemed like hours,' remembered Matt Maer,

the sweetest sound I have ever heard came to my ears as the Warriors rumbled over the bridge, followed by the next-sweetest sound, their chain guns opening up. However, it was not, as I said on the radio at the time, 'over till the fat lady sings', and the disparate groups had to be assisted to safety in priority order. My team was, despite our casualties, in a more secure location compared to the others. I gave instructions that the Warriors were to engage the enemy in the OMS office while the other, Land Rover-borne, teams were to move to my location where we would marry up and exit together. At this stage I was down to two Land Rovers only as Sgt King had broken out of the encirclement in the third Land Rover with LCpl Phillips and Pte Gray, all of whom were wounded.

One of the teams from the bridge duly met me on the street and, the Warriors having made the turn off the fly-over, we duly mounted up to move out. This was a slightly tricky business as the team at the bridge had lost a Land Rover of their own and we were now squeezing into too few vehicles. But you can fit a lot of people into not a lot of space under such circumstances . . .

As a team we had been in contact for two hours and

suffered 30 per cent casualties. It was only tea time on the first full day of our tour.

When they got back to camp Nick Thasarathar heard that Kev Phillips had been evacuated to Shaiba field hospital; he was to make a full recovery.

> The boys were still buzzing and the outrageous banter that follows a firefight was starting to come out. I got them to place their weapons down in a line, with safety-catches applied. I didn't want to see an ND [negligent discharge] after they had performed so admirably. There were broad grins, a lot of hugging and a few tears. As things calmed down, we did a kit check, unloaded all weapons under supervision and made our way to the HQ buildings for a debrief ... I popped into the ops room to let the CO know that everyone/thing was accounted for and then went straight to the intelligence cell to give them a brief account of the fight ... The girls from the pay office came out to talk to the guys. They were excellent, they brought cold drinks, cigarettes and a smile – it really helped the guys come back down to earth. As one of the guys put it afterwards, 'That was just like *Black Hawk* fucking *Down*.'

The incident could so easily have ended in tragedy, but, as is so often the case with the opening engagement of a campaign, this first major contact set the pattern for what was to follow. The insurgents shot a lot and hit a little; body armour and helmets proved their worth, and individual skills in shooting, weapon-handling and fieldcraft told heavily in favour of the British. The value of the Warrior was quickly identified, and thereafter the battle group had four on immediate notice to move and could field fifteen of them in thirty minutes. The importance of medical training and casualty-handling was re-emphasized. 'Lance Corporal Phillips was lying face down,' wrote RSM Whyte, 'and it took four of us to lift him into the Land Rover with shots winging all round and it wasn't a graceful movement either.' But he was delighted with the way everyone had performed:

I was extremely proud of the way the soldiers worked that day, not just within the rover group who covered mine and each other's backs but the other troops involved in the contact. The Y Company teams who came under contact initially and the Warrior crews that were . . . from different battalions all showed the values and qualities that make us a professional army.

Sergeant Mills, a man who sets high standards, was also delighted with his multiple, in action from start to finish. 'All men in my patrol reacted very professionally,' he wrote. 'I couldn't have asked for more from them.'

We should, though, spare a thought for Agnes, the CO's interpreter. Until she could be extracted, she was to be stuck at CIMIC House for a further three days without kit, sleeping bag or change of clothing. Matt Maer had known her for only a week, and was not quite sure how she would react to all this. However, 'she was magnanimous, she gave me a big hug and said she was glad I was OK'. So was the rest of the battle group.

CHAPTER 4

———

Taking the Strain

WHAT HAPPENED IN IRAQ in mid-2004 was neither a conventional battle between two symmetrical adversaries nor a peace-keeping operation, for the very phrase implies that there is a peace to be kept. It was instead a postmodern conflict comprising extreme violence and near-normality, formally structured military operations and sheer terrorism, diplomatic negotiations and Mafia-style power-broking, all intertwined like the skeins of a rope.

Although in trying to make sense of events I risk applying to them a greater degree of consistency than would have been apparent to the men and women who lived through them, I will deal with the period April to October 2004 by establishing, in this chapter, a broad chronology of events, superimposed on a thematic account of everyday life. In the next two chapters I shall tighten the tactical focus to examine some selected operations. Events in Al Amarah and Basra were linked because the Mahdi army uprisings coursed through both towns: anarchy ensued in Al Amarah on 2 August, and six days later B Company fought its sharpest and most costly battle in Basra. But throughout the period B Company was organizationally distinct from the rest of the battalion, and although operations in Basra were directed against the same enemy, their setting was wholly different.

CAMP ABU NAJI AND CIMIC HOUSE

The engagement at Yellow 3 on 18 April, the first full day of the 1 PWRR battle group's responsibility for Maysan province, set the pattern for what was to come. There were to be two distinct Mahdi army uprisings, the first in April–May, with an arrest operation, Pimlico, on 1 May, Operation Knightsbridge on 3 May and the large-scale Operation Waterloo, to reassert control of Al Amarah, on the 8th. On 14 May came the Battle for Danny Boy, a road junction on Route 6 south of the city. Then from the 25th the rising began to peter out, though sporadic fighting went on for another two weeks. The second uprising began on 2 August, and Operation Hammer-smith took place on the 10th–11th. This uprising effectively ended on the 26th. The resupply of CIMIC House, Operation Whitechapel, was mounted as required.

The codenames for these operations were mainly gleaned from the London Underground map. The final end-of-tour extraction plan was Mornington Crescent, and few things in my life have given me more pleasure than being telephoned to be told that the train had arrived safely. The ebullient naturalist-cum-explorer commander of Y Company preferred 'some flora, or a bizarre jungle-dwelling creature' for operations carried out by his company. Its ops officer selected the unimaginative name Tortoise for one, and Major Featherstone was distinctly unimpressed.

At least there was a comfortable familiarity with the battle group's selection of codewords. The MOD, in contrast, selects the names of its major operations from a computer-generated list. If this spares us some of the grandiloquence that comes so easily to our major coalition partner, who is capable of sending an unmistakable signal of intent at a time when the preservation of security may still be important, it does inflict shameful indignities on the language of Shakespeare and Milton. The first Gulf War had the merit of being called Operation Granby, redolent of the marquess of that ilk charg-ing the French bald-headed at Warburg in 1760. But the current run of Gulf deployments is called Operation Telic – Telic IV was the

2004 iteration. Winston Churchill correctly objected to the use of frivolous nicknames: he would not have brave men risking their lives on Operation Bunnyhug, for instance. He would doubtless have consigned Telic to the computer that generated it, and he would have been right.

In summer 2004 violence tended to be full on or full off, and it was hard to predict its setting on any given day. When it was full on it could take a Warrior company, supported by the tanks of The Queen's Royal Lancers and air cover from an AC-130 gunship, to get into the city. When it was full off Lieutenant Colonel Maer would drive to the Pink Palace, seat of the provincial government, just south of CIMIC House, in a Land Rover. Discussions with the various Iraqi factions continued almost unabated throughout the process, and both the CIMIC teams and Major Justin Featherstone of Y Company, who had a particular flair for such things, worked on a variety of civil infrastructure projects, and were to be interrrupted only when the fighting was at its height.

As an almost constant back-cloth to this, both Camp Abu Naji and CIMIC House were regularly mortared and rocketed. All this imposed particular strains on the members of the battle group, and Matt Maer proudly acknowledged that

> their restraint and compassion in recognition of the dangers and risks of getting it wrong were as equally matched by their willingness to risk their lives and 'mix it' with those who wanted to take us on. At no time did I ever feel nervous that the lethal force entrusted to these young officers and men was being or even in danger of being abused. It was not unusual for a patrol in Al Amarah to shift from the daily exchange of pleasantries with a shop-keeper or passer-by, and within 300 metres or a moment in time being entwined in mortal combat with a large heavily armed enemy and having to resort to every skill and piece of ordnance available to survive.

For most of the time the battle group based at Al Amarah comprised Y Company 1 PWRR, particularly associated with the defence of CIMIC House (though relieved there from time to time by C Company 1 PWRR, A Company of The Royal Welch Fusiliers, and A Squadron of The Queen's Royal Lancers); C Company, with its Warriors; A Company 1 RWF with its Saxons, A Squadron QRL with its Challenger 2s, K Battery Royal Artillery with mortar-locating radar, an MP detachment, the battle group's own immediate combat support and, at the time of my visit, a company of The Black Watch. A Company 1 PWRR, as brigade reserve, were birds of passage, constantly on the move and living out of their Bergens, but at Al Amarah for some of the bigger clashes like Operation Waterloo. B Company 1 PWRR was, as we have seen, part of the Cheshires' battle group in Basra. Although it never took part in operations at Al Amarah it had its own battles to fight, for violence in Iraq spread in seismic shock waves across the country.

Camp Abu Naji squats about seven kilometres south of the centre of Al Amarah. Maimuna Road forms the northern boundary of the old Iraqi corps headquarters complex, of which the camp now constitutes a tiny part, with a spongy slab of dispiriting marsh between it and the city. Indeed, water is never very far below the surface, and the camp, so dry and dusty for most of the year, would be ankle-deep in water with the winter rains. All around the camp itself is assorted debris of wasted military might, with acres of ammunition bunkers gnawed to hardcore laced with rusty reinforcing rods, picked over by furtive families of burrowers, like ants on an elephant's carcass. Two kilometres to the east runs Route 6 – Route Topeka in coalition-speak – with the Tigris to its immediate east. The airstrip Sparrow-hawk, secured only when C-130 flights were expected, is four kilometres north of the camp; what was in 2004 an Iraqi National Guard barracks is located nearby.

To call the area flat and featureless is an understatement, and even from Sparrowhawk the buildings of Al Amarah, three or four kilometres away, are simply a smudge on the horizon. There are occasional sand berms, and unkempt wire fences which catch the windblown debris that is as recurrent a feature of the Iraqi landscape as jetsam is of a beach. Low hovels draped with power cables dot the roadside and cluster more thickly around the town, where larger buildings, uniformly flat-roofed but for the domes and minarets of the mosques, flank what looks from the map like an orderly gridded townscape but is in fact chopped finer by alleyways and drainage ditches that are little more than open sewers.

The Pink Palace, home of the provincial governor, is one of the town's few essays into corporate grandeur and, like most of the other public edifices of Saddam's era, is an unlucky cross between Babylon and B&Q, with marble façades and dicey drains in equal portions. As most British soldiers were quick to observe in their personal accounts, the town stank of excrement. A brisk wind often gave a small measure of relief from the heat, but hosed dust on to sweaty skin and sopping uniforms. I have an abiding memory of talking to Challenger crews on the tank park, with too acute a sense of the ridiculous to allow me to risk a shimargh (an Arab-style scarf, 'ally' in Gulf War 1, naff in 2004) but acutely uncomfortable in what seemed like a sand-blasting furnace running at low velocity but full heat. 'The wind in Abu Naji put a continual layer of dust on everything,' recalled James Driscoll. 'Every building, despite being occupied, had an abandoned feeling to it because of the dust. Vehicles, buildings and people belonging to Abu Naji Camp would all be slightly yellow.' Corporal Mark Wesley of the QRL thought that stepping off a Hercules at Sparrowhawk 'can only be compared to opening an oven door to check on your food'. As Colonel Tim Collins so eloquently reminded his men of The Royal Irish Regiment in 2003, Mesopotamia, the land between the Rivers Tigris and Euphrates, is indeed the cradle of civilization and the site of the Garden of Eden. But a visitor to Al Amarah in the summer of 2004 might have been forgiven for thinking it a land that God had forgotten.

Camp Abu Naji formed a rectangle almost a kilometre from north to south and half as much from east to west, surrounded by a wire fence and covered by seven sangars which had overhead cover but were otherwise open to the elements. The sangars were normally the responsibility of one multiple, which would rotate between them. Sometimes it was a shadow guard of cooks, clerks, intelligence personnel and other 'echelon lurkers', but more usually it was a rifle company multiple. Soldiers on sangar duty had to wear full CBA

Al Amarah from the roof of the Pink Palace

and helmets; they would climb the stairs into the sentry box, where they took over a GPMG and a pair of binoculars. They had a photograph of the ground ahead of them, gridded to correspond with an identical photograph in the ops room so that recorded incidents could be accurately plotted. Sangar duty was generally described by soldiers as 'shit' or 'the worst part of the tour'.

The sangar logbooks, regularly checked for items of intelligence interest, revealed that sentries usually got to know shepherds and their flocks by sight, and tried to mitigate boredom by occasional excursions into humour: 'I saw a smiley camel trot by wearing a jumper.' 'When I was on guard,' wrote Trooper Ken Boon of the QRL,

> I would start tapping beats with my fingers, sing, mark time, do push-ups off the wall, see how many bugs I could kill, and think how to sort all the world's problems out, just to stay awake. The second stag [watch] – 3 a.m. to 9 a.m. – was the worst, and used to drag the most. Sangar 6 would come alive at night and it got so bad I wouldn't lean on the sides.

Another lancer, Trooper Paul Martin, reckoned that

> stagging on [sentry duty] was probably the worst thing I did in Iraq ... Sometimes you would wish for something to happen to make your stay go quicker but it rarely did when my troop was on, but that's a good thing in the end, because it was great to see all the squadron come back safe and sound, it's just a big weight off everyone's shoulders because we all looked out for each other.

James Driscoll tells what he swears is a true story, and though the company commander concerned is nameless the list of candidates is a short one. He was visiting his sangars one evening and after chatting to the sentry for ten minutes reached across in the dark to the sand-bagged wall, picked up a half-empty bottle of water and took a big gulp.

> The company commander in question said that as the water passed across his tongue and down his throat he thought it

Sangar at Abu Naji viewed from inside the camp

tasted odd but assumed that someone had added some flavouring salts to it. Moments later one of the soldiers, realizing what bottle their company commander was swigging, grabbed it from him and, trying desperately to keep a straight face, pointed out that with the constant drinking of water to keep hydrated and not being allowed to leave their sangars during their duty they had to piss somewhere.

The guard commander had an unenviable job. He had to keep his men on their toes during long, boring and painfully hot hours, and, in controlling the camp's main gate, would be inundated by a steady stream of the good, the mad and the indifferent:

One moment he could be reacting to the sighting of a dicker, the next he could have some barking old woman demanding recompense for a dead family member. The translators available to the guard were the worst (translators were always in short supply), and even if he could follow what she was saying there was no way of telling whether she was lying or not. Then there were the nutters. One man tried to get into camp dressed as a policeman. One might think that this was an enemy agent but the police assured us he was just plain barking. He was the Iraqi equivalent of those people in Britain who turn up at road accidents in paramedics' outfits and try to help, but he was doing it in Iraq where policemen are frequently killed. The genuine local visitors were no less hassle; expecting to be treated like VIPs, even though for the most part they were nobodies.

The fields of fire around the camp were clear apart from tank hulks and ditches, and there was little chance of an attacker getting to within direct-fire range. Sentries were chiefly on the lookout for mortar teams and dickers. The latter is an expression originating in Northern Ireland and referring to individuals who observe patrols or static locations. They were very active at Abu Naji, often using motorcycles that could outrun pursuit cross country. It was hard to justify shooting one of them, for the rules of engagement required a man to be able to demonstrate 'hostile intent'. One team dicked the route from camp to Sparrowhawk in a red Range Rover. Even if they were detained it was hard to prove what they were up to and virtually impossible to convict anyone.

CIMIC House was altogether different. It stood at the northern end of the Al Mahmoodia area of central Al Amarah, just north of the Pink Palace, wedged into the confluence of two rivers, the Tigris to the west and the smaller Al Kahla to the north. It was a large compound with several buildings, housing the operations support group and controlling all CIMIC activities for the area. Initially Molly Phee had hoped to keep it non-military, so that local people could meet to discuss infrastructure issues without soldiers around. Once the decision was taken to garrison the place, room had to be found for a company, which was not easy.

When he arrived in April Steve Brooks of Y Company spoke there to a young lady whom he remembered and who allocated him accommodation for twelve men, which he knew would be nothing like enough. He decided that the conversation was going nowhere and determined to allow Major Featherstone to 'bat out the details with her'. As a parting offering he asked what her concerns were.

She seemed shocked that I should ask, but immediately answered in a shrill voice: 'My concerns? My concerns? My concerns are that this used to be a nice place to live, now everything is broken, there is barbed wire everywhere and the place stinks of squaddies' . . .

Private Graham Wateridge tells us:

The complex had three main sangars, one at the front gate, one at the back gate and one on the roof. The guard multiple's rotation was normally an hour in each and then a break, but during certain periods the roof sangar was manned by the sniper multiple . . . Collocated at the other sangars, at least until they left at the end of June, were civilian security personnel. They were mainly from the Philippines but their commanders were either British or American. Having these civilians working next to our guys took the pressure off as they didn't have to double-man the sangars. Guys on stag would normally be wearing helmet, CBA and webbing along with carrying their individual weapon and plenty of water. At the stag positions you had normal guard equipment – binoculars, field phones and of course a GPMG.

At both Abu Naji and CIMIC House enemy mortar teams were very busy during the two major uprisings, and the threat they posed was never wholly absent. The sangar guards were charged with identifying the firing points of the mortars and the impact points of their rounds. Although the former would not be directly visible from the sangars, it was often possible to take a compass bearing on their flash and smoke, and the triangulation of three such bearings enabled the firing point to be plotted with some confidence. It was also important to count the number of rounds fired and the number of impacts: if the former exceeded the latter then there was an unexploded mortar bomb which would have to be dealt with. Mortar bombs that landed outside the camp and failed to explode were often visible by the dust cloud raised by their impact. The arrival of

A rooftop sangar at CIMIC House

K Battery with its sound-ranging equipment helped enormously: this identified the firing point, time of flight, trajectory and impact points, enabling the ops room to work out whether the incoming missile was a mortar or a rocket and to calculate its calibre. Mortar crews rarely hung about long enough to be intercepted at their work, but there were occasional terminal exceptions.

Within the camp the most annoying thing about being mortared was the siren, which went on when the attack began and remained on for some time afterwards, letting any mortar bombs that had not detonated on impact ('blinds') detonate of their own volition ('soak time') before clearance searches were carried out in camp. Then the siren remained on, with personnel under cover, until clearances were completed. Despite the most efficient searching, this could take an hour and a half. Matt Maer decided that the effect of this regimen was 'debilitating our ability to carry on essential work and any form of life as well as grating in the extreme'. He eventually decreed that if the number of launches coincided with the number of bangs or blinds seen to land by the sentries outside camp, then the siren would stop as soon as the attack was over.

Rounds turned up in the most unlikely places. Steve Brooks's most treasured image of Justin Featherstone followed a mortar attack on CIMIC House:

> He had been on the roof and had, in consultation with Pte Ads Somers, concluded that a blind had been fired. Ads believed that it had landed in the compound, but Justin disagreed. Justin came via the ops room to confirm the consolidated report to be sent and then announced he was off to bed. We were shocked to see him five minutes later as he walked in and reached for the handset stating: 'Yeah, I found the blind – in my fucking bed space.'
>
> It had come through the roof and was sat neatly like a 60mm dog shit behind his door.

The canine analogy was provoked by Justin Featherstone's furry companion, the mongrel bitch Tigris – of whom more later.

Blind mortar bombs or rockets were supposed to be dealt with properly by a qualified ammunition technical officer (ATO), because they might explode if handled. While this was possible at Abu Naji it was not at CIMIC House, where there was not only no ATO but often no chance of getting one, or there was only one for the whole province.

In July, Captain Charlie Curry was replaced by Captain Dom Sweny as the battle group's Ops Officer. Charlie had just been picked up for promotion to major, had a place at Staff College, and seemed the ideal replacement for Justin Featherstone of Y Company when he went off on leave in early August. 'Charlie rocked in on the Warriors and Justin went out on the same move,' recalled Steve Brooks, 'no handover.' By that stage the CIMIC compound had been hit by mortar fire and there were numerous cordoned-off blinds lying around, gravely restricting movement. Charlie had soon systematically cleared all the blinds (fifteen to twenty of them) by personally chucking them into the Tigris, for he knew that there was no chance of getting an ATO to clear them formally. Steve Brooks:

That night Charlie came into one of the sangars on the roof where I was and we sat there, getting mortared and chatting. I wondered why Charlie had done what he had, maybe seeking a medal or reputation, but I concluded he had done it to make sure we could fight the compound when the time, and the enemy, came. It was the bravest and most selfless thing I have ever seen.

The constant mortaring made people jumpy. When the battalion arrived in Abu Naji, the Northern Ireland habit of closing doors quietly had been lost, and there was initially much irritating superfluous banging and crashing. The shutting of a Warrior door resembled the thump of a distant mortar, as did the door of the fridge outside the ops room if it was closed too quickly. 'Jumpiness itself was interesting to observe,' wrote Matt Maer.

> While, when we first arrived, somebody jumping was a source of merriment, as time went on and most people succumbed to it at least once it was no longer commented on. Your reaction to an unexpected noise was a result of a number of factors, including tiredness, unfamiliarity with one's surroundings and the acoustics of a particular room. The worst 'jump-maker', however, was at CIMIC House, where an internal metal door banged with a sound which wakened the dead and caused those who were not to almost join them.

Mortar bombs arrived by both day and night. Trooper Ken Boon was

> trying to sleep at CIMIC House when a mortar round hit our building. All I remember is opening my eyes and seeing flames and smoke all over the ceiling. I could hear people screaming so I got up to get my body armour and helmet, then I fell on the floor. I felt my leg and it was wet, so I knew I'd been hit. Two TA soldiers carried me out of the building but I wasn't worried about myself: I was thinking I'd been hit – so what about everyone else? They got me to hospital where they found a piece of the mortar round

in my right knee. I had one bounce off my shin where most of the pain came from and another on my right leg which just cut me. I had only one dream about it but spoke to the padre and welfare officer, which sorted me out. It was upsetting phoning home – it took me two days to phone home just because I didn't want to worry anybody. After all I was well looked after, and I owe a lot to the hospital staff that looked after me. After six weeks I went back to work.

Private Jackson, who was a clerk in the admin office at Abu Naji, noted at one point in the summer:

> Over the past two months Camp Abu Naji has been bombarded with rockets and mortars night in, night out . . . It's difficult to understand what the surrounding people are telling you until you've experienced it for yourself. The noises are most frightening, it was best described to me as 'sitting ducks', there's no way you know where it is going to land, you just have to wait for the bang – then you know you are safe. As soon as you hear the explosion the flood of relief is amazing . . .
>
> As strange as it may seem you actually become used to the sound of the rockets and although the fear still remains inside you, you carry on as though it never even happened . . . The mortars were just blips in your normal working day. Every time it becomes more and more tedious. 'Not again,' everyone would say. 'When will they ever give up?' Then it'd be forgotten about, with everyone laughing and joking again . . .
>
> I believe that 1 PWRR's admin office has some very strong characters who have helped the less experienced through some very hard times.

Some soldiers attributed narrow escapes – and there were many – to luck or something more powerful. Private Lee of the Mortar Platoon was just taking over sentry duty on Sangar 3 at the rear of CIMIC House:

As I climbed the ladder to get into the sangar on my final tour I said hello to Ben the Filipino and then did my exchange with the off-coming guard ... I noticed on the wall at the front of the sangar a white bird which apparently Ben had put there because the bird couldn't fly. I told him that he had to move it because if I had to use the GPMG then it would be in my way, so he placed it on the back wall of the sangar ... The next thing I heard was pop, pop, pop, which all of us knew to be the sound of the [enemy] militia firing the mortars. I think there was only two explosions, I heard a dull thud that must either have been on the other side of the wall on the bank of the Tigris, or behind me in the camp ... I knew there was a blind ... The company's Quick Reaction Force [QRF] was deployed to search inside the camp for it, and as they approached the area around Sangar 2 there was another couple of pops. I don't know why, but on this occasion I got down on one knee and told Ben to do the same. Time seemed to stand still for a moment and then 'BANG' an almighty explosion happened. I realized within seconds that we had just taken a direct hit. A member of the QRF, LCpl Deano Deane, saw us scrambling out of the entrance and dragged us into some hard cover ...

The next day I went to look at the miracle that had happened. The sangar had been hit by a 66mm mortar round ... There were potholes from shrapnel on a solid metal bar and some link [ammunition] from the Filipino's machine gun was torn to shreds. Ben was there as I arrived, he also wanted to have a look at the damage. In his hand was the bird, still alive and well.

I look back on that day and remember that Ben had said that GOD was looking down on us that night and he kept us alive ... I'm not a great believer in religion but I constantly thank GOD for letting me live to tell this story and I'm sure Ben does as well, and we both felt at the time that this was a miracle and not just luck.

A Company of The Royal Welch Fusiliers relieved Y Company in CIMIC House in August. By then, as Lieutenant Neale admitted,

> the company was tired, felt like it had done enough but took the challenge of relieving Y Company in the spirit necessary, as they too had had a hard time and needed a break more than we did.
>
> Moving into CIMIC I was shocked at the devastation. I had been there three weeks before when it was all quiet and had swum in the pool. Now the makeshift sniper screens had been blown down, mortar craters and shrapnel scarred everything and damaged vehicles and equipment lay strewn around like in a scrapyard ... Even this late in the tour I found the intensity of the contacts throughout this week surprising and shocking. The militia had come a long way since the sporadic shoots of the early tour and we now faced a prolonged period of mortaring followed by prolonged shoots and RPG attacks.
>
> It was during this period that the last major firefight of the tour was fought, on 24 August 2004. Events conspired that once the contact began I moved under mortar fire to the front sangar where two of my Fusiliers were pinned down. I felt the same sinking feeling there, as rounds hit the sangar from three sides, as I did on my first contact, but eventually managed to get up and firing. I became a casualty [hit in the neck] along with Fus Francis 76 [the last two figures of his regimental number] when an 82 mm mortar landed one metre from the sangar. Being injured was a terrifying and humbling experience and I pay all credit to all involved in my evacuation from the sangar floor back to the field hospital, especially those in CIMIC House with me, who crossed the compound under heavy fire to get me treatment or to check on my condition.

One of The Royal Welch Fusilier medics who treated him was of a similar opinion:

This was a scary time for me. A mortar had landed just metres away from the sangars and blew the three guys off their feet, two were injured. While still under contact, another medic and I ran to the sangar and treated the casualties. After a few hours, they were stable and no cause to worry.

The vacant sangar was then occupied by Lance Corporal Lavelle with Fusiliers Greggan, Smith and Gomez.

They spotted enemy positions and started to engage. The GPMG started to have stoppages until Fus Greggan poured a whole bottle of oil into it and it started firing again. The enemies were very sly as they were firing a burst from one alleyway and then popping up on the roofs. Then LCpl Lavelle engaged enemy who were in a pile of rubble with the GPMG. He gave a target indication for Fus Smith to engage with the UGL, who sent two into the rubble. Then Fus Williams [the only unwounded occupant of the sangar's original garrison] came back into the sangar and spotted enemy firing from a balcony 100 metres away. Everyone engaged them but could not hit them as they were behind the concrete balcony. Fus Smith was again tasked to fire the UGL and fired two. One dropped short but the second landed perfectly in the balcony.

There was no more firing from that balcony ... All throughout the attack there were mortars landing and RPGs being fired. The Warrior callsigns got sent out and started engaging with the chain gun and HE rounds. Two F16s then flew very low over the city letting off their chaff. Gradually the fire stopped and the enemy were seen with white flags coming out to pick up their wounded.

'Back in February of that year we were at Lydd ranges,' observed another Fusilier, 'and one of the shoots was a defensive shoot from a building – we all thought at the time, what a waste of ammo. Looking back in hindsight it was a warm-up for CIMIC House.'

The episode was another Fusilier's first experience of mortaring at CIMIC House:

> I put on my combat body armour and helmet and lay under a very small coffee table. The CSM came in and laughed. He said 'Get up, you dickhead.' I laughed back but inside I was really scared. I thought, 'Oh no, the CSM thinks I'm a right wanker now.' We then started getting small arms firing at us as well but there was nothing being fired back. I went on to the roof and another mortar round went off just on the top of the roof again.
>
> I told the CSM that there were only snipers up there and he said get some men and get up there. I thought, 'Yes, I can show the CSM that I'm not a wanker after all.' We engaged pockets of enemy on Green 4 and Tigris Street. It was one of the first times that CIMIC had given OMS a bit of fire power back. I like having firefights but I still hate those mortars.

Because it had been assumed that this was a peace-keeping operation, when 1 PWRR arrived most personnel in Abu Naji ate and slept in tents, so when mortars and rockets began to arrive daily there was little protection against them. To start with, offices, storerooms, corridors, workshops and anything with a solid roof became sleeping accommodation, although, as the penetration of the roof of the admin office by a rocket was to show, all this offered little real defence. Norwegian engineers installed a number of container huts, basically rectangular containers of the type used by long-distance lorries, with air-conditioners fitted at one end and mattresses and sandbags on top, the former to initiate the fuse of an incoming projectile and the latter to absorb its explosion. Royal Engineers, working twenty-four hours a day seven days a week despite mortar attacks, installed 7.5 kilometres of HESCO in two weeks. The squat cylinders of wire-framed hessian filled with sand resembled vast sections of the sausage roll so affectionately described by James Coote. They offered significant protection against blast, even if they did give

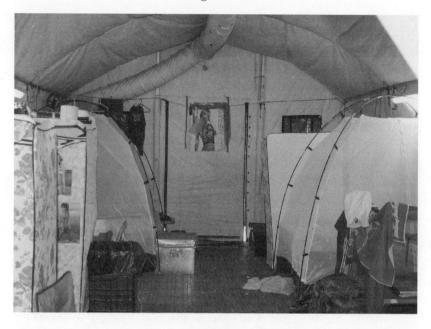

Tented accommodation at Abu Naji

Container accommodation at Abu Naji

Y Company lines at Abu Naji
with a HESCO anti-blast wall on the right

parts of the camp more the feel of shoreline anti-erosion defences. 'Join the army and see the world, join the engineers and put HESCO round the fucker,' quipped the infantry.

Eating arrangements also had to change. There was only a single-tented kitchen and two large tents for eating in, and it was clear that soldiers were very vulnerable during mealtimes, when most people took the long walk from their offices and accommodation to the cookhouse at the far end of camp. Mealtimes were therefore staggered, with only 25 per cent of any company or department allowed to be at the tents at any one time.

> We also started to eat from containers. CQMSs would arrive at their companies' places of work and dish out food from Norwegian containers [large, green, insulated boxes] to soldiers, who would then head directly to an area of hard cover where they would eat in shelter before they headed back to work. It wasn't much of an existence in those days. The chefs could never hope to replicate their superb food if it was going to be served from Norwegians, and there was

little joy to be taken in mealtimes, which were usually the highlights of most people's days.

When I ate at Abu Naji I thought that the food was of excellent quality and abundant choice, and I later enjoyed a restaurant-quality steak in B Company's cookhouse in Basra. But that was well into the tour, when the chefs were in full swing, the heat had abated and the problem of flies largely solved. This is Major James Driscoll's opinion:

the food in CIMIC House was never very good but the food in Abu Naji was, in my opinion, excellent . . . one would always have to wash one's hands and then cover them in quickly evaporating alcohol gel for hygiene reasons. The smell of alcohol gel or neat alcohol now takes me straight back to queuing for food in Iraq. Each of us would eat off a plastic mess tray, the ones that are divided into compartments for various courses. We would use plastic knives, forks and spoons that came in a little clear plastic bag along with a paper napkin. Everything was thrown away at the end of the meal . . .

We never ran out of cheesecake, never ever. Cheesecake, mostly fruits of the forest flavour, was a dessert option no matter what the security situation – amazing.

Private Graham Wateridge, on the other hand, was very impressed with the cooking at CIMIC House:

The chefs were military and known to the blokes in the company. They would do a three- to four-week rotation, which I think the majority enjoyed as it got them away from the bullshit of Camp Abu Naji. They managed to provide three meals a day all of a high standard. They even managed to knock up a barbecue for evening meal on Fridays. During the hostilities in August scoff consisted of rat[ion] packs with one meal of fresh rations a day, but the blokes didn't complain apart from when they got cornbeef hash . . . Prior to August you were allowed to sit on the veranda outside the cookhouse overlooking the river [Tigris]. The view was incredible eating lunch on the veranda, the concertinaed

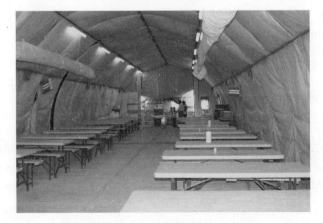

The cookhouse at Abu Naji

The kitchen at Abu Naji: Lance Corporal Kay and
Corporal Shread in the foreground

barbed wire at the water's edge however was a stark re-
minder of our situation. The view was short-lived ... as
when the Royal Engineers turned up they made some alter-
ations to the camp defences. They moved the front sangar

156

and put tarpaulin around the camp's perimeter, and did other things.

Back in Abu Naji, though, Corporal Mark Wesley found that

> eating in camp was torture. Massive queues for food, not just queuing behind fellow soldiers but flies, in huge numbers. There were thousands of the little bastards, and just when you thought you'd won the battle against them for your lasagne and chips; it was that hot in the cookhouse you didn't feel like eating.

'They seemed much more persistent than British flies,' agreed James Driscoll. 'Once they had decided your meal was their target you could not get rid of them. Most of us developed a technique of eating with one hand whilst waving the other constantly over our plate.' Lieutenant Tom Prideaux of the QRL and Trooper Eric Bristow, a soldier of the TA's Royal Yeomanry called up for service in Iraq with the Lancers, submitted a joint report which affirmed that

> no article discussing camp facilities would be complete without mention of food and amenities. Suffice to say, both had a close relationship with the outside temperature. Nowhere in camp could one escape the scent of a thousand people living together in 50°C – the smell at times was almost overpowering but became part of our working day. Likewise the cookhouse – none will remember it fondly, not for any lack of quality in its products, but for its comfort or total lack thereof. Whilst the food was edible, we could spend no longer than ten minutes in the cookhouse to eat it.

We should also spare a thought for the chefs, the hottest men and women in Iraq, trying to serve a varied and interesting menu and running the same risks from mortars and rockets as their clientele. Steve Brooks was enjoying 'a particularly fine chicken korma' in the CIMIC House cookhouse when

> first rounds landed in camp; helmet on, keep eating. Rounds continue to drop with about five- to seven-second intervals; nowhere to hide; keep chewing. After about

twelve to fifteen rounds it all stops. Then the screaming, then everyone is shouting and the chef (Ollie?) is dragged in. We are clearing the floor and he is there bleeding. Corkie [LCpl Corkett] the company medic is there cutting off his trousers, me and another are holding him, washing away the blood. There is a lot of blood and he is being so calm, he even thought twice about the morphine. What strikes me, looking back, is how calm he was as there was so much blood, but also how I thought it did not seem too bad – just a deep laceration – but how he needed several ops to save his leg. It strikes me how delicate our bodies are . . . Corkie saved his leg, and to have seen that feels good.

One of the chefs (his account, sadly, unsigned) had always regarded cooking 'as the most safe trade in the army'. He was work-ing in the CIMIC cookhouse, doing his best to get a meal ready between power cuts, and

it must have been about 1330 hrs when the power went out so myself and LCpl Slasher Whitlam decided to take a break, so Slasher said that he would get the cold drinks from the fridge, so I decided to get the radio from the kitchen. So when I had grabbed the radio [and] I was walking to the exit I heard the first pop of a mortar round and then the sound of the round coming in, not a nice sound. Being in such a small area you know that it is going to be close . . .

As I was walking out of the kitchen towards my room there was this almighty bang . . . I turned to see parts of the kitchen going past me. It was like something out of the movies. You see this big explosion, then you see all the shrapnel go past you at such alarming speed but to me it was all in slow motion. All the time I have been in the army, including tours to Afghanistan, NI and Macedonia, that feeling will never go away. After the whole thing was cleared for us to carry on, all of Y Company helped to rebuild the kitchen, which to me is nice to see so many people help, only for the CSM to come and say he hoped the scoff was not going to be late which I just bit my tongue and said it is never late, sir! . . .

People would not imagine what lengths we go to get rations to the guys at CIMIC – the back of Warriors and Snatch, we had rations come to us in the middle of the night and just thrown over the front gate, to my horror. By the time I got to the rations they were all over the place and Tigris the dog got a good feed that night.

There was a small Expeditionary Force Institute (the name given to the NAAFI when deployed on operations, with its normally civilian personnel transformed into soldiers) at Abu Naji. This did a roaring trade in cold drinks, chocolate bars and Pringles, and cleared $5,000 most weeks. 'It was basic but a godsend,' thought Corporal Wesley, 'when its shelves were stocked.' 'Morale in a container, selling Pot Noodles,' agreed Trooper Boon. 'When passing through Abu Naji it was great to use the NAAFI,' wrote the CIMIC House-based Major Driscoll.

Often a visiting individual from CIMIC House would be carrying a big list of required items from everyone else . . . At CIMIC House we would fill a fridge with chocolate bars and pop and work on an honesty system. It was not unknown for vehicle patrols leaving Abu Naji for CIMIC House to have their top-cover troops stood on crates of Coke whilst big Spar bags of quickly melting chocolate bars were stuffed under ammunition tins at their feet . . .

Even though you knew what was on sale from the last time you were in the NAAFI people still enjoyed wandering around this little shop – I believe it was the association with doing something 'normal'. Sometimes people would buy things not because they really wanted them but because they could afford to and it was nice to own something new like a CD player or camera, almost like a toy to a child, difficult to describe but I've seen it on all operational tours.

Extras could be obtained from an Iraqi, Dodgy Bob, who was boss of the locally employed civilians (LECs) at the beginning of the tour, when he ran a little shop that sold old bayonets and Saddam-era banknotes, but he could usually lay his hands on furniture and fridges. At a price, however. 'He tended to take an unhealthy interest in the younger, fresh-faced soldiers,' recalled Captain Chris Yates of the QRL.

> One under my command, Tpr Wade, described how Bob would hint at the possibility of a drink from his private store of beer or whisky, and having enticed the young soldier into the shop, would put some hardcore porn on his DVD player. Bob would then pick his moment to lunge. The soldiers seemed to view this with some tolerance, although I gather Tpr Wade had to be rescued on one or two occasions ... Despite his proclivities Bob could be very useful, as far as sorting out problems with the locals for the guard commander ...

Contact with home was a real morale-booster. At Abu Naji there were banks of telephones in Portakabins, near battle group headquarters, and in the same row of buildings was a cabin with eight Internet computers and the cabin in which the civilian administrator lived. Time was three hours ahead of the UK, which meant that calling one's relatives in the morning was rarely feasible, and in consequence there was a long queue for phones most evenings. Every man was issued with a phonecard which gave twenty minutes of free calls and was recharged every week. This was not enough for many people, but for extra time it was possible to buy cards for ten or twenty dollars. Captain Rands recalled:

> It was difficult to speak on the phone as we had to assume that foreign intelligence agencies would be listening in. Speaking about future operations was strictly forbidden ... The greater worry was how to tell family and friends what was going on without panicking them. Some soldiers lied outright and said it was quiet and peaceful. It was difficult to maintain this charade when the news teams started reporting from Amarah. One quick-witted soldier did tell

his wife that the 'Amarah' mentioned on the news was a different place to the 'Al Amarah' he was based in.

Private Wateridge of the intelligence section, ensconced in CIMIC House, noted:

> There were sat phones located in the ops room, they weren't too bad provided you could get a signal and the battery hadn't been run down . . . When you did manage to get loved ones, seemed as if they were in the next room, the impacting mortar rounds nearby having to be masked as slamming doors so as not to worry them. They must have thought it was the windiest place on earth.

The phones had to be cut off immediately a casualty had been suffered so as to prevent rumours from spreading at home. RSM Whyte observed that after the first contact at Yellow 3

> a number of rumours and half truths soon started to circulate around the married patch . . . One was to cause unnecessary worry to a wife who was told by a third party that it was her husband who had been hurt. The wife, who was understandably frantic after being told this, had no contact to any injured party except that she, through marriage, shared the same surname . . . people who spread rumours and half truth, no matter how well intentioned, can do more damage than good . . .

The Internet was a godsend for many. At Abu Naji, soldiers could book in advance on a sheet outside the Internet Portakabin a half-hour slot for their emails. There were far more terminals at CIMIC House because the operations support group needed them to work from, and soldiers could use these when they were not busy. James Driscoll thought that 'there were some fledgling relationships formed via "Messenger" and "Hotmail" between some soldiers and girls back home. WO2 Falconer conversed with the lady who is now his fiancée on the Internet for months before ever meeting her. It was certainly good for soldiers to know that they were able to chat up chicks even whilst thousands of miles away in Iraq.' Eventually, however, the satellite dish on which the Internet depended was hit

Abu Naji internet terminals

by mortar fire, 'and suddenly the troops went from non-stop access to nothing, families became worried and soldiers really felt the loss, they had become too dependent on it'.

Neither the phone nor the Internet could rival letters and parcels. 'Letters were always welcome,' said James Rands,

> and DVDs and sweets were often included. I used to get huge pieces of Parma ham sent out. The outside would rot slightly on the three- or four-day journey, but well wrapped the majority of it was almost always edible. The soldiers were convinced that it must be poisonous by that stage.

CIMIC House received its post at irregular intervals, and, noted James Driscoll,

> this meant that when a patrol or convoy came in carrying a big blue mail sack there would be a rush of soldiers to where the sack was unloaded, all hoping that the parcels that toppled out were for them. A bluey [email letter] was good, a 'fat' letter was better and if one of the parcels was for you you'd excitedly take it off to a quiet area and savour

the opening, hoping it wasn't just more sun cream from your mother.

'Letters always brought morale,' agreed Trooper Ken Boon.

> At one point I was writing to twenty-seven women and the mail system was brilliant. The Internet was very difficult to get on because it was always full of airmen or firemen. I usually went to the computers after a late patrol, about 2 a.m. As for phone calls – we got twenty mins a week but we needed more. Sometimes they were upsetting because there were problems at home, and I was stuck in Iraq and I would feel helpless.

One of The Royal Welch Fusiliers clerks commented:

> The main thing was getting the mail. I used to go back and forth to get mail for the boys to keep them happy! I enjoyed that as well because it meant that I would not be in one place too long and at least I was getting out a bit! The first and last question of the day would be, 'WHERE'S THE MAIL!' or 'IS THERE ANY MAIL TODAY?' It's always disappointing to have to say no, there's no mail. It's really good for us when we do actually get mail as it makes our day brighter and reminds us that someone is thinking of us.

Before setting off to Iraq Captain James Jeffrey was directed by Major James Coward, commanding A Squadron QRL, to organize some female pen-pals for the soldiers of the squadron. He composed a letter saying that the squadron was going to Iraq, and sent it to numerous newspapers and magazines, asking them to publish an advert asking for pen-pals. Although both the *Sun* and the *Daily Mirror* complied, Captain Jeffrey was 'slightly bitter' about the fact that some magazines which devoted so much page space 'to "vital" sex tips and advice for "improving your orgasm"' had not run his ad. Undaunted, he returned to the charge in the great tradition of the light cavalry, and *Take a Break* magazine duly put a pen-pal appeal on its back page.

Private Oliver relishing a 'bluey'

This was to prove a turning point in the pen-pal fortunes of the squadron . . . as if a small seismic shift had occurred, a batch of fifty letters arrived on one Chinook [helicopter] postal drop. This was quite a shock and when it was followed by an even larger batch of seventy letters, one suddenly got the feeling that the winds were changing. They changed so much that on one particular day a tornado of a mailbag blew in with over four hundred letters! . . . *Take a Break* magazine had not printed exactly what I had sent in and had not provided 'A lonely soldier' as the addressee for any letters to be sent to, as I had intended. Instead, my name had been printed right next to the advert so 99 per cent of the letters that came through were addressed to me!

Thus the squadron went from famine to glut. Soon some of its soldiers had ten lovely correspondents, and Captain Jeffrey decided that the bounty should be shared more widely. He 'started to hand

Left C Company canoeing on adventure training in Bavaria.

Below A recce platoon patrol on the Tigris.

WO2 Falconer (*centre*).

A view from the roof of CIMIC House.

Training for a petrol-bomb attack.

A view from the top sanger of CIMIC House, looking east.

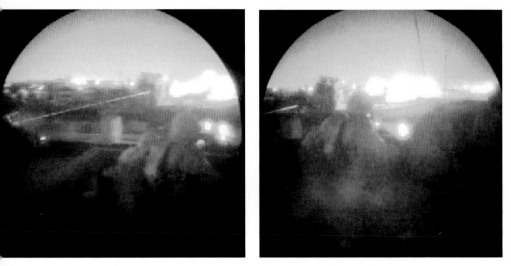

Night fighting from the roof of CIMIC House, August 2005.

An 81mm mortar in action.

Stand-off in Al Amarah. This photograph probably shows 1LI, from whom
1PWRR took over in April 2004.

Left Major James
Coward QRL
and an Iraqi police-
man.

Centre Corporal Palmer
QRL training Iraqi
police recruits.

Bottom Iraqi police.

Hearts and minds.

Private Lee O'Callaghan's body is repatriated from Basra.

Major Coote and WO2 Falconer of C Company.

A soldier of the Household Cavalry Regiment scans the horizon
on the Iraqi border.

out the pen-pal letters to the other subunits in the battle group: the companies of the PWRR, A Company RWF, the RMP, K Battery and the medics'. The range of ages and personalities writing in, observed James Jeffrey, was remarkable. There were grandmothers who had known soldiers in the Second World War, or who had had husbands or boyfriends in the forces and just wanted to write to wish the boys luck. An angry mother wrote to complain that a soldier had asked her eighteen-year-old daughter for a 'more revealing' photograph: 'This was the one letter of its kind, and the only time I am aware that a soldier's literary charms seemed to fail.' One lady sent in photographs of herself and her pet tigers – very appropriate in view of the PWRR's nickname – while Diane, 'who was just beginning to break into the world of glamour models', sent some of her auditioning photographs, which were especially bountiful.

When Captain Jeffrey returned from his post-operational tour leave he found yet more letters in his pigeon-hole in the mess, redirected all the way from Abu Naji. 'The kindness of everyone who wrote in,' he declared, 'was greatly appreciated by the soldiers of all the different subunits of The Princess of Wales's Royal Regiment battle group, who spent six months being "lonely in Al Amarah".'

The presence of female soldiers went some way towards puncturing the balloon of testosterone that hung over the camp. Men behaved better and swore less when there were women about, although several officers confessed to what I might best term wistful speculation about the wondrous Captain Liz Sandry. If they hung around too long, she would politely enquire whether they had met her husband, then a captain in the Parachute Regiment, and admirers would recall urgent appointments on the tank park.

A Company Royal Welch Fusiliers had a female company medic:

> I basically have to go everywhere and do everything the company does. Being a medic and a female, I have to prove myself to the boys. Obviously being attached to an infantry battalion, I have to work that little bit harder to gain the respect I deserve. I have been with A Company over a year

and a half now and I get on very well with all ranks in the company. I always have a go at everything the boys do. If I do it then it's a bonus, but if I don't then at least I can say I tried. I like to think I am respected throughout the company. Because I am not a typically girly girl, I don't moan about breaking a nail or getting dirty! As you can imagine . . . I can't do some things like the boys can. Like going to the toilet as easy as them . . . Whilst we were in Iraq we became a lot closer as a company. We went through a lot for each other and we were always there for each other. It is an incredible relationship that you have with these people.

When she first came under fire she was delighted to discover that 'I reacted just the way I should. The adrenaline rush was amazing.' She was present when Fusilier Stephen Jones (little Stevie to his many friends) was fatally injured in a traffic accident.

This was the first time I had to treat a friend with major life-threatening injuries. I hope I will never have to do it again. We all know that all of us involved in the accident did everything we could to save Stevie but his injuries were so extensive it just wasn't possible. That day we as a company shed at least one tear. Even the big hard men of the company. It was a day none of us will forget. He may be gone but he will always be in my memories. Never forgot.

Military language has been famously fruity ever since, as an eighteenth-century diarist tells us: 'The army passed over into Flanders and swore horribly'. Many officers and soldiers are bilingual, with two languages – one flecked with obscenities which gets used at work, and a politer version for use at home. But it is probably true that while military English remains salty, civilian English has caught up with it. The language used by the average rifle section chilling out behind a Warrior is certainly no worse (and often a good deal better) than celebrity chef Gordon Ramsay's televised strictures on some of his professional colleagues.

But the battle group's world was still innately blokey. Men lived cheek by jowl: 'At times living in such close quarters, with seven other blokes, tempers were a little short and the room smelt of sweaty bollocks,' affirmed Mark Wesley. Once when I peeped into an accommodation container I found it full of soldiers stripped to their boxers, lying on their beds with an assortment of devices plugged into their ears and a lifetime's supply of Pringles and Coke to hand. All was silence but for the suppressed hiss of heavy metal. An anonymous Lancer admitted:

> One of the biggest problems I felt was the lack of privacy. There were about ten of us in each room and if you wanted to have a wank you had to go to the Portaloos. They were very hot and smelt pretty bad, and squeaked and rocked easily, so it wasn't the nicest environment. Just down beside the seat was a slot that people left porn in. When we took over from The Queen's Royal Hussars there was some great porn, as they'd come from Germany, but gradually it all went missing. The LECs took it sometimes, because you'd see them sitting down reading it, as if they were amazed or had discovered a secret stash of treasure.

'The accommodation and living area ... were pretty poor but what can you expect in Iraq, a five star hotel? I don't think so,' reflected Trooper Martin. 'We made the best out of it and bought TVs, game systems, stereos and more to make it livable.'

Men did their best to keep clean, though it was never easy. At Abu Naji, as Captain Yates tells us:

> The laundry service was run by LECs from Basra, who would come up for a month or so at a time. When the camp would run low on water, the laundry would reduce their turnover, which would invariably lead to hot and bothered confrontations with sweaty soldiers, with bags of stinking clothes, being turned away. A few words of Arabic would often work wonders to calm the situation. They didn't seem to have much detergent, and the clothes were dried near a generator, which led to an assumption that all the laundry did was to boil the clothes in diesel ... the laundry also ran a sideline in paintings, which they would produce from

9 Platoon C Company relaxing while on QRF

photos of soldiers' girlfriends, pets etc. – with varying results. The artist was obviously committed to a policy of representational fidelity.

There was originally a contract laundry team at CIMIC House, but this quickly disappeared when the fighting stepped up in April, although soldiers could do their own washing in the two or three machines left behind. 'The sweat-soaked uniforms would be stuffed into army-issue white net bags and piled up waiting sometimes for days before they could be thrown into a machine,' wrote James Driscoll. 'Alternatively we would wash our own kit in a sink or in the showers while showering.'

'Washing facilities were not up to much,' remarked Corporal Wesley of the ablutions at Abu Naji:

A 200-metre walk from our building to several Corrimec structures which housed eight showers and eight sinks in each building sounds all right until you see them – they were never in the best state maintenance-wise and were

Private Kenny Bosch on QRF

absolutely filthy. Most of the time, turning the tap revealed a distinct lack of water.

The officers shared two Corrimec [portable] ablution blocs, from time to time confusing the unwary when either might bear the sign 'Females Only', which was not reassuring for middle-aged visitors on nightly tasks. Some lavatories were in Corrimecs, but most of those at Abu Naji were single-unit Portaloos,

> small plastic cubicles that had their own septic tank in the base. These things heated up to an incredible tempera-ture during the day and the smell was atrocious. However, squaddies being squaddies would have 'hard man shitter competitions', where they would deliberately go for a dump at midday in the fullest Portaloo they could find and then try to outdo each other by staying in there the longest; everyone should have a hobby, I suppose.

Despite the heat, men played football, jogged and worked out. The helipad at Abu Naji doubled as a football pitch. 'What a laugh,' thought Trooper Martin, '50 degrees plus, sweating our tits off, but it was good for morale between the boys, plus we got to know the other regiments better by playing them; we always won of course but it definitely passed the time away.' Euro 2004 was played during the

Corrimec ablutions

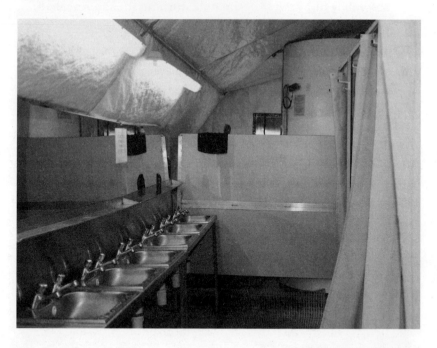

tour and became a real focal point for the camp: soldiers dashed in to whatever room provided a large-screen TV and slumped on to any available surface until the match was over. Captain Rands:

Virtually all English soldiers are [interested in football] and a lot of the Welsh soldiers turned out to be as well. And the Iraqis loved football. During the Olympics we were told by a number of locals that we were assured a quiet night as Iraq was playing and the locals would be far too busy watching and talking about the match to shoot at us. There was a lot of celebratory fire [from Iraqi civilians] on match nights as people emptied magazines into the sky to mark the result.

The battle group's version of Euro 2004 was a mini-tournament between the PWRR, RWF and QRL elements of the battle group. The England v Wales game caused a particular stir. Helicopters had to be removed from the helipad and large numbers of people turned out to watch. A PWRR officer recalled the game:

Fusilier Mitchell was the goalkeeper for the Welsh A team led by Sgt Hulse. He regarded it as the national honour of Wales which was at stake and was ecstatic when Cpl Gavin scored ten minutes into the game after a pass from Cpl

The gym at Abu Naji

Redfearn. The match carried on with a series of stop-overs from Cpl Gavin which the English couldn't deal with. Eventually one of the English players gave away a penalty from which Cpl Gavin easily scored. The second half saw renewed pressure from England. Sgt Plimley, Lt MacAvan and LCpl Roberts formed the put-upon Welsh defence which broke twice in the face of the English assault, but Mitchell saved both shots at goal. Wales beat England 2–0, but as LCpl Finnegan says it wasn't the same result in the real World Cup qualifier.

James Rands believed that the game reflected a wider national tension:

> During the tour there was a real desire among Welsh soldiers to better the English. They often expressed the feeling that they were being shoved up on a rooftop somewhere to get shot at because the English either weren't up to the job or preferred to give the Celts the crap taskings. Some Welsh soldiers were convinced that they were sent in to CIMIC House because Y Company was being overwhelmed and only Taffs could stem the flood of attacks. Some genuinely believed that when ten days later they were relieved this was an Anglo-Saxon plot to steal the glory from them. I don't know if those who believed this were aware that the CO who made the decision was married to a Welshwoman.

Both Charlie Vere Whiting and James Coote, however, detected far less friction. The former believed that 'one of the things that Matt Maer achieved was a very unified team despite the diverse backgrounds,' while the latter was sure that the banter – inevitable with Englishmen and Welshmen living cheek by jowl – was always good natured, and never spilled over into animosity.

There was a well equipped gym tent at Abu Naji, busy in the evenings and always very hot. 'The facility that saved me was the gym,' reckoned Corporal Wesley. 'If I ever had more than a couple of hours to myself it was spent pumping iron. It enabled me, for a short while at least, to forget where I was.' Sergeant Chris Adkins, initially vexed to be allocated a camp-bound job, consoled himself by settling into 'a routine of fitness' and memorizing any intelligence details that might help his old company. Trooper Bristow recalled:

> Many spent an hour or three in the well equipped gym, and most who worked out with any regularity reaped the benefits on returning home, to comments that stoked the vanity coals. To a man, we all lost a pound or two, with the most impressive cases losing two to three stone, most of which by now will have returned.

There were a few items of gym equipment at CIMIC House, but all were eventually destroyed by mortar fire. Nevertheless, observed James Driscoll,

> troops could be seen maintaining their fitness by running dozens of laps of the small base or sprinting up and down a 15-metre stretch of road until they were suitably knackered. Fitness in CIMIC House was taken when [you were] able to and the mortar threat allowed. In the ops support group I insisted a group fitness session take place every Sunday (when safe to do so) so that I could check a standard was being maintained and give some structure to the week.
>
> Abu Naji had much better facilities, with a mile circular track that had people plodding around it carrying camel-baks in the cooler morning or evening periods.

The binary character of violence meant that when the switch was off most people had some free time despite punishing schedules. The first Mahdi army cease-fire coincided with the Olympics, allowing soldiers to watch many of the main events. 'The period of the cease-fire was so quiet that it even allowed time for people to just sit and chill and for people to get together and shoot the shit,' recalled James Rands. Many soldiers were actually very busy in their free time. Captain Chris Yates was struck by

> the variety of multimedia recording devices owned by individuals. Most soldiers seemed to have a digital camera, often with a video function or even a separate camcorder. Between every five or ten persons there would be a private

laptop, and most senior ranks had their own. Most laptops were used primarily for playing DVDs, but could also be used to store and montage film and video clips. Within the battle group, a large amount of material was quickly amassed. The command element rightly kept a concerned eye on this one, and inspections were carried out to make sure that nothing too ghoulish was being recorded. Even so, thanks to simple editing software, the tour saw a proliferation of startling presentations featuring footage of mortar bombardment, small-arms contacts and pieces to camera. As the techniques became more advanced, these would include slo-mo, artificial grain and colour desaturation, rock soundtracks or maudlin dirges, nods towards *Full Metal Jacket* or *Apocalypse Now*. There emerged an almost competitive spirit between subunits to produce the best version.

Captain Yates wondered whether the relative absence of the media – 'their lack of interest, or ignorance, or unwillingness to visit Al Amarah' – encouraged soldiers to fill what seemed to them to be 'a void of unrecognition'. He was, I think, right to suggest that this must be 'the ultimate postmodern combat experience: returning from combat to immediately create a media product'. Given the evident unpopularity of the war at home, and the widely held feeling that the reality of Iraq did not conform with the official image, perhaps soldiers needed to make their own cultural context, 'of bravery, danger and triumph on a screen with titles, explosions and music'.

Many of the CDs I saw featured remembrance too. When the body of Private Lee O'Callaghan of B Company was flown back to Brize Norton I was there to pay my respects. And when, not long afterwards, I visited B Company in Basra, I was struck by the fact that the company CD showed his body being loaded on to an aircraft at Basra with all proper military ceremony. He was their mate, and deserved remembering. Previous generations might have sought immortality in graven stone or written word, but it is the moving visual image that strikes a chord with the young of today.

BASRA

Although the situation in Basra was markedly different from that in Al Amarah, B Company 1 PWRR had deployed to the city in precisely the same way as its sister companies. There was the usual less than inspiring flight from Brize Norton, followed by a short period of acclimatization and training at Shaiba. The remainder of 1 PWRR had already moved north, and Lance Corporal Jodi Tuvak of B Company's 6 Platoon was made 'aware that this tour would be very different to any other tour I had been on' when one of his friends arrived at the hospital in Shaiba after having been wounded by an RPG in one of the first clashes in Al Amarah. However, the assessment by the experts at Shaiba was that the situation was 'relatively benign', the main threat being posed by IEDs; this proved to be 'slightly out of touch with the reality of the situation on the ground'.

B Company's advance party spent only three days at Shaiba and then moved up to Basra to begin the process of taking over from The Royal Regiment of Wales (RRW). However, the Warriors, which had been landed at the nearby port of Umm Qasr, had not travelled well. Lieutenant Hallam Scaife of 4 Platoon noted: 'They had been emptied of sea water and a great deal of maintenance had to be completed on them before they would be operationally ready. This was proved by the firing on the ranges, which created some concerns over the state of the weaponry.' The company moved into Camp Cherokee, just south of the Shatt Al Arab and north of the old Ba'ath Party headquarters.

Major David Bradley, the company commander, found his role heading the Warrior company in Lieutenant Colonel John Donnelly's Cheshire battle group 'both exciting and disappointing'. Disappointing, because after its return from BATUS, 1 PWRR 'had a confident "buzz" and it felt a great organization to be part of'. But it was exciting too, because

> as the only Warrior company we would have an interesting part to play, and it would probably involve a great deal of autonomy. I had been surprised by the amount of autonomy

I had as an OC, and this would continue as an attached sub-unit to another battle group. The role that 1 Cheshire battle group had been given, as Basra city battle group, was also exciting. Basra was the capital of southern Iraq and would therefore be at the forefront of any developments in the area. In addition it was a predominantly urban environment and having served in Northern Ireland in both rural and urban roles, urban was always the most fast-moving and exciting.

David Bradley's recce took place in early December 2003 and, like so many other new arrivals, he was struck by the incongruities of what proudly announced itself as Basra International Airport. 'We stood in the arrivals lounge, watching a creaking carousel turn round on a pitted concrete floor,' he wrote. 'What was once a symbol of Saddam's power was now the arrival point for the British army.' He got his first view of Basra city while riding as top cover to Major Dinger Bell, commanding B Company of The Royal Regiment of Wales, the Basra battle group that the Cheshires would replace.

> The drive back to the RRW battle group HQ was fantastic. The picture painted by the media was of a broken city with no services, high unemployment, and little food and water. It seemed to be the complete opposite. The place was absolutely buzzing. The roads were chaos. There was every sort of car, from expensive Western imports to the most dilapidated jalopies, battling for space on the crowded roads. The main streets were lined with shops or market stalls piled high with consumer goods or fresh produce. In one particular street there were so many white goods for sale that they were stacked four high on the pavement: fridges, microwaves, air-conditioners imported from Kuwait and ready for sale to the 'impoverished' people of Basra. There was certainly poverty, but not on the scale implied by the press . . .
>
> The sounds and smells were particularly vivid. Only a quarter of the city had a working sewage system, with the rest relying on open drains leading into the Shatt Al Arab waterway. This method relied on the tide emptying the

Corporal Monty Bath on patrol

drains twice a day, but over the last ten years they had become silted up and blocked. This meant that whenever you crossed one there was the most incredible stench.

Another officer described Basra as

the . . . Venice of Iraq, at least in terms of stinking canals at every corner, which vary in colour from an almost acceptable green to a frankly disturbing pink. The smell is at times sufficiently strong to navigate round the city on dark nights. The homes vary from reasonable to slum around the city, but the filth remains fairly constant, up to the point that a newly arrived Warrior commander ignored the advice to 'stick to the path' in Al Qibla, and a cunning short cut ended with a Warrior up to its armour in generations of human filth. It is fair to say that during our time the city has become noticeably cleaner, street life is picking up and there is a wave of building around the place, which helpfully leaves lots of rubble for improvised bombs to be concealed in.

Basra has a population of some 1.2 million, 85 per cent of them Shi'a, with 10 per cent Sunni and the remainder Christians, Jews and Zoroastrians. The city is comparatively rich in Iraqi terms: the majority of oilfields lie in Basra province, and proximity to Kuwait makes it the focus for imported goods. The Shi'a population had been brutally repressed under Saddam, and were 'clearly grateful for what we had done for them. I saw more hate from the local population in one day in Strabane or Belfast than I ever experienced from the people of Basra,' commented David Bradley, soon to be badly wounded there. Nonetheless, there were always problems in the city. The power supply was intermittent, and imported white goods had imposed a further strain on the electricity grid. Similarly, the growth in car ownership had increased the demand for petrol, and there were long queues at the petrol stations. The disbandment of the Iraqi army had created unemployment, and there were riots on police and border guard recruiting days as young men fought to secure a place.

As elsewhere in Iraq, political power in Basra was complex, a mixture of secular politics, growing religious influence and tribal loyalties. There was active opposition to the coalition's presence from former-regime loyalists, generally Sunni Muslims who had done well out of Saddam and wanted to destabilize the occupying powers. They generally favoured radio-controlled IEDs, planted beside main roads in the hope, occasionally fulfilled, of catching a military convoy. Next, although Al Qa'eda was not popular in the Shi'a south, on 18 April 2004 it detonated suicide bombs outside three city police stations, killing or injuring nearly fifty people. 'An important consequence,' thought David Bradley, 'was the obsession of the local police with force protection.'

The third dissident element in Basra was the Mahdi army, militant arm of the local Office of the Martyr Sadr. This was significantly less popular in Basra than it was further north, but lack of widespread support did not stop it from mounting mortar and rocket attacks on coalition bases, and sometimes launching ambushes against coalition patrols in an effort to take over the city. However, its relative lack of muscle can be gauged from one incident. In May one of its mortar teams tried to hit the Shatt Al Arab Hotel, headquarters of the

A Basra street from a B Company vehicle

Cheshires' battle group. One bomb went through the roof of a nearby house, killing four members of the Eden tribe. The tribal sheikh at once demanded blood money from the OMS. The latter paid no attention to the initial demand, and when it was repeated threatened retribution against the tribe. The tribe at once responded that if the OMS did not pay up, the whole body would immediately descend on the office and take revenge. The OMS apologized and paid forthwith.

The Basra city battle group provided a security framework within the city and mentored the police within each district. B Company 1 PWRR was at first given its own area of operations, but within three days it was allocated the task of operations company, losing its zone of responsibility but retained for surging into an area on demand. Lieutenant Scaife recalled: 'A number of tasks came our way in those first weeks. I had the task of training the traffic police, whilst Lieutenant Ian Pennells [5 Platoon] set about the same task with the checkpoint police.' This proved short-lived, and 1st Regiment

Royal Horse Artillery (1 RHA) was tasked with leading on security-sector reform. The brigade commander and the CO of 1 RHA led on political negotiations, and the importance of Basra meant that, in contrast with Al Amarah, there was more high-level interest in the city, with the provisional authority, the Foreign Office, non-governmental organizations and a number of private security firms all having an input. One officer felt that the media had an effect on the military approach to security in the city:

> Basra being the second city of Iraq, and the only place the British media are aware of outside Baghdad, has added a continual requirement for a softer political approach to all problems than the average infantryman would like. This has meant that during the tour there has been no fire-support potential from Challenger 2s or the air, which did at times cause a lot of frustration, especially with air recce reporting, in great detail, enemy movement we could do nothing about.

For the first month of its tour B Company felt themselves to be in 'a sleepy backwater, listening to the war stories from Al Amarah and attempting to set the world record for sitting in a Warrior on a random road junction while nothing happened (9 hours, 6 Platoon, Red 6)'. 'The company continually heard reports from Al Amarah of the fighting that the PWRR battle group were involved in,' added Hallam Scaife. 'Needless to say most individuals wanted the company to be moved up there, so that we could do our share in the conflict.' There was a sharp burst of fighting on 8 May, with 6 Platoon seeing the lion's share of the action.

Towards the end of June the company moved up from Camp Cherokee to a tented camp just behind the Shatt Al Arab Hotel, a gaunt building in the omnipresent concrete, towards the northern edge of the city. 'This was close to the Al Hatha region,' wrote Hallam Scaife,

> where the fierce Garamsha tribe lived. Their arsenal of weapons was awesome. We were often treated to nightly firefights, only a kilometre or two away, and it was better than any fireworks display. One of the long-running operations was . . . [to mount] regular patrols, both day and

night, of the Iranian border. For any military tourist it would have been heaven, regularly moving through the old defensive positions of the Iran–Iraq War, littered with abandoned and destroyed armour, traversing the safe lanes through the existing minefields. Despite our best efforts, and endless nights staring at the lights of Iran, the total haul of confiscated weapons was one AK-47.

On 5 August, however, there was a major clash with members of the Mahdi army on Qarmat Ali Bridge. This turned out to be a curtain-raiser for the battle of 9 August against the Mahdi army during which Private O'Callaghan was killed and both the company commander and company sergeant major were among the wounded. The company 2ic, Captain Pete Williams, an attached Royal Marine officer, was on leave, and so the senior platoon commander, Captain Mike Reid, took over the company until the rapid and well timed arrival of Major Andy Carré, actually bound for Al Amarah but hijacked to fill the gap. 'The worst part of my brief spell in charge,' noted Mike Reid,

> was the half hour on getting back into our own operations room to discover that one of the soldiers left down at the other camp with Hallam had been killed in action. It was then down to me to tell the company, who thought that everybody was roughly OK, that Private Lee O'Callaghan had been killed . . . and then, in the next breath, that we now had to ensure that we were ready to go back into the city if we were needed again. That is one element even the training can never prepare you for.

It was a hectic time, as Hallam Scaife remembered.

> All convoys had to be brought into the city under escort by armour, and we had the responsibility for the northern city, The Black Watch for the south. Over the next few weeks, crews worked round the clock, sleeping only a few hours a day on the floor of the hotel. There were regular contacts, and plans were even made for the evacuation of forces from the city.

The hardest time was in the aftermath of Lee O'Callaghan. I was forced to write piece after piece about him and the events of the day, when all I really wanted to do was grieve alongside my blokes. A week later there was the repatriation of his body at the airport. I remember having a moment alone with him, tracing my finger over the brass plaque on his coffin, the outline just visible through the Union Jack draped over it. The sight of that coffin being carried by members of my platoon on to the Hercules is one that I will carry with me for the rest of my life.

On 17 September Lieutenant Scaife led an attack on the OMS headquarters, breaching the wall with his Warrior and spearheading an assault which resulted in the seizure of 15 tonnes of weapons. 'The following days were a little surreal,' he wrote:

> Everyone that we met congratulated us on the operation. Locals started to offer their thanks, indicating the public support that we had. The OMS were furious and demanded the return of their weapons . . . The biggest effect was that direct attacks on the coalition forces stopped almost immediately, and it became obvious that we had severely dented their supply chain of arms and ammunition.

'Like every tour,' commented Mike Reid,

> for every expanding war story there have been hours of the less glorious but always important tasks. Sangars have been well and truly bashed, areas cleaned and permanent vehicle checkpoints manned. Possibly one less glamorous operation that will remain for ever in the minds of B Company is the longstanding effort to prevent the transit of terrorist materials from Iran via the nearby desert. This has been a particularly effective operation, as in hundreds of hours observing the desert absolutely bugger all has been seen.

One factor linking Al Amarah and Basra was concern about leave. Every person in the battle group was entitled to two weeks. Some were able to choose when they went home; others had to take the vacancies they were given. The process was particularly stressful for

Mourners at the repatriation of Private O'Callaghan's body from Basra

Men from Y Company with Private Rayment's coffin

soldiers in Al Amarah, who had to get to Basra with a convoy down Route 6 or by a C-130 out of Sparrowhawk. You were never confident that you would actually get home until you were on a plane and out of Iraqi airspace. I left in a darkened C-130 by night, with everyone wearing helmets and body armour and 81mm parachute-illuminating rounds popping over the far end of the airfield. I was lucky enough to be sitting up front, behind the pilots (the drama of the moment has burned their names, Greg and Pete, firmly into my memory), and it was a majestic moment when the armour came off, the lights went on and a loadie asked me how I took my coffee.

Many found the sensation of actually getting away from Iraq to be the highlight of their tour: one experienced soldier, with a number of operations to his credit, thought that it was the best rest and recreation he'd ever had. The way people spent their R and R varied enormously. Some crammed all they could into every moment; others capitalized on long lie-ins and lazy afternoons. A few soldiers did not get leave until they were five months into a seven-month tour, and many agreed that the experience taught them not to take their wives, girlfriends and families for granted. However, many found that leave had its own particular tensions: the mind flicked back to the boys in the Warriors, ordinary noises provoked extraordinary responses, it was hard to relate the normality of England to the abnormality of Iraq. And the departure lounge at Brize was always there, like a death's-head at a feast.

Apart from leave and a chance for a brief period of local standdown there were still occasional quiet moments, both at Al Amarah and Basra, when soldiers got a chance to relax; sometimes, anything that could take people away from where they were for a few minutes was good. Fusilier Tarrant remembered the best moment of his tour coming when he was on guard. His multiple was placed on dishwashing duties after dinner, and for a short time they were just a multiple doing the washing-up and chatting as if they weren't in Iraq. But it was hard to escape from the hot, gritty, brooding presence of the place, hard to forget that rockets or mortar bombs might arrive at any moment, or that a sudden alarm would see the QRF, armed and dangerous, turning out to ply its trade.

CHAPTER 5

Round One

No SOONER HAD the PWRR battle group deployed to Al Amarah than the security situation, already on the slide, slipped from bad to worse. The ambush at Yellow 3 on 16 April gave an early indication of the strength of the Mahdi army in the town, and over the next few days there was an increase in the use of IEDs against patrols and Route 6, although many devices happily failed to function as intended.

'Daisy chains' were a local favourite. In April these often consisted of three 155mm shells laid a short distance apart and detonated remotely; by August significantly larger versions were being used, with three shells laid together but attached to four other similar bundles, fifteen shells in all. Intelligence was often of high quality, and in early May a combination of frustration at a deteriorating situation and a large batch of comparatively good intelligence encouraged Lieutenant Colonel Maer to move on to the offensive.

THE FIRST UPRISING: FROM PIMLICO TO WATERLOO

By the end of April almost every patrol was being ambushed, and the police were now, at best, absent from their posts or, at worst, actively shooting at the British. The lack of any effective response made the attackers bolder: Majar Al Kabir and Al Kahla were no-go areas, and coalition credibility across the province had all but collapsed. However, intelligence was able to supply the battle group with the names and addresses of many bomb-makers and insurgent commanders. 'When we looked at the map,' remembered James Rands, 'it was clear that there were a lot of targets concentrated in the south-west of the city in the Kadem Al Muallimin [residential] estate. The plan was simple – go in and grab them. Obviously there was some refinement needed.'

Operation Pimlico was to be launched in the early hours of 1 May. A Company 1 PWRR would carry out the arrests, the Warriors of C Company of the RWF would stand ready to seize key junctions if there was indeed a Mahdi army counter-attack, and C Company would be on QRF at camp. It was obvious that getting the right suspects arrested would not be easy. James Rands remembered that

> We had real difficulty identifying individuals because at this stage our photography was poor, as were the descriptions (about five foot seven, black hair, dark skin, moustache, Arab appearance described about every suspect on the tour – ginger terrorists beware, we have you in our sights). If the arrest teams snatched every man in the house, then the prisoners could be processed back at Abu Naji and again at the detention centre at Shaiba.
>
> The teams would also be looking for evidence. At that stage we could intern without trial but we knew that . . . eventually . . . this would end. We needed to find the evidence so that at a later date they could be tried. Also, evidence was always useful to the interrogators at Shaiba. Suspects caught with an RPG would always try to claim that they knew nothing about it, but eventually they would have to start talking . . . If two were caught together they were far more likely to crack as they raced to grass on each other.

Once prisoners had been arrested they would be loaded on to Snatches under command of The Queen's Royal Lancers and returned to Abu Naji, where the RSM would supervise their detention. Preliminary interrogation would enable some suspects to be released, and the rest could be taken down to Shaiba. At this stage the local police should have had primacy and carried out the arrests themselves, 'but given that they kept shooting at us this wasn't much of an option'. Nevertheless, it was important to prevent an arrest operation from turning into Stalingrad, and an officer pointed out:

> We knew that the OMS was jumpy about coalition oper-
> ations. If the operation went noisy we were concerned that
> the Mahdi army would mobilize. The OMS itself was a
> legitimate political party hijacked by a gang of thugs . . . We
> thought that we could assure them that this was not an
> operation aimed at the OMS . . . The chief of police seemed
> to be an OK sort of bloke. As the operation went in he
> would phone the OMS office and tell them that this was an
> arrest operation aimed at criminals, not at the OMS itself.
> This was intended to prevent a major Mahdi army counter-
> attack. It could also add credibility to the Iraqi Police Ser-
> vice position. In retrospect, fat chance.

Because Matt Maer spent much of his time working with Molly Phee and local leaders, many of whom were anxious to avoid being dragged into a confrontation by their armed and impulsive young, he gave broad-brush instructions to the planning group. Major Toby Walch, with the assistance of Charlie Curry, ops officer at the time, and the subunit commanders, thrashed out the detailed plan. The CSM of the Royal Welch company describes the first stage:

> We all RVd at the cookhouse at 0100 on 1 May 2004, the
> vehicles were all lined up ready to move in order of march.
> The commanders had carried out final checks and everyone
> went in for an early breakfast and some much needed tea.
>
> At 0200 I gave the order to mount up and I called in
> the commanders – the OC wanted to speak to them before
> we left. He only said a few words but it made the hairs on
> the back of my neck stand on end. He said: 'The Royal
> Welch haven't carried out an operation like this for many
> years, and if it goes wrong it will go horribly wrong. Good
> luck.'
>
> We mounted up and soon we were driving into the
> outskirts of Al Amarah, the vehicles were going to be

dropped off next to the prison [codenamed 'Broadmoor'] and protected by the QRL . . .

Out of the vehicles we shook out, carried out a head count and away we went, making best speed towards the Kadeem estate. The OC stopped short and launched the teams on to their various targets. If we were to get in and out without any trouble, surprise and speed were of the utmost importance.

The arrests and seizures of arms and explosives generally went well, though not without unusual hazards. Fusilier Andrews tells how

we had to walk down through the streets of Al Amarah when we found the house. I was one of the cut-offs when my multiple entered the building. They came out success-ful, and walking back down the streets all I heard was gun-fire . . . All I saw was tracer coming from a house, and there is a trench in the middle of the street full of sewage etc. and I had to go and jump into the trench. I was not happy because it stank. Well, that was it for me. It came up to my waist. On my way back to the vehicles I heard gunfire so I ran from one part of the city to the other just to get back to the vehicles.

Fusilier Coverson saw the CQMS, Colour Sergeant Roberts, pitch head first into another open sewer: 'It was like watching a cartoon.' Despite these malodorous interludes, the CSM recalled:

The teams were having great success and the operation was going according to plan, suspects arrested were brought to a central point and collected by the QRL and RMP and taken away for questioning. The teams moved through the estate coordinated by the OC and eventually we arrived at a bus depot, which was the last target. Lt Neale's team went in and made a substantial find: we needed a few Snatches to pick up all the ordnance; the OC and his group moved back to send the QRL callsign up to the bus depot to collect the ordnance.

Sgt Greg Plimley's team secured the immediate area

while Lt Neale's team got the ordnance ready to be picked up. Time was ticking by and Greg and I were getting quite worried, it was an ideal opportunity for the enemy to hit us. We discussed escape routes and which houses we could take cover in in case we got hit. Thirty minutes later the cavalry arrived in the Snatches to collect all the kit. We got it loaded up in double quick time and as they pulled away we came under contact from the rooftops to the north. A rapid rate of fire went back in the direction of the enemy and I pulled the troops back into the bus depot.

Lieutenant Neale had just finished loading the captured items on to the vehicles:

A feeling of a job well done rises within me and I stand in the entrance to the compound ready to reorganize my troops to patrol back to the vehicles [at the pick-up point south of the estate].

Suddenly the air about me seems alive with noise and movement. We're being engaged from across the road and this is my first contact. I dive for the cover of the wall and see my multiple doing the same. I spot one of the Fusiliers still caught in the open, frozen to the spot. The noise is unbelievable and I grab him and pull him tight in next to me. There are three of us caught behind a pillar of the wall a foot and a half wide. Slowly my mind starts to catch up and the firing stops briefly. I peek around the wall determined to follow the format I've been taught – locate the enemy, that's what I know I must do.

As I look across the road I see a gunman no more than 75 metres away, with his weapon pointed directly at my head. While this thought is still registering he fires and misses, but not by much, and I feel stone chippings splash against my face from where the round hits the wall beside me. My right ear bursts with pain and rings uncomfortably. It seems all wrong. I realize that this is what is called being 'pinned down' and hate it. I see the CSM trapped behind the wall with the remainder of my multiple. They too are stuck, as this is the only way out. I manage to shout a rough target indication but my head feels fit to burst and it does anything but follow the sequence that has been drummed into me since day one. Somehow the guys on the CSM's side manage to get up and start firing and this gives us the momentum to start moving.

The CSM takes the story on:

LCpl Parry tried to give a contact report but the comms had gone down. I assessed the situation and the only thing to do was to move to the outskirts of the Kadem estate. I sent Lt Neale's team to lead us out with Sgt Plimley's team with myself bringing up the rear; we also had the medic, LCpl Miles and the CQMS with us – he had taken cover in an open sewer and was covered in human shit from head to toe.

As we fired and manoeuvred towards the south of the estate we came under constant harassing fire from different areas. We had a few rallying points to make sure we had all the men and to try and establish comms, which LCpl Parry eventually did. This also gave us a breather; it was hard going, you didn't know where the next burst of fire was going to come from . . .

Falling back with the Fusiliers was Quartermaster Sergeant Instructor Craddock, the ammunition technician who had checked the arms and explosives in the bus depot and certified them safe to move. 'The QMSI withdrew with the men, making history,' said one eyewitness. 'He was the first ATO in the history of his trade to fire his weapon in anger. He actually fired so many rounds that he changed magazines on the move, hurling the empty magazines over his shoulder Hollywood style as he went.'

The CSM resumes his narrative:

We made it to Route 6 and the Warriors were waiting for us, it wasn't over yet, the intensity of fire increased and a number of RPG rounds came in our direction. We put down a fire base and moved everyone about 200 metres

C Company Warriors cover Yellow 3 as the dismounts
assault the OMS at dawn on Op WATERLOO

down Route 6 where we were met by the OC who had
brought up some Land Rovers to get us out of there ...
Some of the men had managed to get themselves in the
back of some of the Warriors and the OC and myself ended
up going to the back of each Warrior to retrieve our lads,
we needed to make sure we had everyone before we left. It
took some shouting to get some of them out of the Warriors
and on to the soft-skinned Land Rovers but we managed it.

'The Land Rovers drive up under fire and pick us up,' wrote
Lieutenant Neale:

I wait for my guys to get on and ride out laid across the
bonnet, as there's no room in the back. As we stand in the
car park at Abu Naji I feel scared, still excited, and upset
in a confusing order, but this subsides quickly and turns to
relief that we were lucky this time.

Back at camp there were difficulties with the prisoners. In order to defuse the inevitable allegations of ill-treatment, it had been decided that all prisoners would be given a full medical on their arrival at camp. Once they had dressed again, they would be photographed with a name board. This was not in itself a bad idea, but its results were not helpful. 'We were an unknown quantity to the prisoners,' admitted an officer, 'and being told to strip for his medical made one think he was about to be raped. This was an incredibly strange experience for all involved and made no sense to us.' And, despite all the early emphasis on quality of evidence, it proved hard to tie finds to suspects.

Despite what Matt Maer called 'its less than textbook ending', there was a general feeling that Pimlico had met its aim. He had been out on the ground all night, and after returning to Abu Naji he spoke to both Molly Phee and CIMIC House on the phone, then had breakfast before making an embarassing admission.

His rifle's night-sight had fallen down the turret of his Warrior, and had been gobbled up by the 'turret monster' when the turret was traversed unexpectedly, catching the sight between the turret cage and the vehicle's hull – a frequent cause of crushed feet and ankles. He was on his way to seek a replacement from the quartermaster ('and to apologize for my carelessness') when the ops room runner arrived to tell him that he was urgently required.

The news was bad: the Mahdi army had not only taken three Iraqi policemen hostage, threatening to kill them unless the morning's detainees were released, but had also secured all entrances to the town, effectively taking it over. The police were too frightened and underequipped to deal with the situation. This was alarming in itself. What was worse was that there was now a pressing need to get ammunition and food through to CIMIC House. Henceforth this would usually be done before an operation was launched. 'However,' admitted Matt Maer, 'we were still learning and it was about to be a costly lesson.'

The replenishment of CIMIC House would be carried out early in the afternoon by C Company's Warriors, with Y Company pushing out of its perimeter to provide a 'foot on the ground', securing a safe route in, just before relief arrived. Captain Paul Hooker led off from CIMIC House with his multiple, 30A, and occupied the western side of the Majidayya Bridge. He was followed by Colour Sergeant Clifton Lea, whose multiple, 30B, passed through 30A and crossed to the eastern side of the bridge. Corporal Darren Wright, who was part of 30B multiple, recorded:

> 30A had already left by the back gate and were on their way to Blue 11. As we came close I could see 30A in position, they were spread between Blue 11 and Green 9. We moved over the bridge and half my callsign took up position on the other end of Green 9 and we were tasked to secure the other end of Green 4. We had just got there when it seemed all hell had broken loose on Green 9. I heard RPGs going off and loads of automatic being fired at this time. We weren't in contact ourselves and I told the rest of the multiple to take cover under the bridge while myself and Cpl Somerset tried comms with CSgt Lea our commander, but we couldn't, so I took four men and tried to get eyes on Green 9. But no joy, so I decided to get on the roofs but that proved too risky at that time – the enemy had pinged us and as a commander I was in my first contact, it all seemed to be happening at a hundred miles an hour. They had come under contact under the bridge as well.
>
> Every time we moved on the roof automatic bursts hit the wall around us. I remember Pte Berson laughing, shouting 'Fuck', which in turn made me laugh. Nerves, I think. I was torn: I had to get those guys away from the bridge or get eyes on to support them – we made a mad dash for it off the roof, and over some open ground between the houses. It was like something out of a movie: rounds hitting the ground and mud spitting up as we ran across. We got into another house and I opened a big metal gate and called the other blokes. I think it was about that time that LCpl Bliss's zap [number] was sent over the net and I knew he had been hit. Casevac was requested but we still couldn't get comms with our multiple commander.

Then I heard a calm voice on my PRR from the Badge [CSM Norman of Y Company] who was in CIMIC House with the snipers. 'All right, Daz, you're doing well, mate, you've got about thirty armed men to the left and running around where you are: try and get eyes on.' I heard the enemy running around but I couldn't get eyes on. At this time the blokes were in all-round defence, we had a six-foot wall all around us, we were in someone's back garden. Three RPGs went over the top of us. I didn't think we were going to get out of this. The Badge told me to sit tight and wait for a Warrior extraction. It seemed that time was now dragging. And they were still firing at us. The thing that pissed me off was that I didn't see a single gunman and didn't fire a single round. I heard the famous sound of the Warrior rockin' towards us and all the firing stopped. I remember thinking thank God, about time. We stopped off at Green 9 to pick up more blokes from 30A. An RPG hit the side of the Warrior but we all managed to get back to CIMIC in one piece.

Corporal Kris Stammers had been close to Colour Sergeant Lea on the far side of the bridge when the firing began.

Rounds started to hit our immediate vicinity and I heard CSgt Lea yell out from 50 metres away 'On me, on me!'

At that stage me and the lads sucked in what air we could, held our breath and high-tailed it back to the round-about. I can remember looking in front of me watching splashes in the dusty ground and tried to judge my speed not to run into the fire but, at the same time, not to slow down to a 'walk in the park' speed.

We got to a small compound which was situated to the left of the bridge but were deterred from entering it as there was a burst of sustained fire cutting down our right-hand side which made me shout out some extremely choice words. The team split: well, I actually split the team. The three boys took cover behind the smallest wall in the world 10 metres from the smallest open guardbox which was similar to those outside Buckingham Palace. I still can't understand why but that's the place I chose to take cover. Rounds started coming in from everywhere. It was at this stage of feeling the same as a battery hen ready for slaughter that I spotted a lone gunman on the roof to my front, no sooner I saw him than he opened fire . . . the rounds smashed into the box and I was forced to crouch and try and form myself into the floor as the white pieces of dust and brick fell on to my head.

The rounds seemed to stop coming into my position. 'Come on, Kris, get up . . . but I don't really want to, though!' I was finding out I had multiple personalities at this stage, one telling me to do my job and one saying 'Fuck it, stay where you are, he won't hit you.' What seemed like minutes was probably seconds. I forced myself up off the floor and looked to my front seeing the gunman flapping to get another magazine attached to his AK-47. At this stage, like my instructor in training once said, in battle seize the initiative. I returned three double taps at his position; the gunman fell below the roof wall. I thought 'Have I hit him, though?' Seconds later he popped back up. 'Necky wanker,' I thought, but this time I had the advantage: I pushed out of the box five metres and fired four rounds and saw them impact in his chest, the AK fell to the ground and the gunman slumped on the wall.

Corporal Stammers managed to join Colour Sergeant Lea, who was on the radio, trying to find out when the Warriors would arrive. Privates Bowler and Hall saw two enemy trying to sneak up on 30A on the other side of the river, and shot them both. Then:

the Warriors turned up, time stood still and it seemed to take for ever for our guys to be picked up. At one stage the only people on the far side of the river were CSgt Lea, LCpl Natumeru and myself, but we were shortly picked up by Maj Coote of C Company. We crammed in like sardines and extracted back to CIMIC House.

Right Private Flemming of
Y Company on patarol
in Al Amarah

Below A snap VCP is recovered
by Chinook helicopter

Lance Corporal Barry Bliss had not been so lucky. He was in Captain Hooker's multiple and remembered approaching Blue 11:

> It seemed unusually quiet which was our first combat indicator. We didn't get another. The enemy opened up in force – they seemed to be all around us. They were. I noticed a splash mark in front of me and saw it went from left to right from the opposite bank of the Tigris, so I crawled up behind the concrete pillar of a brick wall and popped my head over to see if I could see any of the enemy . . . As the firing was becoming more intense the front two soldiers started withdrawing and got into position, then me and [LCpl] Dave Larkey got up to withdraw and then, as I was running into position, 'thump' I lost my footing and stumbled but managed to keep my footing as I looked down to see a red mist and body armour fibres floating into the air around my chest. 'FUCK' I said as the realization hit home that I had been shot! Dave grabbed me and sat me down and I looked at my watch – 2.17. I didn't look at it again . . .
>
> After a while I felt myself slipping in and out of consciousness: Dave gripped me and started telling jokes . . . I heard Warriors approaching for my extraction then boom one of the Warriors was hit by an RPG. My stomach came up to my mouth as the thought of not getting extracted quick enough was rattling through my head. The next thing I knew I had been picked up and thrown into the back of a Warrior. It seemed to take for ever to get to Abu Naji but as soon as we arrived I was put on a stretcher and . . . on to a Chinook where I was stabilized and felt a hell of a lot better. My last memory was being wheeled into a field hospital at Shaiba, my clothes being cut off . . .
>
> After coming out of hospital I was told by workmates that it was a sniper with a [Russian-made] Dragonov who shot me, who's now a lot worse off than me, myself missing the right lower lobe of my lung with some impressive scars, demoted to Silk Cut cigarettes and a long Christmas card list.

While protecting him Dave Larkey had been shot through the web-bing, 'seriously injuring his camera'.

'Baz Bliss was evacuated and the remainder of the guys sat in silence with mixed emotions and partly on a natural high,' remembered Kris Stammers. 'We all have our own thoughts on the contact that day and we talk about it occasionally, and occasionally we laugh about it, taking the piss out of each other, but we all are here now to do that, which is the most important thing.'

'I have had lasting thoughts about that afternoon...' mused Captain Hooker.

> Whilst being stuck behind a wall under fire and Cpl Raynsford deciding that, as we were not going anywhere, he would have a cigarette, only to discover that he had forgotten his lighter, and both of us finding it highly amusing. That having been in contact for two and a half hours, the order for us to go back out again, within the hour, was met with a shrug and a nod from the men.

Major Justin Featherstone was impressed by the bravery of the Scots Territorials he had committed to the fight.

> Even with C Company on their way, the seriousness of the situation meant that I ordered my Territorial Army mul-tiple, from The Lowland Regiment, to make an extremely hazardous link-up along Baghdad Street, in order to secure the casualty for evacuation. The multiple was all TA, bar Sgt Cornhill and Cpl Marsh, who I had embedded from my recce platoon. Their teams, with CSgt Ivine's, then fought their way along this kilometre-long, narrow street, whilst under fire from RPGs, small arms, medium machine guns and grenade attack. Even as they were told the enemy was sealing their entry point with a burning barricade, they never faltered.
>
> For forty-five minutes they pressed on, engaging the enemy all around them and entering a number of houses, often running across one rooftop and then descending into the street through a different building. Even in such a

precarious situation, Cpl Marsh still took time to find out the latest football results from a family watching football on television ... The actions of these men [the Lowland Territorials], whether butchers, mechanics or unemployed only weeks before, was simply stupendous. Their bravery, aggression and drive forced the link-up and ensured that Bliss was protected until C Company's Warriors could extract him and my other callsigns ...

While the firefight was in progress, Second Lieutenant Richard Deane, commanding 8 Platoon, was clattering into the town from the south-west when he ran squarely into an ambush:

As W20 callsign approached Blue 7 in Al Amarah it was struck with two missiles and a number of RPGs. I was knocked out by the blast in the turret. The driver, Private Beharry, took the initiative and led the rest of the packet [of vehicles] out of the killing area in the damaged and burning Warrior to safety at CIMIC House. He then got out and helped casevac me out of the burning turret before collapsing ... Later a 7.62mm bullet was found lodged in his helmet.

Pte Samuels, the gunner, did very well indeed as he managed to return fire with my rifle from the turret even though we were under very heavy fire. He had also sustained burns to his face and neck ... however, he still managed to maintain his discipline and return appropriate fire. LCpl Wood was a dismount in the back of the Warrior. He managed to put out the fire before administering first aid to the remaining dismounts even though he himself was injured. He also helped with the casevac at CIMIC House whilst under fire.

Pte Crucefix was also a dismount in the rear of the Warrior and was injured with shrapnel to his face. He got out at CIMIC House and was not casevaced straight away. He returned to the Warrior a short time after the rest of the callsign was airlifted to hospital and collected all the equipment and ammunition he could carry. He returned

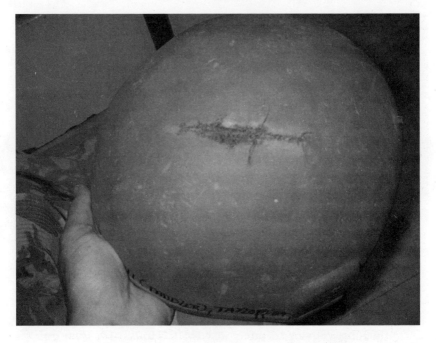

A narrow shave: Private Johnson Beharry's helmet

to CIMIC House with this kit, thereby denying it to the enemy, all the time still under incoming fire.

Johnson Beharry had in fact driven the damaged Warrior through the first ambush position, and was now without any means of communication with the others in it or with the rest of the multiple. He had halted short of a barricade in an effort to establish communications, but, when the vehicle was hit by another RPG, he decided that the surest way of saving the lives of his comrades – all of whom seemed to be wounded or dead – was to crash on through the barricade and to head for CIMIC House. Another RPG wounded Private Samuels, and Beharry drove on for 1,500 metres, with his hatch open so as to obtain a better view and escape from the smoke in the vehicle's interior. He dismounted again to drag the wounded Richard Deane from the turret, under fire all the time, and put him safely in the back of another Warrior. He then negotiated the chicane at the entrance to CIMIC House before dismounting for the third time and collapsing with sheer exhaustion.

C Company's Private Tatawaqa after a heavy contact

The vehicle had come to a halt in the compound with its rear door facing the gate. New Zealand-born Private Crucefix, a big, quiet man with only a few months' service, later removed all the weapons and equipment from the back, all the while with an RPG fragment the size of a credit card embedded in his face.

Meanwhile 7 Platoon pushed on, as Private Cham recorded:

> . . . we have to go and evacuate the dismounted troops on the ground. This was my first personal experience of live bullets coming inches close to me. As a dismount in the back of a Warrior the most disturbing thing is when you hear one of the crew shout RPG! All you can do as a dismount . . . is to try to cover your ears, make yourself smaller somehow and wait for the worst outcome while sweating more than usual.

Major Coote, emailing his friends at the time, thought that, all in all, C Company had been 'very lucky'. All his casualties had been evacuated, and Private Beharry had become 'something of a local hero'. He himself recorded a near miss:

> During the battle my gunner was engaging an RPG man when I looked out to the side to see another fire from 75 metres away. The missile left the launcher, swirled a bit and then dropped to the ground about 20 metres from our Warrior. Whatever thoughts or prayers you have been saying – keep it up!

C Company duly got through to CIMIC House with rations and ammunition. 'It's not every girl that has her groceries delivered by Warrior,' said Molly Phee.

'Having recovered C Company,' wrote Matt Maer,

> it seemed as if the day was at last starting to reach some form of equilibrium. While the Mahdi army still had a large number of ambush parties on the streets of Al Amarah we had at least got through to CIMIC House and it was resupplied. It was under attack intermittently but it was strong enough to hold and we had proved that we could get through when we chose to do so, if we amassed sufficient strength. However, there was still a roll of the dice left to come.

It was late afternoon when Agnes, his interpreter, took a telephone call from the chief of police in Al Amarah asking if there were any Americans in the area. He replied that there were not, and thought no more about it. Then, at about 1800 hours, a patrol to the south of Al Amarah reported vehicles burning on Route 6. Further investigation revealed that there were several US army vehicles in flames on the road, and the Lancers' 6th Troop was immediately detailed to escort two ambulances to collect casualties. Lieutenant Tom Prideaux recalled:

> We sped south, Land Rover engines screaming. In the distance we could see an ominous glow. As we drew nearer, expletives slipped out from under the breath of even the

The wreckage of the American convoy

most experienced members of the troop. Our lead vehicle, commanded by Sgt Mark Brewster, reported that the south-bound carriageway was blocked with burning vehicles. Never had any of us seen anything burn as fiercely as the decimated remains of the convoy. There was no sign of life. No sign of movement. Did the entire convoy cop it? Where were the survivors? Where were the casualties? The realization that this was for real finally hit home. Cpl Mark Stevens said what we were all thinking: 'There's no survivors there, boss.'

The troop continued a few kilometres further south, where it discovered the American survivors, who had met a patrol of The Argyll and Sutherland Highlanders, operating to the south of Al Amarah, who had advised them to turn back. 'Back to where?' was their first response, for they did not know that there was a British base in the area.

It turned out that an American engineer unit, at the end of its tour of duty, had headed south for Kuwait with an assortment of soft-skinned vehicles including low-loaders, trucks, some HUMMVs and a petrol tanker. It was not aware of the local tactical situation and had apparently made no contact with the British. As Matt Maer explained:

On entering Al Amarah the convoy saw little to arouse suspicions but then they weren't expecting to see anything suspicious. They proceeded across the bridge at Red 13. Once the first few vehicles were across they started to receive fire from their left – the eastern side of the route. There are a number of large buildings there such as the court and the police station and the enemy were firing from all levels of the buildings. The convoy was large . . . and so stopping and reversing was not really a feasible option. The commander decided not to become split up and so every vehicle was forced through the ambush. They returned fire with fifty cals [.50in machine guns] but were taking a hammering at the hands of the enemy . . .

North of the Purple Route the Americans were subjected to a number of concentrated and intense ambushes focused on individual junctions or road sections. To the south they felt the intensity of the fire lessen considerably, however it was constant for the next two kilometres until they broke clear of the city.

The Americans went into a hasty leaguer south of the town, and their commander decided to destroy some of his seriously damaged vehicles so as to deny them to the enemy, and to continue with the remainder. Two of his men had been killed and several more wounded; two were missing in action. James Coote observed that this was, in itself, an index of the Mahdi army's early inefficiency, and it soon emerged that four of the attackers had been killed by 'friendly' fire, the result of one side of the road hitting ambushers on the other. 'The US soldiers were in a daze,' thought Tom Prideaux:

They didn't have a clue what had hit them. At least ten vehicles were still burning fiercely . . . The convoy had started out with thirty-five vehicles, only twenty-two were recovered . . . we had some difficulty in working out how many men still had to be accounted for.

As 6th Troop was dealing with the American wounded, a platoon of C Company Warriors arrived and fanned out into covering pos-

itions. 'We were lucky that no further complications arose,' wrote
Lieutenant Prideaux, 'enabling us to get the wounded loaded into
the ambulances and head back to camp, leaving the Warriors to
escort what remained of the convoy.' There was good news back at
camp. The two missing US soldiers had appeared at the Iraqi police
checkpoint at Red 2, having been left behind by the convoy after
their vehicle was disabled in the ambush. Their escape was little short
of miraculous, and speaks volumes for the courage of some Iraqi
police.

> The two men . . . had run through the city trying to get
> clear of the danger area and being pursued by a large crowd
> . . . The two soldiers knew that the convoy would end up to
> the south, but that was all they knew, and their flight
> through the Kadeem Al Muallimin estate, one of the most
> dangerous areas of the city and where we had earlier that
> day conducted Op Pimlico, must have felt hopeless at times.
> A police car drew up and the crew ushered the two men to
> get in. At this time a very significant number of the local
> police were fighting for or collaborating with the Mahdi
> army. The soldiers were lucky that the crew were decent
> honourable men who just wanted to get them out of danger
> and who, at considerable risk to themselves, delivered the
> soldiers to the gates of the camp.

The incident could have been infinitely worse, and the day ended
as a qualified success. Matt Maer recognized, however, that 'qualified'
was the right word. Operation Pimlico had sought to sever the head
in the hope that the snake would die, but 'we had not achieved that
effect. The Mahdi army was still able to assert its violent will in
Al Amarah.' He needed to regain control of the town for two reasons.
First, his primary aim was to train the Iraqi security forces so that
they could take over from the coalition, and this could not be
accomplished with the Mahdi army in control. Second, it was evident
that, although the insurgents

> found their support amongst the unemployed, disaffected
> and dangerous male youth, for whom liberation had

brought little positive change . . . for the majority of Maysan-
ites there was a desire to carry on life in a peaceful manner,
to gain what could be gained from liberation (even if it was
not at a pace expected) and to move on to a new Iraq.

It was entirely characteristic of the conflict that negotiations had
been going on in the Pink Palace, seat of the provincial government,
while the fighting was in progress. Molly Phee had maintained the
support of the moderate majority in the Provincial Council and
amongst the wider Iraqi leadership. But nothing could be taken
forward if gunmen still ruled the streets. The police would never
improve; the moderates would lose faith, and the coalition's credibility would be called into question. Matt Maer concluded that 'the
Mahdi army had to be taken down in Al Amarah', and began to plan
how to do it.

His opening move, on 3 May, was to launch Operation Knightsbridge. This involved another resupply of CIMIC House, but this
time the battle group advanced with tanks leading, hooking round
from the west and north to the area of the Majidayya estate. Although
there were sporadic clashes, the tanks clearly overawed the insurgents, but intelligence indicated that the story put about by the
fighters was that they had been asleep when the convoy arrived. This
information provided the genesis for Operation Waterloo. For this,
there would not simply be a thrust and recovery to and from CIMIC
House, but C Company 'would sit on the junction at Red 11 which
had good fields of fire and wait for them to have a go. If they bottled
it they would lose face in front of the local community. If they fought
they would lose. Either way we would win.'

The result of the planning was unveiled on 7 May when Lieutenant Colonel Maer issued his orders for Operation Waterloo. The
C Company notes recorded:

The orders group had given some hint of the scale of the
operation, with the crews of 12 Warriors, 4 Challengers,
Forward Air Controllers, Medics and Recovery teams,
amongst others, crammed into the small briefing room.

C Company soldiers in the police station (Coot)
at the end of Operation Waterloo

Despite the heat and lack of air there was not a hint of anyone's concentration wavering. Forty minutes later and following the Commanding Officer's last word the assembled masses departed for their final checks; when deploying into battle for real there is no need to remind even the newest privates of their responsibilities.

A Company 1 PWRR would fight with the battle group in Operation Waterloo. It had previously been in brigade reserve in Basra, where it had first been based in Basra Palace. On the day the company took over responsibility from a company of The Royal Regiment of Wales there were three massive explosions at the three main police stations in the town, which 'really gave the company the eye-opener it needed'. For a long time this was the most significant incident to occur in Basra. These were suicide bombs, mercifully rare in the south but hideously lethal and indiscriminate. Bodies were strewn around the streets and some angry locals accused the coalition of having fired on the crowds from helicopters; there was to be more of this nonsense as the tour ground on. Those who witnessed the explosion were sickened. I saw one photograph of a man's face, peeled away from the skull by the blast, lying mask-like in the street.

A week later, A Company was ordered to move up by road to Al Amarah to work with the PWRR battle group, and although there were some difficulties persuading the drivers of the low-loaders to proceed up the dangerous Route 6, they had all arrived in time to join the battle group for its biggest operation to date. Captain Richard Jones remembered:

> I quickly became acquainted with the logistics of moving an entire company, together with its [vehicle fleet and] combat service support elements, 150 kilometres north on minimal notice to move. It is amazing how quickly the cogs can turn when the heat is on and things have to happen. The company was given sixteen hours, we needed only thirteen.
>
> The guys had mixed emotions. There was a sense of anticipation, apprehension and a healthy dose of excitement. A lot of people at home find it difficult to understand how we could be excited about being sent into the thick of things. It was simple, we were doing the job we had all trained to do. For us not to have wanted to go would have been like a lawyer studying law, passing their bar exams and then never wanting to step into a court room. Abu Naji was a world away from the relative comfort of Basra Palace. It felt almost like a different tour. At SLB and the Palace it was a common occurrence to see people walking in shorts and T shirt without a care in the world. At Abu Naji it was the highlight of the week if you got to walk around without your body armour for half a day.

The first phase of the operation was to be the well rehearsed resupply of CIMIC House, carried out by the whole of C Company with a troop of four Challenger 2 tanks, with the whole of this combat team hooking in from Sparrowhawk. At 2.00 in the morning of 8 May the C Company combat team shook out into assault formation on Sparrowhawk. As it moved past the Iraqi National Guard camp the lights flashed on and off: the whole town knew that the British were on their way. With the Challengers leading, the group moved steadily to Red 11, the main intersection in town. This was in full view of the Office of the Martyr Sadr, and so far all seemed quiet, although experience already indicated that engine noise meant that shots could only be heard when they hit the sides of vehicles.

The Warriors then leapfrogged through with the tanks and moved north on to Red 14, and then across to Green 5 and 4. The Challengers were too heavy to cross the bridge at Green 4, so moved to positions covering the last leg of the advance and the resupply of CIMIC House, each supported by a Warrior with its dismounts. As soon as the position was firm, the eight remaining C Company Warriors began to move through this fire base and to cross the bridge.

Corporal Edwards of 7 Platoon recalled:

The plan was simple. Two tanks and two Warriors complete with two sections were to secure the bridge. W12 commanded by LCpl Laird on the left with W13C (myself) and six others in the back. On the right, W23 was commanded by Sgt Llewellyn with W32C (Cpl Difford's section) in the back. The funny thing about Warriors, other than requiring more maintenance than a Chinook, is that, when you're in the back, even a journey from the sheds to the POL point feels like you're doing a run into an attack. So when we debussed to the sight of the tracer from the rooftops, with a random passing RPG and not a safety supervisor in sight, I knew the pressure was on.

As was agreed, I cleared my side of the bridge first before Diff's section cleared theirs. As Diff went forwards there was a contact, and fire was returned. The next thing I heard was Diff on the PRR stating that he had been shot . . . reality check time!

Like the other CSMs, Company Sergeant Major Falconer had swapped his old lightly armoured 432 (whose survival in an armoured battle group doubtless makes more sense to accountants than to tacticians) for a Warrior, callsign W33A, which he had effectively converted into an ambulance, with stretchers, oxygen, fluids, chest seals, dressings, painkillers, spare morphine and a good medic . . . The soldiers needed to know that when things had gone wrong I would be there through thick and thin, that I was going to get them off the ground and back down the chain.

A quarter of his company became casualties in the first few weeks – with everything from 'heat injuries, gunshot, blast and shrapnel wounds to severe burns'. The only time he doubted himself was when Corporal Difford, over the radio, sounded as if he was announcing that he had been hit in the throat:

> Within what seemed like a week but was in reality about two minutes I had located Corporal Difford who was being treated by a number of his section. 'Out with the stretcher, medic stand by in the back of my Warrior, driver full speed ahead for the ambulance exchange point, wait a moment! A gunshot wound to the foot, calm down' went through my head in seconds.

'Foot' had been misheard as 'throat' and 'within two minutes Corporal Difford was smoking fags like there was no tomorrow in the back of my Warrior . . . within thirty minutes he was asleep for the next two to three hours as . . . the battle for Al Amarah continued'.

Corporal Edwards had also been concerned, because he, in turn, thought that Corporal Difford had been shot in the 'front'.

> I offered to take my team medic over . . . Then, just as quickly as the Challenger was getting through 1B1T 7.62mm [machine-gun belts loaded with one round of ball followed by one of tracer] . . . the voice on the net changed to the very reassuring tones of W33A who appeared, just as he had promised in every O Group [Orders group – a pre-battle briefing], 'I will get you.' Without wishing to sound like an American, I felt proud as the CSM's wagon, 'the Millennium Falconer', thundered forward and casevaced Diff. Section 2ic crack on!

The battle gathered intensity, with tracer curling across the sky. The eight Warriors pushed on and secured Green 9. Barricades across the road made it hard to identify the bridge at Blue 11 and a blizzard of incoming fire from the Majidayya estate made it too risky to open turrets. Nevertheless, Major James Coote in W0B took the lead, crossed the narrow bridge with the remaining Warriors following on – unexpectedly joined by some REME recovery vehicles – and followed the bend of the river to CIMIC House. No sooner had they come to a halt outside its blast walls than a swarm of men poured through the gates; supplies were heaved out of the Warriors to those waiting, the tracer overhead reminding all concerned of the imperative.

Captain Marcus Butlin, the company 2ic, controlled the troops on the ground, moving the Warriors on as soon as they had disgorged water, food, ammunition and the occasional passenger. When the business was completed, the troops remounted and the packet fought its way back to join the Challengers and the Warriors on the far side of the river. The Challengers pulled back from their over-watch positions and led the combat team back to Red 11. Instead of falling back on Camp Abu Naji, however, the team took up a loose defensive position, awaiting counter-attack on ground of its own choosing. Over the next hour or so scores of attacks were repulsed by an aggressive defence; vehicles and dismounts repeatedly engaged parties of insurgents until the weight of the assaults fell off and it was clear that the battle was won.

An RAF Nimrod MR2 and an American AC-130 Spectre looked down from above in touch with air controllers attached to both company and battle group headquarters. When an enemy mortar team with infantry support came into action from close to the OMS, it was hit by two rounds of 105mm airburst from the Spectre. 'The effect,' noted the C Company account, 'was breathtaking and final.' More crew-served weapons appeared on the roof of the library and in the back of pick-up trucks, and were destroyed from the air: 'Dealing with them with infantry would have been a risky business: Spectre proved to be a battle-winning asset.'

Just before dawn Matt Maer gave orders to advance on the OMS. He had worked hard to ensure that all the leading political figures realized that this was a targeted operation, aimed specifically at the Mahdi army's gunmen. The Challengers eased their way towards

Yellow 3, and as they and the Warriors nudged up on to the exposed ramps of the bridge they were assailed by sporadic RPG fire, but the firing points were neutralized by mutually supporting vehicles. The enemy around the OMS declined to engage the Challengers as they crested the bridge, and the CO gave the order to 'go and knock on the door'. The Challengers pushed on, and 9 Platoon shook out to cover the final leg of the advance. W0B drove down the far ramp of the bridge, turret traversing as its crew looked for signs of life. Corporal Edwards had done a five-week Arabic course, but

> it was the last weapon in the company arsenal I was ex-
> pecting to use. So you can imagine my feeling when Zap
> Echo Delta [his personal zap number] was called forward
> to the company commander's Warrior. As I climbed in a
> loudhailer was thrust into my hand.
>
> So, as [W]0B pulled up outside the OMS, I couldn't
> help feeling a little ironic . . . with my loudhailer and com-
> edy Arabic voice. Needless to say, I became one with the
> back [storage] bin in the hope that four jerry cans of water
> would have the same protective qualities as a sandbag wall.
> It was with great relief and much amusement for my section
> that I returned to W13 having found nobody at home.

As dawn broke Corporal Byles's section dismounted to storm the building – 'they went through it like a dose of salts,' recalled Corporal Edwards, who accompanied the assault in case translation was required. The OMS was empty but for a vast haul of weapons – 'from your average AK to aircraft-mounted missiles'. The ATO was summoned to ensure that they were safe before they were removed. Other dismounts then moved in to secure the area. As they did so, a grenade was thrown by a passing motorcyclist, wounding Private Hartnell. He thought it unnecessary to inform anyone, and remained on duty until his section commander noticed that his uniform was soaked through with blood: he made a full recovery. Clearance patrols sent out into the gardens west of the OMS found grisly evidence of Spectre's handiwork: 'Dismembered bodies lay around on the ground, their rifles and RPGs beside them.'

A baton gunner, almost certainly 1 LI,
engages a rioter

A Company, under Major Simon Thomsett, supported by another four Challengers, was initially held in reserve, with a number of possible tasks. It could be used simply to reinforce C Company or, if the latter became bogged down short of CIMIC House, to conduct a 'forward passage of lines' and move on through C Company. But its primary task was to provide a block east of the Tigris, cordoning off the central area so that it could be searched by C Company, and at the same time to prevent the Mahdi army fighters known to live around the Sadr Mosque at Blue 8 from entering the fray. Simon Thomsett proposed to advance up Blue Route from the south-east, avoiding the known ambush position at Blue 7 by cutting in via Blue 14. 2 Platoon would secure the southern part of the area between Yellow 2 and Blue 8; 3 Platoon was to seize the police HQ, and 1 Platoon was to go firm at Blue 9 before moving north to Blue 11. This was the older part of town. The wide boulevards on the west bank of the Tigris favoured the use of armoured vehicles, but the narrow streets on the east bank lent themselves to the hit-and-run tactics popular with the insurgents.

Lieutenant James Robinson and 2 Platoon led off to Blue 6 and secured a break-in. The rest of the company rumbled on, heading for Blue 14, coming under sporadic small-arms fire as it did so, so that turrets had to be closed. When the company reached Blue 14, Lieutenant Robbie Hicks was ordered to hang back there with 1 Platoon, while 3 Platoon moved on. His men dismounted and there was a brief exchange of shots, but they soon mounted up again and headed for the platoon objective at Blue 9, squarely in the centre of the town:

> I led the four Warriors around the edge of the soft marshy wasteland between Al Muqatil Al Arabi and Al Husayn estates and crossed the bridge on to the main road heading north. About 200 metres further up the road I heard an almighty crash, as I looked back I saw callsign N13 had misjudged the bridge and crashed quite badly into the open sewer. Callsign N13 was jammed tight and could not self-recover. I informed callsign N0B Major Simon Thomsett and collected the REME recovery wagon commanded by Corporal Mason to extract N13 from the sewer.
>
> As I returned to the crash site things had gone from bad to worse. Callsign N11 had tried to find another way round the sewer and got stuck in the south-east corner. As soon as N11 had crashed it came under fire from three

C Company's W0C from the rear window of W0B, on the
way to action at Danny Boy

sides. I told Corporal Wardle to dismount his section and
provide cover to the north and east. I then took the Warrior
to the south-east corner and parked it across the junction
to create some cover for the men of N11 and N13 who had
already dismounted. I tried to find out what was going on
but was unable to get any comms with Sergeant Epton, and
Corporal Ransley's comms were difficult to unworkable.

This was it, time to earn my pay. I handed command
of the Warrior over to Private McAllister my gunner who
although still a private soldier had commanded a Warrior
for two months in Canada and was more than capable. As
I pulled my 352 radio on to my back in the rear of the
Warrior I took a second to calm myself down, opened the
door and jumped out. As I closed the door what looked
like a firework came flying towards me at about head height.
I dived to the floor but warned Corporal Wardle that an RPG
rocket was flying towards him. The rocket hit the ground
but did not explode. I stood up and Corporal Ransley
vocally guided me on to his position. As I approached what

looked like a slightly marshy area Corporal Ransley started shouting at me to stop. I thought something really bad was about to happen but he was just saving me from the same mistake he and Private Edris had made, the marshy area to my front was in fact just the drying-out crust of another open sewer.

Robbie Hicks now put his platoon into a triangular position of all-round defence. After another half-hour of firefight he seemed to have the situation under control, and tried to tell his company commander this on the radio – but, bizarrely, he could not reach him, although he was less than a kilometre away. However, he was able to speak to Steve Brooks in the ops room at CIMIC House, four kilometres off. He was sending the report when the platoon was taken on by a 13mm anti-aircraft gun, but happily 'they were not the best shots in the world'.

Corporal Mason and his REME recovery team, meanwhile, were working under constant fire and up to their waists in ordure. 'I cannot stress enough the role played by Corporal Mason and his crew,' wrote Simon Thomsett. 'For six hours they fixed lines, effected tows and changed tracks in order to get vehicles moving. All of this was compounded by the need to work in raw sewage. They deserve our praise, although getting too close was not advisable.' Whenever Major Thomsett asked how long the recovery would take, he was told 'twenty minutes', and as dawn came up the plight of 1 Platoon, now clearly visible, attracted increasing hostile attention. Major Thomsett sent a Challenger down to cover their left flank, but 1 Platoon fought a private battle with all the weapons at its disposal, using the Warriors as mobile fire support while the dismounts took on the gunmen with accurate small-arms fire.

Corporal Mason's stalwarts managed to retrieve N11 from the sewer, and by 4.15 Lieutenant Hicks was in command of three work-ing Warriors, one of them rather smelly. But N13 was still firmly jammed, and Corporal Mason had to summon more help before, at midday, it was at last dragged clear. It transpired that it had thrown a track, and so it had to be towed to safety. Robbie Hicks cross-decked as much of the ammunition and manpower as he could, then went to join the rest of his platoon, who had now taken over at Blue 11. He reached there to be told that the first phase of the operation was complete: elements of C Company were escorting several truckloads of weapons and equipment captured in and around the OMS.

Much earlier, with 1 Platoon effectively out of action, Simon Thomsett took over its task at Blue 9 with his headquarters group – N0B, N0C, the CSM's Warrior and the remaining REME recovery vehicle. He soon realized that the fire station building gave him the best position for a strongpoint and its roof had the added advantage of height. Company Sergeant Major Wood posted the group's dismounts in the building and sent snipers up on to the roof, while Major Thomsett collected reports from his platoons and began to make a rapid plan. At this stage the men came under heavy attack from groups of gunmen and RPG teams. They could reply only with small arms, rather than with the Warriors' turret weapons, because the enemy fired from buildings evidently containing women and children or from behind groups of bystanders. Staff Sergeant Smith, the company's REME artificer, and Lance Corporal Kasaiwakya, one of its medics, were both wounded by an RPG which bounced off N0B and exploded on the wall of the fire station. Both were evacuated in the CSM's Warrior, which was itself hit by two RPGs on its journey out.

2 Platoon, meanwhile, was working its way up Blue Route, dealing with ambushes as it met them and pushing aside the enemy, most of whom fell back into the blue estate. The Challenger accompanying the platoon hit mines hidden amongst the debris, but they damaged only its armoured skirts. More surface-laid mines were discovered close to the Sadr Mosque. Here 2 Platoon met both 3 Platoon and some forward troops of C Company, and soon Major Thomsett was at last in a position to fight a company battle. The enemy concentrated their fire on the tank to the detriment of maintaining a proper all-round defence, and the dismounts of 2 and 3 Platoons began to fight their way through the alleyways towards and across Blue Route. 'This was a classic advance to contact in a FIBUA [fighting in built-up areas] environment,' thought Simon Thomsett,

and the training A Company had completed at Copehill Down [the 'German village' on Salisbury Plain] the previous summer paid dividends. The platoon commanders used fire and manoeuvre at team level to engage and destroy multiple enemy positions despite having to contend with a three-dimensional battlefield. 3 Platoon were bogged down at one point by small-arms fire, but accurate sustained fire by Minimi and the use of the UGL as a close support weapon allowed them to win the firefight and clear positions without having to enter buildings. Eventually the advance was complete and the enemy had been cleared to a line roughly north/south along Blue 14. 1 Platoon had been recovered and the OC rebalanced the company for what was bound to be a long day.

Not far to the west, the ATO had by now arrived at the OMS building, and under his supervision an unbelievable three 8-ton truckloads of mortars, rockets, bombs, rifles, mines and ammunition were recovered. Crowds were beginning to gather, and were less than enthusiastic about the redistribution of assets, but a well timed low pass by an RAF Tornado reminded them who was in charge of Al Amarah now.

The crowd thinned out, allowing the troops to clear both the library – there was a Russian AGS17 automatic grenade-launcher quite correctly shelved in the non-fiction department – and the labour exchange. Attacks from the west were now infrequent, allowing C Company to reorganize into a defensive position around Red 11. Troops were rotated through the jail building to get them out of the sun and to let them take on water. 'The police guards looked somewhat bemused,' recalled Major Coote. 'They had looked on with disinterest as we had fought through the night, presumably not wishing to take sides until the victor was known. They now accepted our presence with little more than apathy and continued with their daily work of watching the world go by.'

With the enemy defeated, the battle group moved on to the next phase, the domination of the city. C Company now went to the central police station and established a patrol base there in concert with A Company of The Royal Welch Fusiliers. Platoons patrolled the streets in Warriors,

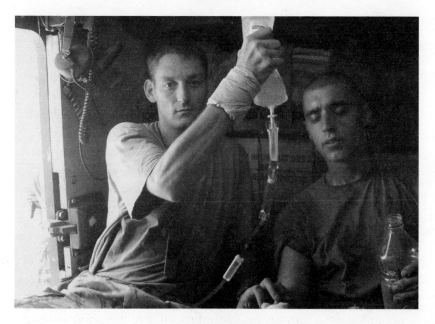

Private Pritchard gives first aid to a dehydrated
Private Crawshaw

generally unmolested save for the occasional have-a-go hero
who was sent to meet his maker if he hung around long
enough ... Soldiers slept wherever they could find floor
space, being eaten alive by insects and kicked by policemen
as they stumbled along the corridors in the darkness of power
cuts. Compo rations were sufficiently hot to eat without cooking and tea was made directly from the water bottles. Several
soldiers braved local cuisine, dispatching policemen or one
of the army of children to local shops to fetch soft drinks or
kebabs in return for US dollars. However, the exhaustion of
the night's exertion meant that few couldn't sleep and there
were no complaints. That no one had been killed and that
our casualties were so light was the only thing of concern.

A Company also began to wind down, as Robbie Hicks recalled:

Things were starting to look up but the extreme heat was
starting to take its toll and Pte Annis started to throw up

and drift in and out of consciousness. His temperature was through the roof and I knew if I did not extract him straight away he could be in really serious trouble. I took him in the Warrior to the fire station at Blue 9, which following some serious fighting had become company headquarters. The sight that greeted me once there was not what I had expected – the building had taken a real hammering, there were scorch marks and bullet holes all over the walls from this morning's attacks. I returned to the rest of the platoon to find that 2 Platoon had been sent to co-locate themselves with us. It was great to see Lt Robinson and Sgt Fitzgerald again and we decided to move into the local school to give the troops some cover from the afternoon sun. We rotated a stag outside in the Warriors, and I even managed about half an hour's sleep. We stayed there till late afternoon when we pulled back to CIMIC House.

We were now in the final phase of the operation – the transition back to normal life. We were to go out on mobile patrols throughout the night, providing an almost constant presence in the town. There was not enough room in the compound so whenever we were not on patrol we would park up outside and try to get some sleep. We were all so tired that the tarmac felt as comfortable as any bed I have ever slept in, and as soon as my head touched the ground I was out like a light till my next patrol. The night was very quiet but I will never forget the look of horror on the faces of the recce lads when they left the compound for a morning patrol and saw where we had slept, as they called the area opposite our open-air bedroom RPG alley as that was where most of the attacks came from. After a quick wash and shave we had more patrolling to do before C Company arrived to relieve us.

The Royal Welch Fusiliers had been waiting in the wings while the fighting flared on. Lieutenant Neale reflected:

The main thing that sticks in my mind about Op Waterloo was the uncertainty. A Company sat with its vehicles lined up in packets waiting for the CO to deem that the armoured battle had reached a stage at which he could take a sensible risk by allowing the soft-skinned vehicles into the city. We were sat from midnight on and could hear the sounds and see the flashes as the fight progressed. Time seemed to drag and slowly daylight broke.

When the call came the atmosphere was thick with mixed emotion. At this point all had been involved in a number of contacts and were loath to do so again but the choice was not ours to make. We knew that we were going into hostile territory without either the benefits of good protection or heavy firepower that the armoured callsigns possessed, and we did not know how long we would be deploying for . . .

There was a definite feeling that we were doing an equally dangerous task but all knew that it did not carry the same kudos as the armoured battle. Also, as the Warriors reached their limit and pulled back to camp we knew that our task was only just beginning.

Matt Maer began to pull his Warriors out of the city. He was delighted:

> Operation Waterloo was a success. The feeling of driving into Al Amarah to meet up with James Coote outside the OMS building was one of the highs of the tour. To be sitting back outside the building that I had last seen through a cloud of RPG smoke was pleasurable. I then moved up the road to see Molly Phee in CIMIC House. She was full of praise for what the battle group had achieved. Not only had it relieved, I hoped, some of the pressure from her and her team, along with Y Company, in CIMIC House, but it also gave her the political capital to carry the Provincial Council.

But Operation Waterloo had a sting in its tail.

On 9 May C Company's 8 Platoon, accompanied by a Challenger 2, was turning west at Blue 8. Sergeant Llewellyn was commanding W23, the penultimate vehicle, when a petrol bomb was thrown, by a boy of perhaps eight to ten years old. The platoon commander, Second Lieutenant Deane, now recovered from his injuries incurred on Operation Pimlico just over a week before, describes what happened:

> The petrol bomb smashed on the front of the turret and the flaming petrol engulfed Sgt Llewellyn in the commander's turret. He managed to get out of the Warrior and was rolling about the street on fire. Sgt Broome took the initiative and jumped out of his Warrior W22 with a fire extinguisher and put the flames engulfing Sgt Llewellyn out. He then proceeded to put the fire out in W23. Pte Hughes also assisted Sgt Broome with helping to douse the flames with a fire extinguisher.

Sergeant Chris ('Stick') Broome knew Sergeant Llewellyn very well:

> Sergeant Adam Llewellyn is a good friend of mine, he is an excellent soldier, robust and a solid man to stand by. On the day he got petrol-bombed, this attack was carried out by children. A child you would think could not do damage to someone as robust as Lewy. But when petrol is set alight all over your body, it doesn't matter how old or big the person who threw it is. The moment I saw Lewy on fire, time went into slow motion for me. A thousand thoughts went racing through my head. The first was to jump out of my Warrior and run to him. Before I could do that, I had to stop the vehicle. I was shouting on the intercom at my driver, who could therefore not hear me properly. This caused him to hesitate and question what I was saying. The dismounts in both Warriors were oblivious to what was going on as they could not see what was happening. You may say that all of this took only a few seconds, but when your mate is rolling around on the floor screaming in pain, tell him that!
>
> When I finally jumped out of the Warrior and ran down the road to him, I had to grab him and put him in the back of his Warrior. The dismounts were now aware of what was going on and moved to help [Privates Vuetanatokoka and Sewell were well to the fore]. Straight away we gave Lewy

morphine. I did not know what to expect, but it didn't work as quickly as I thought it would. Here was my mate who was screaming in pain and the morphine didn't seem to be working. His screams were going straight through me, but he desperately needed our help. We used the fresh water that we carry with us on the Warrior to put out his burns. However, due to the fact of the heat inside the Warrior, the water was piping hot. When we poured the water on Lewy, this just seemed to be burning his skin even more. It was not until then that I got a really good look at his injuries. His shirt was completely burnt from his arms and the skin was hanging off in a terrible mess. The best way I can describe the state of his hands was raw flesh . . .

I needed to get him to an IRT. I could hear someone shouting that the turret was still on fire and petrol had gone all over the ammo. Along with the dismounts, I grabbed a fire extinguisher and jumped into the turret and put the rest of the flames out. I quickly returned to Lewy to reassure him that we were getting out of this situation now. I remember thinking that this is my mate sat there with his skin hanging off his arms. It's at this point that I felt very alone. I was trying to do my best for my mate as well as assess what was happening around me on the ground.

Just up the road, Corporal Eddie Edwards of 7 Platoon was told that a casualty was coming in.

The 8 Platoon Warriors rocked up and I was told he's in the back. As the door opened my eyes searched the back for the casualty but all I could see was Lewy sat staring back at me shirtless. It probably took a few seconds to dawn on me that he was the casualty: it was disbelief that caused it, a good mate of mine who if truth be known I look up to as a natural *infantry* soldier.

It wasn't just the state of his injuries, he was badly burned and his skin was hanging off his arms and especially his hands. What got me was what he was saying which I will not repeat as it is hugely personal. Treating him was easy, lots of cold water, mopping his brow with my sweat rag that I had soaked in cold water. I made my team medic inject him with morphine, it seems stupid to me now but I knew the needle would hurt him and I couldn't bear to cause him any more pain . . .

Second Lieutenant Deane led the packet back to the police station where C Company was currently based, and was met by 7 Platoon with cold water for Lewy's burns. By this stage Sergeant Broome was having breathing difficulties because of the smoke and fire extinguisher fumes he had inhaled, so he was casevaced with Sergeant Llewellyn. Major James Coote was frank in his admission of the incident's impact on his company:

> We had been stoned by kids before, seen the gunmen using women and children as human shields and as carriers to take weapons across the street from one fire position to another, in themselves cowardly acts, but this was the first time someone had sent a child to physically attack us. It was extremely difficult for me to calm myself and the company down, particularly as one or two of the younger lads were understandably traumatized by the experience. My initial reaction was to go back in and hand out some retribution, but that would have countermanded our earlier success. After a very difficult talk to my soldiers we went back into the area as peacefully as we could.

There was a wider feeling in C Company that 'the young boy who threw the petrol bomb is responsible for the deaths of many of his countrymen, as the company are no longer reticent to make full use of their weapons whenever they feel it necessary to protect them-selves. Within the rules of engagement, clearly.'

Despite the incident, James Coote emailed his friends, saying:

> The Company is fantastic to a man and woman (my clerk is female and engaged to a soldier in the recce platoon) . . . They are reacting better than I could possibly have hoped for and with calm professionalism throughout. Morale is high and we have well and truly bonded. I have

little time to myself and so appreciate it when I can get it. My morale is maintained by the smallest of things, for example ice cream at supper when the food convoy gets through, clean clothes when there is enough water for the laundry to function, walking into an air-conditioned room, or just cold drinking water . . . I manage to speak to Sarah [his newly married wife] most days, which is the best tonic of all; I am looking forward to seeing the house improvements when I get home, and to spending two weeks of relaxation with her (if the puppy will let me into the house!). In the meantime I am arranging a barbecue with a couple of beers for the lads in the next few days . . . I have a feeling that a sniff of the barmaid's apron might be enough to floor me at the moment, so no change there you might say.

Sergeant Chris Adkins, that unwilling denizen of the intelligence cell at Abu Naji, wrote:

I was distraught at missing out on the largest operation so far, as each contact buzzed over the radios. It was chaos on the ground, with . . . casualties coming in at a rate so fast that it was hard to keep up and ensure we had the correct assets, flying, driving and securing safe areas to ensure a speedy casevac. I felt as if my life depended on it . . .

It was when the casualty reports came in from my very own 8 Platoon (W20s), which had taken the brunt . . . as the zap numbers began to roll in I knew them all by memory and I could see each young man's face as I wrote them down – this was a massive low point for me and extremely emotional. Once I was sure all the casualties were in and being treated I was relieved and sat outside on the floor watching the helipad. I watched as they loaded my soldiers on stretchers on to a waiting Chinook. I didn't realize it, but tears began to fill my eyes.

Sergeant Broome was quickly back on duty, but Sergeant Llewellyn, terribly burnt, was whisked back to the UK for treatment. Chris Broome met him when he got back on leave.

We were then able to chat properly and put a few ghosts to bed that day. Lewy has had a few skin grafts on his arms and is now on the road to recovery. He is in good spirits, still he has the occasional flashback. It was good to see him and finally put my mind at ease on how he now looks. All credit to his girlfriend Jo for looking after Lewy. He could not use his hands or arms for some time, so you can imagine some of the tasks she has had to carry out.

The evacuation of Sergeant Llewellyn left a vacancy in 8 Platoon, and Chris Adkins was approached by Major Coote and asked if he would like to fill it. 'I of course grabbed the chance and couldn't believe my luck,' he wrote. 'However, the feeling of guilt flowed through my body, as I had gained from Lewy's bad luck. I felt like shit – the trouble was I couldn't stop smiling like a Cheshire cat.'

THE BATTLE FOR DANNY BOY

Sergeant Adkins took over as platoon sergeant of 8 Platoon on 14 May, although that day both his Warrior and that of his commander, Richard Deane, were off the road. To his frustration, he was to miss an action known, from the codename of a permanent vehicle checkpoint on Route 6 south of Al Amarah, as Danny Boy. It is less than 7 kilometres from Majar Al Kabir, a hotbed of anti-coalition opinion. Thanks partly to the reports by the Arab television station Al Jazeera, on Friday the 14th news spread quickly that the Americans had attacked a mosque in Najaf. Although it later transpired that the explosion there was in fact an 'own goal' by the Mahdi army, 'feelings ran high, whipped up by the imams at Friday prayers'.

Elements of 1st Battalion The Argyll and Sutherland Highlanders were to the immediate south of the 1 PWRR battle group, one of whose platoons was on an airfield codenamed Condor, just south of Majar Al Kabir. This happened to be Captain James Passmore's PWRR platoon, sent out to reinforce the Argylls before 1 PWRR deployed. The commander of B Company of the A&SH, Major Adam Griffiths, with his rover group, in two unarmoured Land Rovers, drove through Danny Boy heading northwards. Fortunately, as it turned out, he met Sergeant Broome en route, whose multiple, on QRF that day, had been sent out to try to catch a mortar team by setting up a checkpoint at Red 1 with W21 and W22. The Argyll company commander had been ineffectively ambushed near Danny Boy, he told Sergeant Broome. About ten men had engaged his Rovers from the bund line west of the road; the Argylls' top cover had fired back and two of the ambushers had been seen to fall.

For C Company's 9 Platoon, which James Passmore had once commanded, the day began much like any other. Its platoon sergeant, Sergeant Perfect, recalled

> a litter sweep, a platoon kit check and then lunch which was followed by a battle first aid lesson taken by the platoon's unstoppable training team made up of its junior NCOs. We were on thirty minutes' notice to move, third in line in the company. This would be a quiet day.

Suddenly, towards the end of the lesson, there was a rocket attack. The platoon scrambled for its Warriors. Sergeant Broome's QRF set off southwards in an effort to catch the perpetrators. At the same time word arrived of a contact in Al Amarah, where a patrol from CIMIC House had been attacked. As it seemed likely that this was where most of the company would actually be deployed, the OC's group, W0B and W0C, at once left to assess the situation. 9 Platoon thus found itself suddenly stepped up in the order of readiness, as Sergeant Perfect commented:

> ... as ever part of the slick and well oiled machine that is C Company we moved our vehicles to the front gate. My vehicle W33 was first in line followed by W31 commanded by Cpl Green and then the boss's two Warriors. It then became apparent that an A&SH patrol had been ambushed around the area of Danny Boy ... and that they had taken casualties. My multiple was ready to go, so I offered our

Corporal Bytes commanding a VCP on Route 6

services over the radio and was promptly told to go and help the patrol in contact and get the casualties out.

Sergeant Broome, who had met Adam Griffiths at Red 1 just after 3 p.m. and been quickly briefed on the situation at Danny Boy, followed Sergeant Perfect as his Warriors roared southwards. What had happened was that James Passmore, hearing of the contact at Danny Boy but, because of the bad communications that would dog operations that day, unaware that his company commander had in fact broken through the ambush, had turned out in support. His platoon was initially pinned down south of Danny Boy by accurate mortar, RPG and small-arms fire, and although it put in a successful dismounted attack, ammunition was beginning to run low and it had suffered two casualties.

James Passmore was unable to reach Abu Naji with his radios, but had a Thuria satellite phone, which looked rather like a chunky 1980s mobile phone, and which could be used to reach an operator

Private Williams behind battle group headquarters, Abu Naji (*above*), and Sergeant Perfect in the turret of Warrior W33 (*below*)

in Whitehall who could then connect the call to Abu Naji – always provided that she was happy about the call, that is. James duly reached Whitehall. 'Is this an official call, sir?' the operator asked. 'It's an official firefight,' he replied, and was promptly connected to the ops room in Abu Naji. This message was responsible for Sergeant Perfect being dispatched from camp.

Sergeant Perfect's two-Warrior group, tasked with rescuing the casualties suffered by James Passmore's platoon, was ambushed well before it reached Danny Boy. The enemy was in position behind a bund line about two to three metres high which followed the western edge of the road for several hundred metres. Behind it ran a ditch, and it was later found that firing ports had been cut to enable men in the ditch to fire on to the road. There were also pre-dug positions on both sides of the highway.

Private Williams, W30's gunner, engaged the enemy to the west of the road with the Rarden and chain gun in his turret until both weapons suddenly failed. 'I was spotting with my rifle,' wrote Sergeant Perfect, 'and hearing the inspiring word "stoppage" from the gunner. I told the two dismounts to open the mortar hatches and return fire as we moved the final 400 metres towards Danny Boy.' Privates Hoolin and Danquah were the two dismounts. The former recalled:

> I heard the Platoon Sergeant ask for me to open the mortar hatches and start suppressing the enemy with my Minimi. As I opened the hatches I could immediately see the enemy so I opened up on them; unfortunately they also saw me and fired back. This continued while we were still moving to the checkpoint and whilst moving around the HESCO bollards looking for the casualties. It was as we moved back to the other Warriors that I saw a blinding flash in the corner of my eye followed by a deafening bang.

Sergeant Perfect, unable to find the missing platoon at Danny Boy itself, had in fact swung back northwards to try to establish radio communications with Abu Naji and thus get a steer. As he did so his Warrior was hit by an RPG which started a fire. The two men in the back had closed the mortar hatches because of the weight of incoming fire, and were in the rear compartment of a vehicle now all too evidently burning. 'I could make out over Danny's shoulders flames coming out from where the day sacks were,' wrote Private Hoolin.

I immediately shouted 'Fire, the back's on fire!' We both grabbed the nearest extinguishers to us and sprayed the fire. It was a bad idea to spray the dry powder extinguishers in the back as they filled the Warrior up with really thick smoke . . .

My sergeant shouted down 'Are you lads OK?' but we couldn't answer as we were choking on the fumes. We saw the back door open as Sergeant Perfect, who we later found out was in the prone position on top of the mortar hatches, was trying to get down to us, but Danny kept shutting the back door. This was due to fierce incoming fire from the ambush. Sergeant Perfect was obviously not happy at being locked out, kept banging hard on the mortar hatches until we opened them, thus letting in the air. Sergeant P crawled back into his turret and told me to pass him up the Minimi (as well as a few words for closing the door on him). The back of the vehicle was quickly clearing of smoke, and we told Sergeant P that we were ready to go on.

Private Williams, up in the turret, had a bird's-eye view of a situation that might have been comic had it not been so dangerous:

At this stage I thought we were goners, the vehicle was so badly filled with smoke that Sgt P had told us to be prepared to debus and leave the vehicle, and with both guns down I was waiting for the enemy to completely destroy us. Sgt P who was still firing at the enemy with his rifle crawled out on top and started banging on the mortar hatches to get the men still choking inside to open them up. The funny thing was that he had told the driver to open the back door but every time the driver did this the men inside shut it, probably thinking it was an Iraqi or something. Anyway, finally they opened up the hatches and Sgt P got back in, amazingly unscathed but looking rather angry. I thought, I'm glad I'm not a sergeant.

Private Pederson in the rear of a Warrior

Corporal Green, meanwhile, had been dealing with positions on the east of the road, where insurgents were firing from the area of a Pepsi Cola factory. He takes up the story:

> By a stroke of good luck my gunner Pte Hans Pederson had traversed over a lead for his radio headset so I shifted places with Hans. Now I was like a big kid with the controls of the BIG gun. One problem we had with my Warrior was a thing called speed, so by the time I reached Danny Boy I was third in line behind W22 (Sgt Broome). With a little help from my friends (as the song goes . . .) I was talked on to the initial contact point. Without any warning the ground all around us was being weeded out by the 7.62mm rounds as they tore the tarmac up (Alan Titchmarsh, take note),

large splashes of dust and sparks exploded in front of us. This was my cue to join the firefight as I saw the militiamen bobbing around in fire positions and with the aid of W22 shot at them with a mixture of 30mm and 7.62mm rounds. The initial contact point was at the Pepsi factory 800 metres north of Danny Boy, my callsign by this time had leap-frogged W22 and was facing directly at the berm line which was crawling with armed militia tooled up to the teeth. We continued to destroy the enemy, firing both armaments, until through the cracking gunfire and splashes of enemy 7.62mm and RPGs came a battered W33 with Sergeant Perfect at the helm like a champion jockey with a Minimi machine gun at his side.

Communications were still patchy, but Sergeant Perfect now received a message, relayed via Sergeant Broome, that the casualties in James Passmore's platoon were actually 4 kilometres south of Danny Boy.

There is a Brecon saying that lets you weigh up your forces against the enemy's: SO WHAT? I now had the Minimi suppressing them, lots of ammo, and I had mobility as the smoke was clearing. The lads were ready to go . . . It quickly dawned on me that we needed to drive back through the ambush and that we'd better hurry. Cpl Green pulled himself away from the battle at the Pepsi factory, so I had my wing man back again. I won't bore you with the drive through the ambush again but suffice to say that we both got through and took a few of them on the way. Once south of the checkpoint there was simply one lonely RPG man exposing himself – he fired and got the favour returned.

As he now expected, Sergeant Perfect found the missing platoon south of Danny Boy and the ambush site.

As we got closer I could make out this heroic figure of Captain Passmore PWRR – James to the officers and Pete Passmore to the sergeants (this was due to him being nick-named after me, his first platoon sergeant). My old platoon commander stood there cool as a cucumber with the enemy defeated just as I would expect. After jumping in the back and asking sarcastically if we had any problems on the way after seeing the burnt-out mess in the back, he took me to where his prisoners and casualties were and gave me one of each. Our two Warriors then faced north with W31 leading . . . and we began to move back to Abu Naji via Danny Boy . . . we neared the checkpoint where to no one's surprise we came under small-arms and RPG fire, both callsigns went firm on Danny Boy [both Warriors halted in a defensive stance] and suppressed the enemy, to allow the soft-topped vehicles [of the rescued platoon] to push on through to the safety of Abu Naji via the rest of the company Warriors now at the Pepsi factory.

Corporal Green recalled:

I was the front callsign with a convoy of disturbed men in Land Rovers, with Sgt Perfect tail-end Charlie at the back. We got to within metres of the first checkpoint when I saw out of the corner of my left eye over thirty armed men waiting in vain for me to pass so they could ambush the Argylls. The first Rover stopped and before you could say 'Sadr's men wear women's underwear' they were in a fire base giving it hell for leather. Luck wasn't on my side as both armaments failed and I found myself with my rifle picking heads off from 100 metres away, covering the Rovers' movements. All dismounts on, the Argylls shot off like a scene out of the gumball rally, leaving me to fend off these militiamen with Sergeant Perfect . . . [they] must have been smoking the herbal vines, because I now had my 30mm Rarden cannon working and an endless supply of rounds with Sadr written all over them. Hours passed looking through my sights many contacts later, and all seemed quiet and still, bodies littered the berm lines . . . I felt kind of sorry for their families but if the lunatics tried to ruin my day this is a just outcome.

Substantial reinforcements had by now arrived, and Sergeant Perfect set off for camp. His Warrior was knocked about so badly that it could only use its reverse gears.

> Well, to an ex-Chieftain tank driver commanding a Warrior in reverse for the 18 kilometres was easy, not so for my driver as I told him 'left stick', 'right stick' the whole way, which is confusing to a driver of the high-tech PlayStation era. But we came to an understanding and got all the way to the front gate of camp Abu Naji when the steering went. Talk about divine intervention. I got the driver to open the back door and we took the casualties and the prisoner to the guard room where we handed them over to the guard, and we also called the REME to tow our hulk of a vehicle. As we were standing there we noticed an RPG still lodged half in and half out of the armour. It turned out that it penetrated the armour, caught fire to the back but didn't explode. Now that's lucky.

While the rescue was in progress, further reinforcements headed southwards. In Al Amarah the ambushed patrol had been safely extracted to CIMIC House, leaving the C Company command group free to head south. As it moved off it was engaged, as Captain Marcus Butlin, in the back of W0B, remembered:

> It was something I had seen many times on TV but now it was real. A puff of smoke on his right shoulder had drawn my attention to the RPG man in the crowd. I could clearly see the RPG being lowered from his shoulder. A quick warning to the OC on the intercom, but there was nothing we could do. W0B and W0C were speeding away from the one-man ambush as we had more important things to attend to.

Before they arrived at Danny Boy, however, the battle there had taken a decisive turn. Sergeant Broome, using his own two Warriors, started suppressing dug-in positions west of the road. He was speedily joined by Lieutenant Ben Plenge, commander of 7 Platoon, in W31, and Sergeant Brodie in W32, who deployed their vehicles at the north end of the ambush and dismounted their troops. Sergeant

Broome gave a quick set of orders to Lance Corporal Wood, who was commanding Privates Rushforth and Tatawaqa, the dismounts in the back of his vehicle; Corporal Byles and Private Beggs dismounted from another Warrior.

Bayonets fixed, the assault began. Private Fowler, W22's gunner, sluiced accurate fire on to the nearest position. Given the nature of the ground and the position of the fire support Corporal Byles and Lance Corporal Wood had to assault frontally, with W22 keeping pace with them over perhaps 300 metres, until it could no longer depress its turret far enough to engage the trenches.

The little group of dismounts then split up and used pairs fire and manoeuvre to break into the position; grenades, automatic fire and bayonets were used to clear it. The first trench contained a number of dead and four men who surrendered when the dismounts closed in. Seeing what was happening, Sergeant Broome left his Warrior to supervise the handling of prisoners and the collection of casualties. No sooner was the first position taken than fire was opened from other positions further to the west, which were themselves taken on by the Warriors, now including W0B and W0C, and two Challengers. Sergeant Major Falconer dismounted to assist Sergeant Broome in collecting prisoners and weapons, and once the situation was under control the dismounts, now accompanied by the sergeant major, pushed on to take two more positions, supported by fire from the Warriors. 'A number of the enemy still hid deep in the undergrowth and trenches,' recalled Major Coote, 'and were only discovered when we were reorganizing. They were still armed but chose not to fight on; in retrospect, they could easily have killed our dismounts had they so wished.'

Major Coote parked his Warrior on top of a berm by the road: it was not tactically well sited, but it was the only spot from which he could maintain even intermittent communications with Abu Naji.

'We pulled off the road behind the cover of a levee that formed one side of a large concrete drainage ditch,' wrote Captain Butlin.

> There seemed to be smoke in the air, I think from some of the stubble that had caught fire. I could also hear gunfire, both small-arms and the Warrior's 30mm and chain gun.

W0B took position on top of the mound, which offered a good view of the ground. I had a look around but couldn't pick out anything – it seemed very empty. W20 then arrived with some PWs. I'd got quite used to the Warriors over the last few weeks, but was still impressed with the sight of 32 tonnes dropping down into the ditch and then powering up the 45° incline. The CSM started to unload the prisoners. They were moved back behind W0C and made to lie face down on the floor . . .

The last one couldn't stand up. It was then we realized he'd been shot. LCpl Muir, the company medic, went to work on him. I centralized the captured weapons and ammunition, then checked that Pte Sullivan had control of the prisoners. Pte Pritchard and I then started to help LCpl Muir. The casualty was very seriously injured with a sucking chest wound. LCpl Muir applied a chest seal to the exit wound. At first it worked. But after a while the small amount of blood coming from the wound meant that the sticky patch no longer held. The casualty was semi-conscious and kept trying to lie down. It was hard work for even three of us to keep him sitting up, with a drip in, oxygen mask on and chest seal in place. We did our best, but after forty-five minutes he finally died.

Matt Maer had had a frustrating day. He had been to a brigade commanders' conference at Basra Palace and was waiting for an RAF helicopter to fly him back to Abu Naji, when reports of the contact arrived.

Initially these were not over-troubling (the first report of any contact is never correct, one way or the other), but as the situation developed it became increasingly evident that this was not a small matter . . . I became increasingly agitated to get back to Maysan but the RAF were later and later with the flight and in the end it was cancelled. The brigade staff pulled hard to secure me an Army Air Corps

Lynx to take me north. The pilot was an American officer on attachment, and despite being on the limit of his flying envelope due to the heat flew me at very low level over the marshes back to Abu Naji. The flight was, with refuelling, to take approximately an hour and a half, during which time I was completely out of communications with the battle group.

On his arrival Colonel Maer found that 'the troops were coming in off the ground and the Warriors were on their way back'. The atmosphere was generally upbeat: there was a feeling that the enemy, having picked a fight on ground of his own choosing, well and truly lost. James Coote was still out at Danny Boy, taking fire from the west and

> returning fire where the enemy could be positively identified and were regrouping; this included one round of Challenger main armament and numerous Warrior high explosive rounds, but without doubt many enemy escaped as we could not engage them within the rules of engagement.

He had received orders over the radio to bring all the enemy bodies back to camp for identification; despite his concerns, this order was confirmed by satellite phone. Dismounts were cross-decked to free vehicle space for prisoners and bodies, but collecting the latter was a ghastly task: 'They were badly disfigured as the result of high-velocity hits at different ranges and blood was everywhere.' Some, probably the victims of 30mm hits, had to be collected in ponchos. Sergeant Broome remembered the scene all too well:

> We lined them all up ready to place them in the back. One of the first things we noticed, even though these were not big blokes, was how heavy they were. At first we did not want to make skin-to-skin contact with the bodies, so we picked them up by their clothes. However, due to the fact that they were wearing loose clothing, when we picked them up by their cuffs the clothes started to fall off . . . We were all covered in blood from head to toe . . . the odd shot was still being fired in the distance.
>
> A comment was then made that I will never forget: 'Why are these young lads out here dying like this?' That's right,

some of my lads were feeling sorry for them, now that they were dead. However, if we hadn't killed them they would have killed us.

Killing someone, then looking at them afterwards as you place them in your Warrior, is something I could have done without, personally. Even though this is our job, it still does not stop you replaying the dead faces in your mind time and time again and asking the questions why, and what if? The next time I hear a comment like 'I want to get stuck in and kill somebody', I will remind him of what you may have to live with for the rest of your life. And secondly, if you enjoy seeing a body get ripped open then you shouldn't be in this job but locked up. This is not a game! It takes only one round or one mistake before it could be you getting wrapped up in a poncho.

During this period the C Company group was being constantly dicked by civilian vehicles, which could not be engaged as they showed no unmistakable hostile intent. Major Coote was astonished not to be mortared. The Lynx helicopter that had delivered the CO to Abu Naji flew overhead, reporting that there were crowds in nearby Majar Al Kabir, and James Coote redeployed his Warriors and Challengers to make best use of their thermal-imaging devices. One of the tanks had suffered a complete automotive failure, and a tank-recovery vehicle had been called up; there could be no withdrawal till it arrived. As night fell the situation was surreal, as James Coote recalled.

Normal traffic began to flow along Route 6 . . . the Arabs pay less attention to the scene of a battle than most people pay to a road accident at home. However, movement was continually reported from Majar Al Kabir and sporadic gun-fights ensued, but nothing to overly concern us as we were well placed to defend ourselves. Of particular note was an ambulance moving about. We were suspicious at first, as we knew that ambulances were used to move crew-served weapons around the province. We subsequently discovered that the ambulance was recovering the dead and injured

Private Fowler reflects on Danny Boy

and that the crowds reported in the town were families outside the hospital desperate for news of their relatives.

After what seemed like an age the recovery vehicle arrived, the Challenger was hooked up, and C Company set off back to Abu Naji five hours after the initial contact.

James Coote acknowledges that his company was 'physically and emotionally exhausted' by the time it got back to camp. But there were still tasks that had to be completed. The prisoners were handed over to the RSM, and the company was replenished with fuel and ammunition, and then fed. Private Stuart Taylor arrived back in camp with ten bodies in the back of his Warrior, and drove it straight to the RAP [regimental aid post] where Captain Angus Forbes was waiting to pronounce them dead, with the padre, Fran Myatt, on hand to ensure that they were treated with due dignity. Private Taylor tells us:

> The medics were waiting to take the bodies out of the back. Unfortunately the rear door failed to open and being the driver of the Warrior I had to climb through the turret and over the bodies to open the door. The experience was bad and I still have nightmares on a nightly basis.

Captain Rands searched the bodies for anything of intelligence value, and photographed them for purposes of identification.

> The scene was terribly grim. Fran Myatt . . . said later that it had shocked him . . . One of the dead wore a light blue T shirt heavily stained with blood. He looked like a West Ham fan. Another who was missing a large chunk of his head wore a Firetrap top. Being decidedly uncool I'd never heard of the Firetrap label. It seemed a horribly appropriate logo. When I eventually went home on leave I saw a number of people in my local pub wearing Firetrap clothing. With no other frame of reference for the brand name I was seriously disconcerted the first couple of times.

It took several days to clear the blood and human debris out of the back of Sergeant Broome's Warrior.

The next morning we were told to go and see the medical officer asap. Still in our blood-stained combats, he explained to us that there was a small chance we could have contracted Hepatitis B. We had to undergo a few tests and a course of injections. We were then told that we would be unable to have unprotected sex until we had our results through, which could be six months down the line. From there we were sent to the QMs and stripped of every item of clothing we were wearing and were issued new kit, but not before a good scrub down in the shower as ordered by the doctor.

Happily, all the tests came back negative, but James Rands was amongst those for whom 'the whole issue' made him reluctant to enjoy his R and R to the full.

Nine prisoners had been taken, one of them a police officer, and a count of captured equipment revealed six RPGs, one 7.62mm machine gun, twenty-four rifles of various types and a vast haul of ammunition. There were twenty bodies in camp, and it was estimated that in all about seventy of the enemy militia had been killed. It is impossible to be certain about what they were trying to achieve. Their aim was probably to secure Danny Boy and cut Route 6; they were only partly in position when Adam Griffiths's two vehicles drove through, and had he been a few minutes later the result might have been different. There were eventually over two hundred well armed insurgents, with machine guns and mortars as well as the ubiquitous AKs and RPGs, spilling out across Route 6. Once the initial ambushes had failed – and it is little short of miraculous that the Argyll platoon, in its soft-skinned vehicles, was not harder hit – the advantage swung back to the British:

> Ultimately once the armour was in place and those troops who had been ambushed were out of the enemy's killing area, the battle was ideally suited to us. With our greater range and accuracy and without the fear of hitting civilians in the crossfire we were on exactly the kind of ground we would want to fight on. The wide-open fields provided little cover or hiding places despite the pre-dug positions, and

Danny Boy veterans: (*left to right*) Private Tatawaqa,
Sergeant Broome, WO2 Falconer, Private Rushforth and
Private Fowler

those enemy that occupied bunker positions were effectively fixing themselves in place.

James Coote wrote a quick assessment in the immediate aftermath
of Danny Boy. He regarded the action as an affirmation of British
tactics: the fact that a section of five to seven men supported by
Warrior was able to overrun a strong enemy position without suffering a casualty proved that they worked. Sustained and accurate fire
quickly eroded the morale of a numerically superior enemy, although
the rules of engagement were often inappropriate. Soldiers were
unable to shoot at men who had been in the battle but were escaping
to fight another day. Communications were 'woefully outdated, inadequate, and, therefore, dangerous . . . The two casualties taken could
have been avoided had the follow-up light callsign [James Passmore's
platoon] been aware that the rover group [Adam Griffiths] was clear
of the ambush.' Front-line ammunition allocations should be carried
at all times, even on admin runs. It was vital to ensure that there
were always sufficient weapons: C Company Warriors henceforth

carried Minimi in the turret as a back-up to the chain gun, commanders had rifle, UGL and baton gun to hand, and both drivers and commanders carried pistols for close protection.

Major Coote's last points were inspired by the events immediately following the action. Enemy dead should be photographed and left in place. The press must be welcomed and briefed: 'They will get their story somewhere and it is better that your version of events is published rather than the enemy's.' And finally, local media must be continuously monitored to anticipate likely reactions elsewhere – he wrote this in the wake of the very significant backlash that followed Danny Boy.

Matt Maer was characteristically generous in his assessment of the decision to order the recovery of Iraqi bodies:

> The logic behind that decision was that a particular individual, who we had come close to capturing, was wanted in connection with the murder of six RMPs [military policemen] in Majar Al Kabir in 2003 and it was felt that, there having been a large battle near the village, he was very likely to have been involved. Therefore, if he had been killed and we could identify him it would clarify the matter.
>
> The brigade staff, over 120 kilometres away, reached this perfectly logical conclusion. However, they did not know how many enemy dead there were, and the size of the battlefield. This, in turn, was because battle group headquarters had not informed them, which in turn was due to the fact that *they* had not been fully informed, as few on the ground had a full appreciation of the situation and if they did were engaged and unable to give a clear overview. Indeed, it is unlikely that any one person had the full picture, as the battle had taken place over a number of hours, spread over 8 square kilometres, involved a number of different subunits and darkness was now falling.

Lieutenant Colonel Maer spoke to the leader of the Majar Al Kabir town council at 10.00 the following morning, and told him that he had the bodies of a number of men in the mortuary; aware that they should be buried by sunset that day, he wished to hand them back to their relatives. The council leader agreed that the bodies would be collected that afternoon, and as local people were not happy about coming into the camp, the handover would take place at the Golden Arches, the gates marking the turn-off from Route 6 to Abu Naji. The chief of police would be present, and the bodies would be handed over by British medical staff. The troops found that a large crowd had assembled and when they returned to camp they reported that there was a rumour circulating that the dead had been captured alive and then executed. Matt Maer thought that

It was impossible to gauge where this rumour had come from or how widespread it was, and at this stage it was not regarded as a particularly important issue ... The reason for the rumour was that after thirty years of Saddam's rule, the Iraqis expected that sort of thing to happen. Under his regime Abu Naji had been the scene of various atrocities and people had often entered and then disappeared ... Indeed in the very camp we were occupying mass graves had been discovered following the liberation, and during the previous regime individuals had been detained, tortured or 'disappeared' within our walls. Our argument that things had changed, we represented a new age and we simply did not do these things was undermined by the fact that at the same time pictures of torture in Abu Ghraib were being aired hourly, not only across the Iraqi and Arabic media but globally too.

What happened next remains unclear. But Karem Mahood (otherwise known as Abu Hatim), the provincial representative in Baghdad, his brother Riadh Mahood, governor of Maysan, and a third brother, Salah Mahood (apparently acting as a bodyguard), together with the Majar Al Kabir chief of police, greeted the bodies on their arrival at hospital. Matt Maer thought:

Karem Mahood may always have been anti-British. He may always have been in collusion with the enemy. It is hard to say, but on 15 May he came out as openly hostile to us. He claimed that the bodies had been mutilated and showed signs of torture. He claimed that we had stolen the eyes from the bodies. (One of the dead had been hit in the right eye, obliterating the eyeball, and I can only assume that this was the evidence he put forward.) The accusations grew into a claim that we had captured, tortured and finally mutilated twenty prisoners. The whole event was being videoed by a cameraman for propaganda purposes, suggesting a degree of forward planning.

The chief of police apparently told Mahood that he was talking nonsense, and verbal abuse followed. It is impossible to say who drew a pistol first, but one of the brothers shot the police officer in the head; he died instantly. The police took his body away, and the conference continued, with a doctor being produced, whether voluntarily or under duress, to add credence to the mutilation claims.

A video CD of the bodies was distributed round the souks over the next few days. In Majar Al Kabir a local firebrand demanded retribution against the British but the crowd turned their backs on him, and some of the mothers of the dead even railed against the men who had sent them out to die. 'The reaction to the news of our "murders" was surprisingly mixed,' reflected Matt Maer.

A few of the more educated leaders thought that it was nonsense, but many believed it. Effectively those who wanted to see the British army as mutilators . . . chose to do so, and the rest chose not to. There was no way of persuading people to do otherwise.

AMBUSH AT RED 8

After the action at Danny Boy, the uprising fizzled out slowly with a number of vicious little battles. One of them, fought by a multiple of 8 Platoon, was insignificant in itself but will long be remembered because of the bravery of Private Johnson 'Bee' Beharry, the Grenadian driver of Second Lieutenant Richard Deane's Warrior,

W20, who had already distinguished himself on Operation Pimlico.

In the small hours of 11 June, W20 and W22 (the omnipresent Sergeant Broome) were sent out to Red 8 in an effort to catch a mortar team on its way back from a mission. Richard Deane takes up the story:

> All the lights were out in the city and we were travelling without lights. With this in mind, I remember thinking that it was very dark. I was down in my turret plotting the grid that the ops room had sent us on my map re the mortar firing point, when Beharry . . . stated he wasn't sure if he was approaching Red 8 or not and if I could check it for him it was so dark. I grabbed my rifle with the CWS and stood up in the turret. I knew immediately we were approx 50 metres short of Red 8. Pte Beharry had slowed right down at this stage, however he had not stopped. Within ten seconds of me standing up, I saw the flash to my left-hand side not more than 50–60 metres away and the flash as it hit the front of the Warrior.
>
> The impact of the shrapnel hitting my face stunned me for a few seconds, however when I put the CWS to my eye I saw three men standing in the alleyway. One of them had another RPG on his shoulder. At this stage I emptied my magazine at the enemy position and managed to hit all three of the enemy, thus preventing the RPG man from firing. I realized that I was bleeding badly, as I was having difficulties seeing with the blood in my eyes. I told Pte Beharry . . . to get us out of the killing area asap. Pte Beharry replied OK. The Warrior then started to move backwards across the central reservation and into the waste ground on the other side of the road. Pte Samuels was also engaging the position with the chain gun at this stage, after seeing where my magazine of tracer rounds had struck.
>
> I tried to send a contact report to Sgt Broome in W22, however my radio would only receive and not send. The Warrior reversed approx 150–200 metres into the waste ground before hitting a wall and coming to a halt. I still did not realize Pte Beharry was injured at this stage. Sgt

Broome was still trying to get comms with me and finally said on the net 'If you can hear me, show some white light.' I wasn't able to stand up with a torch, so I used the light in my GPS to indicate where I was and that I could hear him. W22 pulled up beside us and LCpl Wood and Pte Ervin jumped out of the rear. I told them I was cut in the face but was OK and that Sgt Broome needed to lead back . . .

'I told W20A that I would lead them back . . .' Sergeant Broome affirmed.

I must have got about 25–30 metres and their vehicle did not move so I reversed back and told them not to fire as I was going to place my vehicle between the enemy and theirs. The vehicles were conformed in this position with my rear left corner almost touching W20's front left corner – I thought this would ease the extraction of casualties. I then once again dismounted LCpl Wood and Pte Ervin and dismounted from the vehicle myself, handing the turret over to Pte Fowler, my gunner. I did this as I felt the need to assert myself on the ground and deal with the situation where I was needed, fully aware of Pte Fowler's ability to . . . cover any extraction using all weapons systems at his disposal, safely and accurately.

We hit the ground, and we came under contact from small arms immediately. Woody and Erv went left, myself and Cooper started to pull Beharry out of his seat. This was the first time I had the chance to see the badly lacerated face of Bee . . . I pulled him out with the help of big Erv and Jim Cooper and put him into my Warrior with his head in my lap . . .

As I began to collect my thoughts I realized Fowler was engaging with 30mm HE [high explosive]. As we got Bee out I saw the Boss and told him to get back down into his turret. I was going to attempt to drive the now driverless W20 myself, but before I had the chance Pte Cooper, just a dismount, took control, shouting at me 'I have it, let's go . . .' Having no time to cover the niceties of driving standing orders, with rounds passing closely by my head, I was quickly reminded of the situation I was in and had to move quickly. A few hours later I asked Pte Cooper what sort of a driver he thought he was? Pte Samuels responded for him – 'a getaway driver'.

Sergeant Broome shut the Warrior's rear door without realizing that Private Beharry's feet were hanging out of it:

> I swung the door closed and this trapped his foot in the door. With this he leapt up shouting 'AARRRHHH MMEEEE FOOOOTTTT!' in his Grenadian accent. What he was trying to say in English was 'Ouch, my foot...' As injured as Beharry was, he still managed to grab hold of me and ask me in his own way what the hell I was trying to do.

The two vehicles were shot at as they moved south down Red Route towards the new Iraqi prison codenamed 'Broadmoor', a British-held intermediate position near Red 8. Sergeant Broome left Private Fowler in command of the turret, and got in the back of his Warrior, telling the ops room that he would need immediate medical assistance at Broadmoor – he feared that Beharry, with an appalling head wound, might not last the journey to Abu Naji. He declined support from either dismounted troops or Snatch: '1. Snatch would not have had a chance and would only endanger further life. 2. Fowler was still engaging and I didn't want the possibility of blue on blue.' On arriving at Broadmoor, Richard Deane dismounted to guide the inexperienced Private Cooper through the gate – not wholly successfully, for Sergeant Broome described seeing him 'demolishing the wall at the front gate'.

It was the second time that Private Beharry had driven out of trouble. On the first occasion, 1 May, he had taken his hard-hit Warrior through to CIMIC House and pulled its casualties clear. Here, in the action at Red 8, he had reversed clear of the ambush but the RPG had exploded only six inches from his head, not only sending dozens of fragments of hot metal into it but jolting his brain so severely that the swelling nearly killed him, and was to cause him repeated severe headaches. He is still recovering as I write. Richard Deane was also injured. As Sergeant Broome noted:

He had a gash to the right-hand side of his head with blood pouring out of it. This was not the first time for Lt Deane to be injured. Previously he had been blown up and walked away with only minor burns and a sore head, but was back at work after a few days. Plus he had come into close contact with a few RPGs fairly close to his head in similar ambushes on other nights . . . He is a good aggressive platoon commander that you would be happy about following into battle. As he is Irish, we used to say that he had the luck of the Irish and that would get us through the tour.

Sergeant Chris Adkins was now platoon sergeant of 8 Platoon, commanding one of its two multiples. After the action at Danny Boy, 'the reality of seeing the men was horrific – they were like the ghosts of their former selves. I almost didn't recognize them for the soldiers I knew so well.' Here he describes the sensation of hearing his comrades in action, night after night:

> We would usually be in contact first up till 0100, and then 2Lt Deane's multiple would take over and I would sit in my Warrior listening to my friends Richard Deane and Chris Broome . . . my multiple around me. As I would look into my lads' faces there would be . . . angst, as you could see: they were rooting for the safety of their good mates in the other multiple – it was sometimes more worrying than being shot at yourself. We would hear massive explosions which would be IEDs to the south, a mumble from the lads, come on, come on, and then suddenly the radio would spark into life, to all our relief. Then Rich Deane and Sammy his gunner would issue out some recompense: boom, boom, boom the 30mm would go, a loud cheer would start and the lads knew the enemy were getting a taste of their own medicine . . . the night Johnson Beharry was hit beside his head with an RPG which also injured Deano our Boss, I felt sick and totally helpless but had to stay firm due to being on call for further callsigns on the ground in our area of responsibility.

POLITICS, THE MEDIA AND RECONSTRUCTION

There were two specific aspects to the backlash in the wake of the action at Danny Boy. Although the incident's media impact within Iraq passed relatively quickly, its ripples spread wide outside the country. On or about 15 May, a British freelance journalist had failed to get to the main gate at Abu Naji – which was certainly an error in media-handling – and, unable to get a story, had proceeded to Majar Al Kabir. There he had certainly found some copy. In consequence, even some of the 'quality' British press gave space to the insurgent claims, causing enormous resentment amongst soldiers who had risked their own lives so as to adhere to rigid rules of engagement. I had a painful wait until I knew what had actually happened (officers on operations have better things to do than focus on allaying the fears of regimental colonels), but by the time it became clear what had actually happened as far as the Iraqi dead were concerned the damage was done.

Next, the murder of the chief of police left Riadh Mahood in an impossible position. He had been involved (though precisely how remains impossible to say) in the shooting of a senior policeman in front of a large crowd. He was indicted by a central court soon afterwards, but could not be removed from office. The British army could not be seen to be negotiating with a man accused of murder, but for it to arrest him would look too much like colonialism. On the other hand, the local police commander was concerned that if *he* arrested him it would be seen as politically motivated, and the arrest might be followed by an immediate reaction resulting in Riadh Mahood being released or even cleared.

Initially Mahood agreed, through the persuasive powers of Molly Phee, to voluntarily stand aside from office, and the Provincial Council sat without him. But six weeks later authority was handed back from the provisional authority to the Iraqis themselves. When the second Sadr uprising broke out his successor, who had made an encouraging start, resigned, with a speech denouncing both the 1 PWRR battle group and the chief of police. Eventually, probably through his elder brother's influence, Riadh secured a pardon from a Baghdad judge.

The lack of lasting political progress in Al Amarah contrasted sharply with that in Al Zubayr, where The Royal Welch Fusiliers managed to organize the first free elections in recent Iraqi history.

The sharp limitations of Iraqi politics made it hard for CIMIC to function as effectively as it might have done. However, the battle group provided 90 per cent of the Coalition Provisional Authority reconstruction staff in the province. After the transfer of authority to the Iraqis and the departure of the CPA the whole weight fell on the battle group. Most NGOs, understandably enough, could not work in such a hostile environment; after the first uprising only the Salvation Army remained. There was no input from DfID or the Foreign Office, and only very limited UN involvement. Sergeant Eastwood, by profession a mortar-fire controller without any experience of civil engineering or project management, was employed as a civil-military cooperation NCO. He placed contracts worth $7.5 million, in the process regenerating Al Amarah's water and sewerage services. Every estate in Al Amarah received some assistance, and by the end of the tour every person in the town had easy access to potable water. Sergeant Eastwood's contribution was recognized even by the Mahdi army, which guaranteed him safe passage even into the most dangerous areas of the town. It is a measure of the complexities of postmodern operations that this happened even though, in his professional capacity, at much the same time he was directing counter-battery fire on to the Mahdi army's mortar positions.

Operation Kickstart was the brainchild of Major Justin Featherstone of Y Company. The intention was to use the underspent budgets from some of the larger projects to help revitalize the local economy. Most earlier economic rejuvenation projects had been on a large scale, and aimed for big effects. For example, the Bazurgan power station came on line towards the end of 1 PWRR's tour, though it had been one of the earliest projects initiated. The local community had seen no tangible benefits from it, and there was much anger and frustration, increased by the fact that the disappearance of the Iraqi army had resulted in widespread unemployment.

Job-creation schemes were short-term, and the results were often painful. One was in place when the battle group arrived, with thousands of local men employed in relatively menial work. When the project ended all the men were laid off at once. Rioting ensued, apparently stemming from an official's refusal to issue the last of the pay packets. A battle group warrant officer took charge of the finances and ensured that people were properly paid off, but deep resentment remained. There was a real need for projects that would last and that would produce tangible results. The rules for spending UK funds were not helpful, for the money could not be issued to benefit an individual. While it was acceptable, say, to redecorate a school, thereby giving employment to painters and decorators, there was no means at hand to enable them to set up their own businesses.

Operation Kickstart took money left over from various projects and redirected it to low-level regeneration. Local people could apply for a grant of not more than US$500 to start a business. The plan had to be viable; the applicant had to have the necessary skills; and he would have to employ at least two people, one of whom had to be young and one of whom had to come from outside his own family. An attempt was made to distribute the projects both geographically and socially, and checks were carried out to ensure that schemes were being run in line with published intent. In all, 109 projects were approved, ranging from motor workshops through PlayStation arcades to tea stalls. With a minimum of three employees apiece and an average family size of eleven, it was believed that the scheme benefited around 3,600 people. The fact that the projects were self-sustaining meant that this was real wealth generation rather than simply the payment of benefits.

Public reaction was very positive indeed. In one instance a head teacher, acting as a local coordinator for the scheme, was seized by the Mahdi army and accused of being a collaborator. He took his captors to see several of the small businesses that had been created: they agreed that the project was constructive, and permitted him to continue his work. They also allowed British soldiers working on Operation Kickstart to move through their estates unhindered. Job creating and economic revitalization were crucial to breaking the cycle of violence within the province. Most fighters were bored and frustrated young men whose inability to support their families sapped their sense of self-worth. Insurgents of all persuasions fed upon the bitter and unemployed masses. 'Only by killing all the young men or giving them something else to do could we expect to stop them fighting,' observed one officer.

Operation Kickstart did not find favour, though, with the UK Treasury official in Basra, who complained that it did not meet the rules for the distribution of money. After some discussion, however, it continued under the name of Operation Southsea.

Another of Major Featherstone's ideas was the creation of fourteen community centres within Al Amarah. The traditional tribal and village organization had been badly eroded in recent years, and there was often an absence of community spirit and cohesion. This made it very difficult to get anything done within the estates, or for the estates to do anything for themselves. This had suited the old regime, but was a serious obstacle to the creation of a new political system. Existing projects had tended to focus on the more well-to-do living in villas on the fringes of the estates. The new system, by contrast, brought together a dozen or so people who were representative of their communities, and who could interact with their own neighbours better than most politicians.

At first the only place available was CIMIC House itself, which was being used as a storeroom and drop-in centre at the time the battle group arrived. It was speedily turned into a fully functioning community centre with a monthly total of fifty to a hundred visitors. Major James Driscoll, who had overall responsibility for CIMIC, 'quite literally saw businessmen, unemployed Iraqis and local politicians waiting for a pause in the mortaring, as one would wait for a break in the rain, to rush in or out of CIMIC House to see us'.

The creation of community centres took the strain off CIMIC House and provided both a gathering place for the community and neutral ground for its representatives to discuss their ideas. Over $100,000 was spent on creating such centres throughout Al Amarah. Each had televisions, videos, meeting rooms, a library and an Iraqi community worker. The centres ran different projects, but adult literacy for the over-fifties, English language and IT classes were particularly popular. There were sewing classes too, and some women brought in their own products to sell, giving them a small profit and providing

Al Amarah: movers and sheikhers meet Lieutenant
Colonel Maer

the money for more material. Emphasis was laid on drug awareness. Although there was little abuse of alcohol and narcotics, prescription drugs were widely abused. The antidepressant arteen was the drug of choice; taken in large doses it encouraged the user to believe that absolutely nothing mattered, and that he could do anything. It would not be true to say that all the Mahdi army's footsoldiers were routinely under the influence of arteen, but the drug was sometimes used to encourage new recruits to carry out suicidal attacks.

When the youth centre in Majidayya, one of the worst estates, was blown up, it was rebuilt by the battle group. The delighted local inhabitants painted a picture of Muqtada al-Sadr on its external walls to show that it was under the protection of the Mahdi army, and saw no inconsistency in also inscribing their thanks to 'Major Justin'. This fostering of the community spirit helped give people the confidence to confront the guerrillas, and began to spread security bottom-up. When Major Featherstone was about to leave the province he was visited by a delegation forty-eight strong, who wished him well, thanked him for his efforts and gave him a pen set, a painting and a Marsh Arab sheikh's robes. Seven came from the dangerous Majidayya estate – into which the battle group had launched an attack just a month before – and one was an OMS cleric. Justin Featherstone 'was quite simply overcome'.

Significant CIMIC projects sprang up across the whole area. The battle group provided funding for football pitches, to give young men a healthy alternative to petrol-bombing. North-west of the city a small Christian community of date farmers (originally alienated when a patrol raided the area in search of an enemy mortar team) was given purified water, and responded by restoring their plantations' old title, the English Plantations. Chicken husbandry seminars were organized; a milk-processing plant was established in a very rough estate; a publishing house (both a source of employment and a free press) was set up in the north of the city; damaged power lines were repaired, fuel was distributed, thereby averting serious public order problems, and the battle group helped the UN distribute aid to Marsh Arabs left homeless by flooding. Operation Wapping was the codename for re-engagement with local communities in Al Kahla and Qalat Salih, which had been the scene of numerous contacts and had become almost no-go zones. Instead of re-entering these areas with a company of Warriors, the battle group chose instead to embark on CIMIC projects such as filling in what had been pools of stagnant water in town centres, generally creating a good feeling in the local community. This helped to marginalize extremist politicians, and thus to set the conditions for the re-entry of British troops into Majar Al Kabir, achieved by The Welsh Guards after 1 PWRR's departure.

Lieutenant Colonel Maer was the visible face of Great Britain within the politics of Maysan province. He attended numberless meetings, noting with resignation that start times were always sired by fiction out of optimism, and was involved in the agreement of several cease-fires, resolutions and public declarations, most of which came to nothing. He certainly enjoyed certain aspects of his role:

> One of the great privileges of being the commanding offi-
> cer is that I was invited by the tribal chiefs to eat in their

homes. I have rarely met such generous hospitality. While nobody starved in Iraq, as far as I could tell, food was not overly plentiful. However, when eating with the locals they gave all that they could. The table (or carpet) was groaning with sides of lamb in rice, beef, chicken, vegetables, sauces, fruit and a cornucopia of goodies galore. The meat was wonderfully cooked and fell off the bone to melt in the mouth. All was eaten with the fingers (using the correct hand), and more was pressed on you if you looked to be flagging. At times the hosts themselves would not eat until I and those with me had eaten – they always ensured that my bodyguards, prowling the shrubbery, were fed too. Sometimes they would not touch a thing, just in case I could force down another small morsel.

Conversation was light-hearted and free flowing, with opportunities for humour and leg-pulling.

Women were never seen and rarely present . . . Indeed, the only two downsides to these occasions were that the women would not eat until the guests and the men had done so . . . The second small downside was attempting to sit cross-legged on the floor. For a six-foot-three individual with the flexibility of a bedboard this was not the easiest of tasks.

When he explained his guilt about the absence of women to Molly Phee, she looked at him with disbelief. Did he really think, she said, that the women had not, centuries before, learnt to cook more than they sent out, and eat elsewhere at the same time?

The often repetitive process of negotiation and entertainment did help reduce the overall level of violence. While the British could not be seen to be negotiating directly with the Mahdi army, they were able to talk to the OMS, which remained a legitimate political party with many sane and reasonable members. The British were also able to observe negotiations between the Mahdi army and the provincial government, providing the security in which these meetings took place and, by assuring the Mahdi army that there would be no retrospective arrests, encouraging it to agree to a cease-fire after its first uprising.

The Mahoods' grip on power and the events of 15 May inevitably complicated matters. So too did the fact that the Mahdi army was not always able to control its own supporters. When the second uprising broke out in early August Matt Maer was on R and R, and in his absence some Mahdi army leaders actually begged the coalition forces to machine-gun the mob off the streets. Talks continued despite some of the worst attacks yet seen, but it was clear that there could be no settlement in Maysan until there was one in Najaf, the epicentre of Shi'a sensitivities, then under attack by Iraqi and US troops. The eventual ceasefire partly reflected events outside the province, but it also paid tribute to Matt Maer's ability to work with the moderate elements of the OMS. By the time the battle group left, the Mahoods had been prised from power and a moderate OMS politician had replaced Riadh Mahood as governor. As I write the future of Maysan province remains a matter of conjecture – Lieutenant Colonel Andrew Williams of The Staffordshire Regiment, Matt Maer's successor but one, affirmed that policing Maysan 'is like walking a tightrope'. What is clear, though, is that in 2006, as in 2004, the coalition cannot impose a solution by force of arms. It can, within locally varying limits, strive to hold the ring within which Iraqi political groups must reach a solution.

This was always evident to 1 PWRR battle group. The warning order (a brief summary of an operation issued shortly before the distribution of full orders) for Operation Waterloo gave as its end state 'The restoration of Coalition Force control and freedom of movement in Al Amarah city, such that it can carry out Security Sector Reform and CIMIC tasks to further the long-term aims of the Coalition Forces and the Coalition Provisional Authority'. That for Operation Hammersmith, launched on 10 August after the restoration of authority to the Iraqis, announced: 'Operation Hammersmith is a demonstration to facilitate an Iraqi Police Service arrest operation and to mitigate its consequences. This Warning Order also provides a contingency plan for multinational forces to carry out arrests should the environment become less permissive.' Military force was an adjunct to the political process, and we have seen just how complex, violent and unstable that process was in Maysan province in the summer of 2004. It is to another upsurge of violence that we must now turn our attention.

CHAPTER 6

Round Two

THE SECOND UPRISING:
OPERATION HAMMERSMITH

As July drew to a close Matt Maer believed, with some reason, that the province was on an even keel. Although there were some sporadic attacks, things were relatively quiet. Operation Southsea was beginning to have an effect, and police training courses were going well. The battle group was really getting somewhere, he felt, and he had even broken it down into the organizational groupings, designed to facilitate security-sector reform, that he had envisaged on his second recce to Iraq. He himself was now due for R and R, and was rightly determined to take it:

> It is easy for commanders to avoid taking leave. We like to perceive that we are very important people, that our organization cannot function without us, and that it is macho to eschew rest – the 'lunch is for wimps' school of management. I was personally in the 'lunch is a long, leisurely meal' school and was ready to go. Also, Toby Walch, my second-in-command, wanted and deserved a chance at commanding the battle group.

Matt spent the first half of his R and R with his wife Val in Brecon, where he had served as an instructor on the platoon sergeants' course and where Val had a cottage. However, he remained in touch with Toby Walch – 'much to his justifiably great annoyance'. One of the issues they discussed was the death of Private Chris 'Ray' Rayment of Y Company, who had been accidentally killed at CIMIC House when a gate barrier fell on his head, killing him instantly:

> It was a terrible irony that after all those in CIMIC House had been through we were to lose one of their number through a freak accident. We had also lost one of the great characters of the battalion – who had never been shy about giving me advice as to how the battalion should be run! I spoke to his mother from the cottage in Brecon and discussed the funeral arrangements, which I was to attend.

Private Rayment's death made Steve Brooks ponder his own mortality.

> Did I read the Bible? – yes, Psalm 23 which my father had read at my wedding only a year before. Did it help? – well, it felt that I had reminded God that I was around and maybe I was worth a thought. I also prayed for Ray . . . I was his platoon commander and I never wanted to meet a mother and father and say I was sorry for their loss. I put faith in the fact that Ray's time was up, and that God took him to save his suffering later on, but to believe that Ray had gone quietly into that dark night was totally unbelievable – so full of life and energy he must have gone somewhere, and not just ceased to be. Therefore he couldn't be alone and God must have been with him – having his ear bent by Raymondo no doubt.

This death happened against a background of rising violence across the whole of Iraq, and both CIMIC House and Abu Naji were coming under repeated mortar and rocket attack. Charlie Curry, just about to hand over as ops officer to Dom Sweny, saw how finely balanced things were in Al Amarah, and how much depended on the fragile consent of its community leaders:

> Toby Walch was working incredibly hard at maintaining this consent. He was in his element, sweet-talking the movers and shakers of Maysan in atrocious Arabic one moment,

Private Chris 'Ray' Rayment,
killed on duty at CIMIC House

unleashing various sorts of hell on the unsuspecting enemy
the next. He did, though, seem worried that the CO (away
on R and R) would see a connection between the change
of command and the upsurge in fighting.

On 6 August the Mahdi army tried to seize the police stations
within the city. Matt heard of this while walking back with Val from
a large brunch at the Brecon Beacons Mountain Centre. Grabbing
some paper and a pen from her handbag, he scribbled notes while
speaking on the phone to Captain Charlie Curry, still ops officer at
Abu Naji. By the end of the call both he and Val knew that he would
have to go back at once.

Warrior King:
Major Toby Walsh aboard a Chinook

This decision was not a reflection on the ability of others to do the job, but because Toby could not run the hour-by-hour military operations and simultaneously deal with the political situation at provincial level, a role I had now fully taken on with the departure of Molly Phee and the CPA.

He arranged a flight to Iraq, and they drove home to Tidworth. While they were eating a takeaway Chinese supper, Brigadier Andrew Kennett, the brigade commander, telephoned. He spoke to Val, out of Matt's earshot, for some time before being passed on. He had not phoned earlier, Andrew Kennett said, because he knew that Matt would badger him about returning to Iraq, and he wanted to assess the situation fully before arguing with him. In the event, he was prepared to allow him to return to support Toby through the political process. The aim of his lengthy conversation with Val had been to assure her that Matt would be able to return to complete his R and R in due course. (He did: we flew back on the same aircraft in September. This was the time of Val's birthday, and I am assured that she received an even better present than usual.)

The fighting in August differed from that in May, for if the British had learned, so too had their enemy. Yet again the fuse of the conflict in Maysan was lit from outside the province. At the end of the first uprising there had been an uneasy truce in Najaf. Although the city itself was ostensibly controlled by the Iraqi security forces, the Americans held a ring around it. The situation grew increasingly tense, and the Shi'a became convinced that the Imam Ali Mosque, their most holy site, was in danger of imminent destruction by the Americans. Previously Muqtada al-Sadr's support had been relatively limited, but in the hothouse atmosphere of an Iraqi summer with the economy in the dust and little sign of political progress, it grew fast.

Matt Maer found that

> all those with whom I had been dealing, on the Provincial Council, at tribal meetings and across the spectrum of politics and society, wished the potential coalition actions in Najaf to be called off. They were very deeply concerned about the possible consequences of any offensive action. While I attempted to reason with them – the coalition would not damage the mosque, we respected and understood the significance of the holy sites, they must be aware of the true picture, that Muqtada al-Sadr and the Mahdi army were using the holy sites erroneously, they were capturing and torturing people, something needed to be done – it was of no avail . . .
>
> While many did see that Muqtada al-Sadr was wrong in a number of ways . . . they were loath to assist in bringing about a resolution . . . Firstly there was, at some levels, a

dislike of confrontation. Protracted negotiation was better than aggressive action. Secondly, there was undoubtedly a feeling that however ridiculous, dangerous and irresponsible the actions of an Iraqi minority and however logical, beneficial and sensible those of the coalition, the fact was that we were Christian outsiders and not fellow Muslim Iraqis. Finally, there was an element that decades of central rule had enshrined. Generations of Iraqis had grown up being told what to think and what to do by their government. Self-determination was not a natural state of affairs.

Within forty-eight hours of Matt Maer's return to Iraq, Major General Bill Rollo, the thoughtful and clear-headed Household Cavalry officer commanding Multinational Division South East – of which Andrew Kennett's brigade formed a major part – agreed to fly up to Al Amarah to speak to the provincial leaders in Camp Abu Naji. But even before the meeting, there were two incidents that gave a grim foretaste of what was to come. A peaceful demonstration outside the Pink Palace, just south of CIMIC House, was hit by mortar rounds probably aimed at the latter, and several demonstrators were killed. Then, as the first of the delegates were arriving at Abu Naji, the camp itself was mortared. The meeting was no secret, and to have attacked the camp at such a time suggested that the firebrands would have small regard for any message of restraint that might emerge from it.

In the event over 250 Iraqis attended the meeting, including Council members, tribal chiefs, union leaders, politicians and imams. However, it was 'uncomfortable, hostile and fruitless', hijacked by those who repeated endlessly that Najaf was a sacred place, that the Imam Ali Mosque was especially sacred and that terrible retribution would befall the coalition if it was damaged. Afterwards, General Rollo worried that he might actually have made things worse by attending, but Matt Maer felt that the die was cast before the meeting, and at least it had vented a certain amount of steam. And when Matt returned to his office, the television in the corner was already showing pictures of US troops fighting in Najaf. James Coote, himself newly returned from R and R, with visions of his Wiltshire cottage and

Saskia the dog rapidly receding, reported ruefully that 'Al Jazeera, characteristically helpful and accurate, reported this as another attack on the Imam Ali Mosque and everyone picked up their RPG and started again.'

The logic of holding CIMIC House had been clear enough before the transition of authority from the Coalition Provisional Authority to the Iraqis on 30 June. It was the old governor's residence and so had a certain prestige; it was big enough for meetings; was ideally placed to allow people to drop in, and well situated for the distribution of assistance. A company was based there, not only to preserve its security but also to facilitate patrolling and contact with police. There were also disadvantages to the place: it was in the centre of the city, with water on two sides – difficult for the battle group to reach and easy for the insurgents to hit. In addition, the 110 men there eating and drinking and firing ammunition had to be resupplied, and the lack of medical facilities meant that serious casualties would have to be evacuated during a period of attack. When the situation was re-examined after 30 June, it had been concluded that although CIMIC House should be retained for the moment, as soon as the Iraqis assumed responsibility for their own affairs it should be handed back to the population.

The house was still in British hands when the second uprising occurred, and it was clear that the battle group could not pull out while under attack. This would have handed the insurgents a psychological victory, dented the battle group's pride, and sent all the wrong political signals. So, although it was agreed that its utility had in fact diminished, CIMIC House would have to be held. It was unlikely to be overrun as long as its defenders did not run out of ammunition, but it could be attacked by direct and indirect fire from all around. Evacuating a casualty would require the deployment of much of the battle group, and troops were vulnerable to attack both on their way in and on their return. Although the place was, in a way, besieged, the traditional notion of 'raising the siege' by defeating the besiegers made little sense because of the danger of provoking a major clash in an urban area still full of civilians.

Part of the solution lay in the sky. There was a constant combat air patrol over Iraq – in 1 PWRR's experience, pairs of USAF jets that operated a taxi-rank system so that troops in trouble on the ground had access to the next available pair. Major General Rollo had authorized the use of a 500lb laser-guided bomb if circumstances warranted it, and a forward air controller team of The Household Cavalry now arrived in Abu Naji. Over the next few days the FACs developed their tactics. When aircraft appeared over CIMIC House the attacks stopped, but resumed again as soon as the aircraft departed. One of the disadvantages of fast jets is their shortage of 'loiter time', but as aircrew became more familiar with Al Amarah and procedures grew slicker, so it became easier to get jets to the right place at the right time and deter or curtail attacks.

Eventually time and tactics coincided. An enemy mortar team had set up in the shabby parkland south of CIMIC House and opened fire. They had used the site before, and a coalition aircraft, staying north of the city to mask its noise, was familiar with the spot. Lieutenant Colonel Maer called the plane in, but held it at over 15,000 feet to keep it out of earshot. The aircraft acquired the target, reporting that it was indeed a mortar team in action, and was given clearance to drop its bomb but ordered to keep collateral damage to a minimum. The ops room, listening to the radio conversation, fell silent. An officer recalled:

> The bomb took close to a minute to fall to its target . . . If the mortar team moved then the bomb would miss. The hands on the operations room clock were stared at intensely. The radio traffic dried up. The operations room was full: the Quick Reaction Force commander, signals office, company commanders, movement control officers and anyone else who felt they could justify their standing room waited. The aircraft reported the mortar was still firing. The seconds ticked by. The bomb struck. The operations room burst into cheers . . . The radio to CIMIC House carried the sounds of cheering in the background as the commanding officer requested of Captain Nick Thasarathar, the company operations officer, 'How was that?' referring to the accuracy of the strike. 'Better than sex,' came back the jubilant cry.

The bomb had in fact fallen 10 metres west of the mortar, for the pilot, anxious to minimize damage to the flats to the east, had decided that edging it slightly towards the river would deal with the target but not harm the flats. The mortar team was destroyed: one eyewitness saw the weapon's barrel, illuminated by the bomb's flash, departing in the direction of its recently fired round. It transpired that the mortarmen had been the Mahdi army's crack crew, and their demise led to a significant decrease in the accuracy of fire against CIMIC House. But Corporal Chris Mulrine of the sniper platoon had watched it all from the rooftop of CIMIC House, and was clearly unimpressed. 'Is that it?' he asked.

Within CIMIC House the second uprising had much in common with the first: repeated mortar and rocket attacks, and patrols into the surrounding city. Captain Charlie Curry, jobless since handing over as ops officer, was sent there on 8 August to enable Justin Featherstone to go on leave. He splashed straight into the deep end.

> As I got to the door I was surprised to see Justin in full kit. He grinned at me, shook my hand and welcomed me to CIMIC House. Then he picked up his Bergen and ran to catch the Warriors. Movement into and out of Al Amarah was now so dangerous that no chance could be wasted . . .
>
> The ops room went quiet. Everyone looked at me warily. Nick Thasarathar . . . broke the silence. 'The CSM's taking out a fighting patrol tonight across the river. Justin suggested that you stay in the company ops room and get a feeling for the way we do business.' I thought briefly. I had just spent four months in the ops room and I knew just how hard it was to get a feel for things on the wrong end of a radio. I also knew that I had not been out on patrol for a long time, that my skills were rusty and I did not know the ground first-hand . . . I turned to the CSM, WO2 Dale Norman, and told him he had an extra soldier for his patrol. I'd keep my eyes open, mouth shut and take in as much as possible.

The ops room at CIMIC House

For Charlie Curry, part of the patrol was revision:

My kit wasn't quite adjusted right, my torch was in the wrong place, I'd forgotten that you need to take your headset off before you unsling your rifle – these and a thousand other glitches reminded me how long I'd been away from real soldiering. Painfully learnt lessons from patrolling in Belfast came flooding back: how and when to take cover, when to run, how to cross obstacles, how to use shadows. As I listened in on the net I started to remember how to command patrols; how to shuffle callsigns around to cover one another as they move along the patrol trace; how to use the base sangars and snipers to brief you before you cross areas that they can see; how varied clips of chat on the radio can blend to give a picture of the situation all around you.

But there were also new lessons to be learnt, and with them came the keen realization that the rest of the patrol had done all this rather often.

> Swearing comfortably, the guys had already identified an enemy position about 300 metres to our north, the other side of a road and in amongst some buildings. I by this stage had worked out the bottom of the ditch was a good place to be and was beginning to realize that the cracking sounds and the fast-moving lights were connected. At this point, just as I was starting to get to grips with the situation, the CSM leaped out of the ditch and we all started legging it towards the road, covered by the fire of two Warriors that had come up the road from our left. We dived across the road and into the cover of the buildings on the far side, looking for enemy positions. The fire had slackened considerably now, and we started to scan the roofs of some buildings on the far side looking for enemy positions. Our snipers fired twice at enemy seen on the rooftops and we had no more problems from that direction. I took cover behind a truck, caught my breath and took a look around.
>
> Though still pretty disorientated I was starting to enjoy myself. It was still all far too unreal to be taken seriously, and I didn't yet have the experience to visualize quite how lethal all these bright lights and bangs could be. My brain was also beginning to cope with the information overload and I was starting to take in my surroundings again. It was then that it started to dawn on me that I was sheltering behind a fuel tanker . . .
>
> As we started to extract south back into the open ground we again came under fire, this time from buildings a few hundred metres away to the east. I was at last starting to distinguish between incoming and outgoing fire, and . . . to realize the difference between effective fire and random bursts loosed in the general direction. Everyone else, of course, knew this instinctively, and we continued to extract

back across the open ground in the shelter of the dark while the enemy fired high above us.

Steve Brooks had spent the early part of the tour as ops officer at CIMIC House. He was promoted captain on 5 July 'and celebrated by falling into an open sewer and tearing the ligaments in my ankle'. He spent three weeks 'with the dark lords' in the ops room at Abu Naji, and then returned to CIMIC House to command a multiple.

> Warrior was a lifesaver at CIMIC. We used it for fire support, assault, casevac, comms relay, extraction, escorts, VCPs, intimate support – everything. [Warriors] were provided by A and C Companys and the company's own anti-tank multiple under CSgt Cliff Lea. The main boys down at CIMIC in the month of August were Lt Ben Plenge and Sgt Craig Brodie of 9 Platoon C Company and Capt Gary Smith and Sgt 'Fitz' Fitzgerald of 3 Platoon A Company. They were on standby all the time to help us get out of whatever brand of poo we got ourselves in.
>
> At one stage we were relieved in place by A Company 1 RWF, and we had to tab across the dam to the east of Yellow 4 to the Warrior RV on the west bank. We were massively exposed crossing this, but on reaching the other side we were met by Sgt Chris 'Stick' Broome and Cpl Andy 'Star' Brown, both of C Company, leaning out of a Warrior jeering and directing me into the back of their Warrior where they had a bottle of water and a fag on the go for us. It was similar to an unexpected but welcome lift when it has started to rain, and it was excellent to be extracted by blokes you know from the Rifle Companies.

Sergeant Chris Adkins saw the reverse of this image. He describes a double-shuffle extraction to CIMIC House during the second uprising. He first set off with a vehicle full of snipers, leaving Justin Featherstone and another party in action on the ground.

> We were still being hit by accurate small-arms fire. I stayed low until we approached the roundabout. I got up in the

turret determined to get some rounds at the enemy. Then bang – 'What the fuck was that?' 'RPG!' shouted Private Consterdine my driver. 'A0 this is W23 contact RPG wait out.' I was then hit by small-arms fire from the south. Another contact report, and we were moving over the bridge heading north and we then got contacted from across the river in the area of Major Featherstone's enemy. We completed the journey, and dropped off the snipers. They quickly fortified the perimeter of CIMIC, and I turned around to get the rest of the callsigns. 'Power on, left hand down, Mark, let's go get the rest of them – you ready, Huffers?' (my gunner). Once again we were hit at the roundabout by an IED and small arms, then I lowered myself back down into the turret as we again approached Major Featherstone's hostile location. It was time to pull these men out . . . 'Co-ax on, Huffers, see that wall to the right of the school – put some rounds into it and see if we can get the enemy's heads down.' The Warrior came to life: Redit was singing away and the effect had what I wanted, the enemy were silenced for long enough for the Y Company callsigns to squeeze twenty-three men between two Warriors designed to carry seven each, and that is a squeeze! I turned around quickly, ensuring not to neutral-turn and lose a track . . . It was a soft goodbye, just bursts of automatic fire just chasing us all the way along to CIMIC.

Sometimes CIMIC House had to be reinforced in quick time. In early August, Lieutenant Ben Plenge was waiting in the ops room at Abu Naji: as the QRF commander he needed to listen to the net to be sure that he was au fait with the tactical situation. The camp was being mortared, so the ops officer tasked Ben Plenge's platoon to try a two-pronged attack on the mortar's baseplate position. He set off with his four Warriors, but before he had time to carry out the order, he was directed to CIMIC House instead. As the platoon approached Red 9, a well known trouble spot, it saw several dickers, and a green flag had been raised over a house – a warning that coalition troops were on the way. On Red Route, the Warriors were

missed by an RPG, and by the time they reached Green 5 they were
under fire from both sides of the road.

I could hear heavy machine-gun fire from the rooftops to
my left and heard the whoosh of an RPG fly overhead.
I told my driver Private Oscar Nayasi to batten down his
hatch, and rather calmly he informed me he already had,
in his distinctive, Fijian way. LCpl Butler scanned the side
streets trying to locate the enemy, eager to send a bit of
lead back their way. I saw a puff of dust from an RPG firing
point about 150 metres away and swung my rifle around,
standing on my seat, head and shoulders out of the turret.
I fired a couple of rounds before my rifle got a stoppage,
and as I ducked down to clear it in the turret we pushed
through Green 5 . . .

My vehicle started to cross the bridge at Green 4, and
as we did so I saw an RPG man on the north river bank
and quickly fired my UGL at him. The UGL made its usual
satisfying 'pop' and I watched the grenade, almost in slow
motion, arc towards the RPG man. Sadly for me, and luckily
for him, he ducked back into cover just before it struck the
rooftop where he was standing, and I don't know if I got
him. Still, there was no time to worry about that now, as the
RPGs started to increase in their intensity, the whooshes
blurring into one continuous sound. Once over the bridge,
the buildings are a lot closer to the road, and gunmen
occupied the rooftops spraying wildly with their AK-47s.
Our vehicle had been hit numerous times now, and the lads
in the back could hear each round clearly pinging off the
armoured plates . . .

Approaching Green 9 I was planning to go over the
narrow bridge to Blue 11 as I had done many times before.
As I turned right on the roundabout and became committed to this course Oscar stopped the vehicle, and when I
looked at our proposed path I saw why. On the other side
of the bridge were large concrete bollards blocking our
path . . . I decided to back up and take another route. There

wasn't much space, and my wagon didn't neutral-turn very well, and as Oscar swung it around he picked up a large market stall on the front corner of the vehicle. Fruit and veg went everywhere and sparks flew as the metal frame was dragged along the tarmac . . .

All the vehicles were taking a lot of fire, and I could hear the distinctive sound of 30mm firing behind me. It was a good sound . . . Pushing south from the roundabout Oscar stopped again, saying that an RPG had just missed us and it was fired from the front of the vehicle. LCpl Butler swung the turret around and identified the firing point. I gave the order and he let rip. The chain gun worked beautifully for once and a long stream of tracer slammed into the alleyway where we had identified the firer . . . Only a few pot-shots followed us up the road to CIMIC House. The vehicle still had the market stall attached to it . . . On the last part of the road we decided to get rid of the market stall as we wouldn't fit the gate. At this time we also saw a suspicious abandoned car ahead. I was concerned that it might be a vehicle-borne IED, but we had no choice but to batten down for the first time and drive fast past the car. Oscar understood what I meant and buzzed an inch past the car, depositing the market stall through the rear windscreen with a satisfying crunch. A minute later we were at CIMIC House, and miraculously, still in one piece.

Being in the British army we decided that the best thing to do would be to go and get a brew, despite the 48 degrees Celsius heat. It was almost as dangerous as the previous hour, as a concentrated and accurate mortar bombardment came in on the compound. As the first one came in I was able to throw myself under the Warrior into the only puddle for several miles. This was, at least, a good morale boost for the blokes – seeing me emerge covered from head to foot in mud, dust and oil triggered a helpful barrage of comments in a way that only soldiers could.

Sergeant Craig Brodie, just back from his R and R, had also had a perilous journey:

> As we pushed on through the Greens the enemy started to up the ante, pouring a heavy rate of small arms on to us as well as an endless volley of RPGs. At this point, with my chain gun inop, I decided enough was enough and it was once again time for Al Amarah to hear our 30mm Rarden cannon in action. As each street shook from the RPG that had been launched, so it shook again with the impact of 30mm HE: this seemed to deter the enemy from using the same firing point twice and on occasion [we] had the satisfaction of seeing the enemy disappear in the explosion . . .
>
> It's strange to say but through each and every one of the many contacts and battles I have experienced through this tour there always seem to be moments when what is going on round you is just downright humorous. For example, while poking my head out of the turret locating further positions, I was able to reflect on how each RPG man was using telegraph poles which hold their power lines as aiming marks and in doing so was remarkably poor at hitting our vehicles (thankfully) yet flawless at hitting said telegraph poles, always at the top and always shearing the power lines attached. I could just imagine each fighter returning home with a wife waiting to knock his lights out for cutting the power to the entire street. Also cause for reflection is the fighter that we had just laid the gun on to while he squatted with his RPG on his shoulder, and as we were about to fire the driver misheard my command and decided to jockey forward. He will never know how lucky he was.

By contrast, Sergeant Brodie recalled a subsequent occasion when an RPG gunner was plumb unlucky:

> Me and my gunner watched somebody walk out into the middle of the road and squat down in front of us about

250 metres away. I joked to my gunner that it was someone teeing up a shot at us, so we decided to lay the gun on to the piece of cover that had been next to him and see what happened. Imagine my surprise when sixty seconds after he disappeared he came trooping back with an RPG on his shoulder. Imagine *his* surprise when before he even managed to get it into the aim he was on the receiving end of two bursts of 7.62 four-ball-one-tracer . . . there's no religion on earth that could have supplied the miracle needed for him to survive.

Late on 10 August the battle group mounted Operation Hammersmith, with C Company and two Challenger tanks moving out in the darkness to encircle the Majidayya estate – whence many of the attacks on CIMIC House had been launched – followed by search-and-arrest operations by men of The Royal Welch Fusiliers and The Black Watch. For Private Van Zyl of 8 Platoon the operation began with the customary nervous humour. 'I remember that we were all gathered around the back of the Warrior, taking the mickey out of one another, but we all knew that the danger was only a few hours away.' He recalled: 'Our task was a simple one. Move up to the runway, link up with the Challenger callsigns, and then move through the Purples and up the Reds, finally securing a ring of steel around the Majidayya estate in the Greens.'

Lance Corporal Cameron had joined 9 Platoon only the day before, taking over from Private Benion as gunner on W32.

So the order was given and we mounted up in our Warriors at 2230, myself gunning, Sgt Brodie commanding and Pte Lumley driving and of course the dismounts in the back. I looked around the turret as I remembered to turn the power traverse on and eventually managed to get the night-sight on while Sgt Brodie was watching me and giving me plenty of encouragement. We eventually rolled out of the front gates at 2300. I loaded the chain gun and Sgt Brodie loaded six rounds into the 30mm Rarden cannon with our rifles loaded next to us.

We then moved towards the city, the whole company in

C Company 1 PWRR

their Warriors with our platoon bringing up the rear. I remember sitting in the turret thinking 'This won't be so bad', having deployed on Op Telic I the year before; I was to be proven wrong. Suddenly as we pushed into the city [and] the first contact came over the net, I looked through the gunner's sight and the whole city seemed to come to life. RPGs were being fired from alleyways and rooftops at the Warriors: it reminded me of a scene out of *Black Hawk Down*. The turret was now traversing rapidly as myself and Sgt Brodie scanned for gunmen . . . we had a few glimpses

. . . and I returned fire with the chain gun which got into the habit of stopping every thirty rounds, much to Sgt Brodie's amusement. We eventually got into the area of Majidayya and formed our ring of steel, but one of 7 Platoon's drivers, Pte Kenny Hills, had become a casualty after an RPG hit his Warrior . . .

Private Tom 'Fergie' Ferguson was gunner in the Warrior that Kenny Hills was driving. His commander yelled, 'RPG right.'

The wagon had taken a hit but it just bounced off, luckily, so as any gunner would do I traversed right and flicked on to co-ax, not seeing where it had come from I just carried on observing . . . when two more RPGs simultaneously hit us on the left: the entire wagon shook as if it had hit a mine, and instantly filled up with smoke. I had banged my head on the sight but was OK. Ian [Sergeant Page] was shouting at me, but I couldn't hear him properly, in fact I couldn't hear anything until I heard – which I will never forget – Kenny screaming down the headphone, 'Help, help, Tom, help me!' I will never forget how helpless Ken must have been, hatch down, injured and couldn't see . . . So I took my helmet off and just shouted to Ian 'Right, I'm off to get Ken.' From that moment I had no emotions in my body, my only thought was Ken, so I jumped out of the turret; I had to do the usual climbing over the bulky bits of armour to get to the driver's hatch, luckily it had been blown open enough for me to get it fully up. It was weird looking in at Ken, he had his arms up at me and was shouting for help . . . I realized how much of a shit state he was in, he couldn't see anything as his eyelashes were melted shut and his body looked generally mangled. I got him down on the ground and ran with him as quickly as possible to the med wagon . . .

Having shoved Private Hills aboard the Warrior, Ferguson raced back to his own vehicle: 'it was the quickest zoom dash I've ever done'. Although he had never driven before, he managed to get the vehicle under way, with Sergeant Page now in the gunner's position, when they were heavily engaged again.

I directed Ian on to a target and told him to fire, but Lady Luck was not on our side and he got an instant stoppage. The situation was this: our new commander was Eddie [Corporal Edwards], who climbed through from the back and was now in the turret, not a clue; Ian had a stoppage on the chain gun and was flapping, not a clue, me in the driver's seat trying to drive and talk through Ian on how to clear the stoppage, not much of a clue, so there we have four dismounts in the back putting their trust in people who were putting their trust in each other. But as a platoon and crew we did do the job, got the stoppage cleared and managed to get to a safe RV. That night you had to be flexible and I would trust my life with any of those lads, bust.

Private Hills had in fact been hit in what even that stormy petrel, Second Lieutenant Richard Deane, recalled as 'one of the biggest ambushes we have encountered to date', as C Company hooked into the city from Sparrowhawk. His own W20 was hit by four RPGs, and his driver could not open his hatch, so he himself stood up to guide his packet through the ambush.

> The scene was unbelievable! There were numerous RPGs flying through the air, tracer rounds were cutting across the road in all directions. A number of vehicles were burning and the air was thick with smoke. In addition to this, the majority of the Warriors and tanks were returning the fire. The noise was deafening outside the turret. We finally made it to Red 11 . . . Once the driver could see again, I battened down before my luck ran out.

The platoon fought its way along Green Route, although eventually without its tank, hard hit in the ambush. During a forty-minute pause at Green 4, W22 became bogged down, but Private Campbell, driving W21, quickly dismounted, hooked a cable to W22 and then pulled it out. Lance Corporal Wright was wounded by an RPG, but was safely evacuated.

Again, air power proved invaluable, as Richard Deane recorded: 'We were able to use Spectre on the Greens. He spotted five enemy closing in on our position, and after I had taken all my dismounts off the ground and given him clearance to fire, he destroyed them in quite an impressive display of firepower.'

9 Platoon developed the technique of using its Warriors as Spectre bait, inducing enemy militia to attack while the AC-130 was on overwatch, ready to engage. Lieutenant Colonel Maer had now authorized the engagement of 'danger close' targets, which meant that Spectre could take on enemy only 100 metres away from troops in closed-down Warriors. Moreover, the gunship, its callsign Basher

75, was now on the battle group net, and so intimate cooperation was far easier than before. Sergeant Brodie was working very closely with the gunship when he spotted a party of eight or more armed men. Having ascertained that there were no friendly troops in the area,

> I informed Basher 75 as to what I had in front of me . . . as Basher fixed the target I got my gunner to lay the 30mm off to the flank they would be likely use to escape if they could . . . finally, with both of us happy, Basher sent me the message that rounds were on the way. With no more than stone-throwing distance between the target and my vehicle it was time to watch through the sights and see what danger close actually looked like. I can honestly say I will never forget watching as those rounds landed slap in the middle of the militia . . . as expected there were a few of them that were far enough away to try to break for cover, but all they ran into was the volley of 30mm HE that I had waiting for them. Within seconds it was all over and yet it is a memory I can play back as clear as day. As the dust settled it was clear that between my vehicle and Basher 75 we had just killed an entire group of militia who only a minute before . . . were in the process of sorting themselves out ready to ambush us . . .

One of 8 Platoon's dismounts, Private Van Zyl, spent some time out of his vehicle at Green 5:

> I found that I had gone from a closed-down position to being out in the open and feeling very vulnerable. I looked across the road to gain eyes-on with my dismount com- mander Cpl Moore, and as I did I saw a stream of bullets ricochet off the road approximately a metre in front of him. He immediately returned fire and I was now scanning the dark depths of the streets and alleyways to find the firer's position. The lights on the road did not help our night- vision aids so we incorporated the help of the Warrior's raven gunsight. A few minutes later the chain gun began

firing from the Warrior and the light show of tracer bullets lit up the alleyway. With eyes like saucepans we all observed our arcs and let the time fly by.

During the late morning and early afternoon of 11 August, 8 Platoon was rotated between the relative calm of the police station, codenamed Coot (actually in the avian sense, but inevitably known as Coote after OC C Company), and trouble spots from which fire was being directed against CIMIC House. Sent to a possible mortar position at Red 13, Second Lieutenant Deane spotted a gravel lorry whose occupants were in the process of pulling a tarpaulin over two mortars, then sprinted for the cab as he approached. Although he blew the tyres out with his rifle, he dared not risk using his 30mm, which would have clinched matters, 'as the risk was too high of missing and hitting innocents'. With a shower of sparks, the lorry lurched to safety in the Al Iqtisadiyin estate, and he was ordered not to pursue it. Eventually, after repeated battles against determined opponents, Richard Deane's men were showing symptoms of heat exhaustion, vomiting and slurring their words. They eventually returned to camp on the afternoon of the 12th, bringing with them men of A Company 1 RWF, who had been busy in clearance operations on the ground.

Lance Corporal Cameron of 9 Platoon had also been very busy:

We then moved off again at about 0430 back through the city once again, the contacts coming over the net this time a lot more than before. Looking through the sights you could see tracer flying through the air and Warriors returning the fire. As we moved back along the main road we were looking through our sights when we noticed a car approaching us. It stopped 300 metres short of our position and a group of men gathered round the vehicle clearly armed with RPGs . . . The Warrior next to us engaged and we followed shortly after, firing five rounds of HE at the group. Safe to say we definitely got a few of them as we drove past in the Warrior, and saw the bodies on the floor; one was lucky and appeared to be crawling in a bad way to the side of the road. By this time Craig sent a contact report letting the boss know we had destroyed the target.

Almost miraculously, the battle group survived Operation Hammersmith without fatalities, though five of its Warriors and one Challenger were severely damaged. Corporal Nash's Challenger had sustained two RPG hits on its way into Al Amarah, destroying the driver's sight and damaging a road wheel. A further hit destroyed the thermal imaging sight, but, as Major James Coward explained:

> Thankfully the use of a hand-held image-intensifying monocular sight meant that, together with friendly mortar illumination from CIMIC House, he was able to identify and engage the ambush team, as well as guide his driver. This continued for an hour until battle group headquarters decided that they had pushed their luck about as far as was advisable and they were ordered to head for home, pausing only to dismount and replace the various bits of the vehicle which were hanging off.

Tanks usually used their chain guns in action. During Operation Hammersmith a platoon from The Black Watch, detailed to clear militiamen from a school in the north of the city, requested cover from callsign D0B, Major Coward's tank. When the building's militia occupants opened fire on it, 'the chain gun proved persuasive in stopping them'. But, having found a reinforced part of the wall, one resolute gunman remained in place:

> Clearly a more forceful statement had to be made, which was done with the help of a 120mm practice round [essentially, a concrete projectile that has the same flight path as a high explosive round, but no terminal explosive effect]. By virtue of the four-foot hole where [the gunman] had previously been standing, I judged that the argument had been sufficiently persuasive to allow the rest of the operation to take place (and by virtue of the limited effect of the round, the school later to be returned to its intended use). Furthermore, the effect that a tank has in firing its main armament in a built-up area made the point that

we were not afraid to 'up the ante' where required (and appropriate).

Operation Hammersmith did not end the uprising in Al Amarah at a stroke, for the linkage between events there and elsewhere in Iraq meant that there could be no separate peace. Indeed, there were further bouts of fighting in the town, most notably when operations were undertaken to relieve and resupply CIMIC House. But Hammersmith's medium-term effect was decisive, for it had shown that the Mahdi army could not hope to confront the battle group without suffering wholly disproportionate casualties. Although, as Major Coward admitted, armoured operations in built-up areas have 'potential for causing damage but also [for] failing to endear ourselves to the locals', scrupulous attention to the rules of engagement that often seemed absurdly restrictive to the men on the ground ensured that damage to life and property had been limited. Not only was there no surge of popular feeling in support of the Mahdi army, but many inhabitants now blamed it for starting a battle it had all too evidently failed to win. The uprising was effectively over by 26 August, and although there was sporadic violence in Al Amarah for the remainder of the tour, the worst was over.

THE BATTLE FOR BASRA

Major David Bradley's B Company 1 PWRR had remained in Basra throughout all this, and it too was to be caught up in the second uprising. David Bradley thought that the mood in the city was generally more benign than elsewhere in Iraq:

> There was a diverse and relatively well educated population who saw the British as a force for good. Although there were problems, they did not automatically blame the occupying powers and were prepared to wait for the situation to improve. There was generally little desire to see the religious parties prosper, particularly if this was brought about by

violence and lawlessness. No single grouping could rely on the support of the people long enough to mount an overt and concerted campaign. Low-level activity and attacks could last indefinitely, while large forces could be pulled together for a short period, but ultimately without consent they could not be sustained. As with people throughout the world, all the locals wanted to do was to make a bit of money and provide for their families in a safe environment, free from the intimidation of any extremist group.

The handover of power had gone more smoothly than anyone expected, and in late June and early July there was even a break in the mortar and rocket attacks on the Cheshire battle group bases in the city. However, there was a palpable sense that political parties were now manoeuvring hard, usually without a genuine base of popular support. 'The local population either mistrusted the influence from Iran on such groups as SCIRI or were uncomfortable with the radical Islam preached by the OMS,' thought Major Bradley. 'Although good Muslims, they did not want to live in an Islamic state. The tensions started to increase and the overt intimidation by the parties of the people along with their influence over some parts of the police proved very unpopular.' By the end of July the tribal leaders had had enough and, led by the Timimi tribe, produced a broadsheet warning the politicians to stop their nefarious activities or face the (unspecified but assuredly painful) consequences.

Concurrent with all of this was the OMS's desire to stand up to the coalition forces and take control of the city. American pressure on Najaf translated into widespread popular concern in Basra, and, although most of the population remained moderate, this unease encouraged the OMS to try to gain political advantage.

To reduce tension and prevent bloodshed it was agreed that the battle group would remain at its bases, apart from patrols aimed at force protection. Brigadier Kennett continued to negotiate with the governor and chief of police, but the city, most of it now out of bounds to coalition forces, had a new dangerous edge. Fighters were arriving from Najaf and Al Amarah, the number of ambushes increased dramatically, and the coalition base at Old State Building was practically in a state of siege. There was certainly a feeling in B Company that the freshly established Mahdi army local bases and ambush sites should be cleared as soon as possible, for the longer the militia enjoyed the freedom of the city the harder it would be to remove them. And, in the interim, the OMS would gain moral authority and the coalition forces would lose credibility.

B Company, based just behind the Cheshire battle group headquarters in the Shatt Al Arab Hotel in the northern part of Basra, was the group's armoured reserve. It multiples were held at degrees of readiness from immediate to thirty minutes, though Major Bradley reckoned that he could deploy his whole company more quickly than that. Those multiples not on immediate notice to move were kept busy with escort patrols and ambushes on likely mortar base-plate positions. The fact that B Company was the only Warrior company in the city kept it in great demand, although when A Company The Black Watch, also in Warriors, arrived in early August it was able to take over responsibility for the southern areas.

David Bradley spent much of his time in the battle group ops room, keeping up to date with the latest incidents and available for immediate tasking. He enjoyed a good relationship with Lieutenant Colonel John Donnelly, the Cheshires' CO – 'a remarkably fit whippet of a man' – who used to run into the ops room whenever a contact was reported to see what was happening. He had a soft spot for B Company, and its callsigns would rarely send word of a contact without the unmistakable sound of a chain gun sawing away in the background. He would shout, 'Go on, my cockney boys' as he listened in. Sadly, the company's voice procedure – the army's rigid code of practice governing procedure on the radio – was growing somewhat cavalier. Captain Pete Williams, company ops officer, listened to the company net, which during major contacts was routed into the bomb-proof accommodation of battle group headquarters. After every transmission Pete apologized to the battle group 2ic, who generously waved away his concerns: it really didn't matter. Then came the moment when Major Andy Carré, commanding B Company after David Bradley had been wounded, ordered Ian Pennells to move up to his position – Lieutenant Pennells was, at the time, having a little trouble with a rather persistent RPG man. He

B Company 1 PWRR and
(*opposite*) B Company Warriors leaving camp in Basra

responded: 'Yeah, boss, I'm just squaring this prick away now.' 'You might want to have a word with him about that one,' ventured the 2ic.

On 5 August there was a report of militia trying to close Route 6 – the key line of communication to Al Amarah and the north – in the area of Qarmat Ali Bridge. David Bradley immediately went across to the company ops room, and briefed Sergeant Kelly (E30B) to investigate with his two Warriors. Drummer Russ Butler, driver of the second Warrior, remembered:

> It had been another hot sunny day and we had just moved on to our day as duty QRF. We had had lunch, and were just chilling out in our lovely first-class tented accommodation, catching up on a little sleep, when shouting outside caught our attention. Andy Brown flew through our room at Mach 10 saying we had been crashed out, RPG teams at the Qarmat Ali bridge. So we all grabbed our kit and ran up to the Warriors. Our multiple mounted up, and we were out of the gate in five minutes . . .
>
> Our Warriors, spaced no more than 30 metres apart, drove up Route 6, north of Basra, towards Al Halaa over the Qarmat Ali bridge. On reaching the bridge we felt

a shudder on the left-hand side. I asked Jerry [Corporal Maguire, the commander] what it was, as the top cover in the vehicle in front dropped down inside the Warrior. Jerry shouted back down the intercom 'I think we've just been hit by an RPG!' as I caught a lungful of the rifle-range smell of cordite, and realized we'd been struck. Jerry was straight on to Matty [Private Waitawa, the gunner]: 'There, under the bridge, RPG team 200 metres, co-ax, go on.' Following this there was an awesome burst from the 7.62mm chain gun over the back decks towards the bad guys.

We crawled to the crest of the bridge for the front call-sign to receive a volley of rounds in their direction. Corporal Dax Pett and Private Barry Butler in the turret of E33 located their position on the other side of the bridge and started firing 30mm high explosive in return. I could hear the pop pop of rounds over my headset as we had contacts on both sides of the bridge now. Jase Bruce drove E33 to the north side of the bridge once the previous position had been neutralized, to sweep up the rest of them. Our turret was still firing to the rear of the vehicle, while in front of me E33 was scanning in front of them looking for targets, as were their dismounted troops.

Suddenly to my front I observe three Iraqi militia starting to move around the left of a building to engage E33 dismounts. Our turret is still engaging so I had to think what I, the driver, could do. I grabbed my rifle up to the aim. I put the pointer of my sight on the middle of the three enemy and started firing. I could see the splashes and corrected my fire to allow for the wind. A round hit the gunman in the middle and he stumbled to the floor as a second round hit him. One of the other gunmen started to pick up his fallen comrade and his pal still had his weapon pointed at me, so I kept on suppressing, to stop the gunman firing at me. I saw the guy I had hit crawl off, go static and finally stop moving. I shouted up to Jerry, who was now spinning the turret around, 'Jerry, I got one, but there's two more, stick some HE down that alley.' Matty fired three rounds down the alley, obliterating the two gunmen who were still trying to get around to fire at E33.

By this time Jerry had seen another three enemy behind a wall and was firing his rifle. He said over the headset that there was one gunman lying down there, but he did not know if he was dead or taking cover. As he was saying this E33 had driven back over to the southern side of the bridge, and Sergeant Ben Kelly jumped out of the back by the downed gunman, kicks away his rifle and starts searching him.

Having returned to battle group headquarters and heard the first contact reports from the bridge, David Bradley immediately ran back to get his own tactical headquarters up and running:

> As I got out of the door I could hear the fighting: the heavy crash of the RPGs and the staccato firing of small arms. As I stopped and listened there was a short pause before a rapid 'boom, boom, boom' as the Warriors returned fire with their 30mm. It was a great sound and I knew 6 Platoon was giving it back to the bastards.

He took his command Warrior, E0B and two multiples, E10B under Sergeant Marsh and E20A under Lieutenant Pennells, and reached the bridge to find that E30B had won its little battle and was in the follow-up mode. The militia had built some fairly robust sangars and shallow trenches with the intention of dominating the bridge, and as the Warriors had moved on to it they had opened fire from both ends. However, the Warriors had made short work of them. One militiaman – the one shot by Corporal Maguire and disarmed by Sergeant Kelly – lay on the central reservation. He died despite the assistance of Lance Corporal John Drewery, the company medic. David Bradley mused:

> What was interesting about the follow-up was the immediate presence of a large crowd. They seemed to appear from nowhere as soon as the fighting stopped. They were not hostile to us but an imam came forwards and made it clear that we should leave the body. One got the feeling that the locals thought the gunman died in a fair fight and that we were not to blame, as long as we left the body.

A report then arrived that more militiamen were besieging the Wilderness police station in Al Halaaf. Major Bradley left E30B on the bridge and ordered E10B to push north, followed by E0B and E20A. A few minutes later they were in contact again, with gunmen shooting from both sides of the road. 'Trying to identify targets was very difficult,' he recalled, 'as they were flitting through trees and hiding behind women and children. The blokes showed great restraint, but it did not take long before [the enemy] melted away.'

When Sergeant Kelly's multiple returned to camp, Drummer Butler examined 'the damage done by the RPG, just a minor hole on the tool bin on the side of the turret, it did not detonate properly'. He then spoke to Private Mark Patterson, a dismount in the leading Warrior, 'who told me that a guy had fired an RPG at him from 20 metres away, but he had hit him with his Minimi . . . "He didn't fire at us again."'

> We worked out later that we had killed six militia, including the one I had dropped. I've got a bit of a reputation in the company now as the only driver to have fired my rifle, and to have killed somebody. I suppose my actions saved the lives of my mates that day. After that we had a month of fighting in the busiest part of our tour.

Although the company in general, and 6 Platoon in particular, felt pleased with the day's work, the situation in the city continued to deteriorate, with the Mahdi army increasingly dominant. Mortar attacks were now so intense that the soldiers of B Company, normally accommodated in tents, had to move into the Shatt Al Arab Hotel every night, and as they all dossed down in one large room it was hard to get a decent night's rest.

9 August dawned like any other busy day. During the morning there had been a sharp clash between elements of a Cheshire company and a party of militia, who had followed up when the Cheshire patrol disengaged, showing a level of training and aggression not previously seen. The RHA at Camp Cherokee had reported a substantial group of gunmen in front of their camp, and although there were none about when David Bradley arrived, he left Lieutenant Hallam Scaife of 4 Platoon there with 20A in case of further trouble.

Major Bradley had just sat down for a late lunch when he was summoned to the battle group ops room. Reports were coming in of an RHA contact on Red Route, and it seemed that a multiple was missing. When the gunners came back with a grid reference, it revealed that the lost multiple seemed to be in the old Ba'ath Party headquarters building, which had been fortified by the British and then handed over to the Iraqi police. Even more disturbingly, it was right next to the OMS headquarters. Daniel was in the lion's den, and a miracle was urgently required. David Bradley recalled:

> I remember thinking 'They'd better have the location right as this is going to be unpleasant.' The battle group 2ic tasked me to push down to Red 19 while they tried to get confirmation of their location and ensure that the multiple had not actually made it through to another base. I ran back to the ops room and stood to the company [ordered the company to stand to its arms]. E20A [Lieutenant Scaife] was already on the ground just north of Red 20, and the next multiple on task was E10A. As the other multiples got together they would join us at best speed.
>
> We left camp and took the most direct route. I briefed E20A over the net but Ian [Pennells] had already pushed south to Red 20 as soon as the fighting had started. As we got to Red 20 there was the Cheshire multiple securing the road, they pointed in the direction of the enemy threat and stood by to let us pass. The noise of shooting was already deafening. I pushed E20A through first with E0B second and E10A in the rear. As soon as E20A passed Red 20 they came under RPG and small-arms fire. Ian and Cpl Thompson neutralized the threat but it was clear there were other positions further on. In the distance, about where the Ba'ath Party HQ was located, I saw a plume of black smoke, which I could only assume to be the lost multiple's burning vehicles. At this point the battle group 2ic came on the net: 'It is confirmed that 9 British soldiers are lost in the area of Red 18, it is not known if they are alive or dead. You are to use all means at your disposal to get them back.'

Major Bradley passed his information on, instructing E20A to clear the first position while E10A pushed on. As he followed E10A south down Red Route he was concerned that his company was getting too strung out, and told his driver Sergeant Pike to slow down while he tried to raise E20A on the net. The noise was phenomenal: the Warrior was being fired at from all directions, the sound so intense that 'it seemed like a dome all around my head'. Major Bradley was standing up in the turret, holding his rifle and trying to identify a firing point to his right, when the first RPG struck.

> There was suddenly a massive 'bang' and I saw an explosion right in front of me to the rear of the commander's turret bin. I do not remember any pain but I do remember being pushed back by the blast. My first thought was 'This is bad, very, very bad' closely followed by 'I don't fucking believe it. I've been fucking hit, this should not be happening.' Actions and thoughts happened simultaneously. I lifted up my right hand and saw that it was cut in half. I also felt a pressure on my chest and sliding down into the turret which I thought was an RPG coming in (I later worked out that it was my rifle, which had been hit by an RPG from right rear).

He had in fact been wounded by the first RPG, and then his gunner, Private Yee-Lim, saw another on its way and began to tug him down in the turret. The second missile hit his rifle, not far from where he was clutching it in his right hand.

> My first reaction was to get out and I started to climb on to the top of the turret yelling at Yee-Lim . . . to do the same. I ended up lying on the top of the turret looking at Yee-Lim through the gunner's hatch. The noise was even worse. The bullets sounded even closer with ricochets coming off the vehicle, and the constant crackle of high-velocity rounds seemed to intensify as the Mahdi militia tried to shoot me off. Yee-Lim was looking up and shouting at me to get back in, which I realized would be a good idea. As I slid back into the turret I saw that the left side of my body armour was on fire. I quickly patted it out with my left hand but the thought of being badly burned was one of the most terrifying moments.

David Bradley had still not realized that part of the RPG, together with fragments of his rifle, had been blown through his body armour and deep into his chest, and that there were fragments of metal in his right eye. The drive to Camp Cherokee was desperate. Yee-Lim took on targets with the chain gun and tried repeatedly to prevent his commander from slipping into a coma, while Sergeant Pike, who was just standing in as the OC's driver that day, found his way unaided and under fire, unable to contact anyone else in the vehicle but fearing that they were all dead or wounded. In fact the CSM, Lance Corporal Drewery, Lance Corporal Phillips and Private Tallack had all been hurt. David Bradley, receiving urgent medical attention at the camp, wondered: 'If we had been hit already, what would happen to the rest of the company?'

His company was fighting on just as he would have wished. Hallam Scaife of 4 Platoon had barrelled on down Red Route with his multiple, moving through the Warriors of Ian Pennells's 5 Platoon, as ordered. He told Corporal Pepper, commanding his other Warrior, that they were not going to stop till they reached Red 17. They accordingly took Red 19 at speed, killing an RPG gunner as they did so, and reached the roundabout at Red 17 to find the left turn into the Ba'ath Party HQ blocked by a burning RHA Snatch.

I looked out over the far side of a narrow canal, and saw several men all armed with AKs. Again both the soldiers in the back and I fired, dropping two of them. We reversed out, so that both Warriors were just off the roundabout at Red 17, looking down towards the OMS building, with the old Ba'ath Party HQ on our left side.

The firefight raged on for another half an hour . . . By this time Sgt Marsh had arrived in callsign E13 to provide us with some much needed protection back up Red Route. The ferocity of the enemy's attack was incredible, with militia advancing on to the Warriors. We were receiving incoming fire from all directions, as I jockeyed up and down the route, peering down side streets in order to try and identify the RHA's position, which they were marking with smoke. Cpl Pepper in callsign E12 was busy unloading his 30mm into a building that was being used as a firing point, as I saw a militia member run across the street with an AK. Pte Smith, my gunner, was quicker and the Iraqi ran into the chain-gun fire and folded in half.

At this juncture the company commander's Warrior roared past, turned right on to Blue Route and disappeared from view. It could not be raised on the radio; they had no idea that it was full of wounded and that Sergeant Pike was finding his way to Camp Cherokee as best he could. Lieutenant Pennells had now arrived with his two Warriors and there was more information about the lost patrol, which was reported to be in a house 100 metres away. Hallam Scaife was reluctant to send men to search buildings under such ferocious fire, and in any event they were all hard at it, firing from the mortar hatches with rifles and Minimis, covering the vehicle's side and rear arcs. Convinced that the RHA were not going to dash out to the Warriors – and who can blame them? – he decided to find a closer approach to the house:

> As we were manoeuvring out of position, I heard a shout from the back, looking over my shoulder I saw Pte O'Callaghan fall back into the Warrior. My heart leapt into my mouth, and I shouted for Private Tame, my driver, to reverse at full speed on to Red Route. The medic, Pte Crow, shouted from the back: 'Boss, he's bad, get us out of here.'
>
> Up to this point we were invincible. The fact that RPGs had been hitting the sides of the vehicle, and rounds had been pinging off the turret next to my head, had not seemed real. You were aware of them, but they did not stop you from going through the drills that we had practised so routinely. But your mortality is thrust upon you all of a sudden when you see one of your men get hit.

Knowing that Lieutenant Pennells and Sergeant Marsh were on hand to continue the hunt for the lost gunners, Lieutenant Scaife decided to evacuate the casualty himself and, telling his driver to stop for nothing, set off for the nearest aid post at the Old State Building. Almost all the way there they were ambushed, firing back from the turret and mortar hatches. 'Through some awesome driving, a large number of 5.56mm rounds and pure luck, we arrived at the gates of OSB with a few extra holes in the Warrior, but thankfully with no more casualties,' he said. But no sooner was he safe inside the perimeter than he heard the news he dreaded: Lee O'Callaghan was dead.

Meanwhile, Corporal Thompson, commanding the second vehicle of Ian Pennells's multiple, had been told that the missing gunners were inside the former Ba'ath Party HQ. His Warrior was already badly damaged, with its turret jammed and its electrical system shorting out so that touching bare metal administered a shock. Nonetheless he barged the front gates down with it, and then set about clearing several sangars in the compound with his rifle and UGL. He shot fast and accurately, and the sheer high-speed lethality of his onslaught confused his opponents, whose responses grew increasingly ineffective. This was no time to keep score, but he and his men seemed to have hit twenty-six of their enemies in and around the courtyard. However, they did not find the gunners, and Corporal Thompson emerged, declaring that the lost patrol was definitely not there. He was prepared to go back again if ordered, but doubted if they would emerge alive.

Corporal Pepper, meanwhile, had located the RHA in a building behind the Ba'ath Party HQ. He asked Lance Corporal Robson, commanding his dismounts, 'Are you good to go and get them?' 'Fucking right I am,' replied Robson, and disappeared into the buildings. The dismounts duly cleared the building and the gunners were loaded into the back of the Warrior, leaving no room for the B Company soldiers. These dismounts, under Lance Corporal Robson, then fire and manoeuvred, with the Warrior in close support, for several hundred metres and through some well defended positions, all the way back to the main gate. Here the troops remounted, and the multiple withdrew through 6 Platoon.

This had been the last element in the company's order of march, and Captain Mike Reid, its commander, had been briefed only intermittently because of the bad communications that had characterized the day's battle. Eventually – 'and with my gunner Private Ricky Coombes working some size 9 magic on the radio' – he gained a shaky grasp of the situation. There was a platoon still ahead of him, and the RHA had been picked up and were on their way back. As the remainder of the company folded back through his position, he was unsure of what had happened to Hallam Scaife. He knew that Scaife's vehicle had been ahead of him.

This left me with one of the hardest decisions I have ever had to make. To assess the risk of moving forward across a river and into the armour killing area in front of the Sadr compound to look for signs of E10, Hallam Scaife's Warrior. In effect, to balance the lives of my platoon against those of his. To be honest I think my boys would not have forgiven me if we had left our friends in the city alone anyway.

Mike Reid took his three Warriors forward to the site of the main battle, and while two of them engaged the militia there he pulled into cover and tried to raise Hallam Scaife on the net.

The extra helpful bit was that for some unknown technical reason, I could not use the radio, only my gunner could. This meant that when Pte Coombes informed me that he had found out E10 was secure in the Old State Building, the downtown base, I had to trust him entirely that he had correctly understood the message on a distorted and confused radio net. On this trust alone I had to pull back, happy that my mate and his boys were safe . . . Fortunately working with someone seven days a week can build that trust, and I pulled my Warriors back and got the rest of the company back to the Royal Artillery base behind us. After, of course, Cpl Daxius Pett, one of my section commanders, had destroyed an enemy machine gun using the unexpected method of shooting a nearby tree, which then fell on it.

Captain Reid reached Camp Cherokee knowing that the gunners had been rescued, but unaware of the cost. Seeing the company commander's Warrior he 'somewhat rudely asked where the fuck he had been', and heard that 'nearly all his Tac command group was injured'. He realized that command of B Company had now devolved on him.

I also realized that there was a reason why we had been harassed in South Wales streams, and that in the short term at least we can get by without anyone [to assist us], as our training is good enough to let us get by doing someone else's job; and those above us had enough trust in us to let us know what they needed to do so that we could work it out for them when they weren't there . . .

It was then down to me to tell the company, who thought everybody was roughly OK, that O'Callaghan had been killed trying to save the isolated gunners, and then, in the next breath, that we had to ensure we were ready to go back into the city if we were needed again. That is the one element even the training we get cannot prepare you for.

Over the next few weeks the battle group prepared to reopen the city centre by force. There were armoured raids into known militia-dominated areas, which both wrenched the initiative from the insurgents and boosted morale within the battle group. Another large workload was generated by the need to furnish armoured escorts for moves within the city, especially to the Old State Building. When the recce party for The Welsh Guards, who were to take over from 1 PWRR, arrived they were escorted by Sergeant Marsh, who managed to get shot at both on the way out and on the way back, 'probably adding extra emphasis to final pre-tour training plans'. Towards the end of August the situation eased as Grand Ayatollah Sistani, an authoritative figure with a powerful benign influence, returned to Najaf to establish moderate Shi'a authority there.

However, neither continued negotiations nor the improvement of the situation elsewhere – serious violence had ceased in Al Amarah on 26 August – could conceal the fact that the OMS office in central Basra remained a symbol of defiance to the new regime and was apparently full of weapons. One search operation yielded an impressive haul, and on 17 September, in response to a shooting outside the building, the company turned out for a large-scale raid. Drummer Melville, driver of E30, had just come off guard:

> I dropped off my kit in my room, saturated in sweat. A can of cold Coke was in order so off I went to the NAAFI and bought one. On my travels back to my room the company commander [now Major Andy Carré] ran past me in sports kit. He stopped and turned to me and shouted 'You've got to get the Warrior ready, we're going out.' I was miffed as

he must be confused, as I was on guard, and besides he's in civvies. I got back to my room, opened my beautiful ice-cold can, put my feet up and began to chill out. Then I heard footsteps running outside. I went to investigate, there was people everywhere running around. It was like a scene from *Starship Troopers*. I shouted out to find out what was going on. A mucker replied that we were doing a company attack, we were storming the OMS building. Fuck me, this is serious. I dropped off my can, grabbed my kit and done one up to the vehicles. There were blokes everywhere, people sorting out cold water and platoon sergeants running around like headless chickens, accounting for their men. I climbed on to my vehicle and embraced the chaos. This is the shit I am talking about, what an awesome sight.

We all mounted up, adrenaline pumping, and with a last kiss of my wedding ring we were off, a company of Warriors rolling out of the gate. We were the fucking daddies, I remember thinking as we rolled down the street with nothing getting in our way.

The company was hit at Blue 5, RPGs streaking for the leading vehicles and chain guns responding. Drummer Melville continues:

I stopped and went firm to allow my gunner to engage any enemy. It came back over the radio from my boss, Captain Reid, we must push on, so we drove off.

The next junction was ours. Suddenly a burst of gunfire and tracer came cracking past my face, no more than two metres away. Fuck this, for some reason my hatch was still open. In all the excitement I never closed it, believe me it was closed now. We turned left and moved to our objective; we were to give flanking support to all our callsigns. Hours pass, the heat in my seat was intense. I have the engine next to me running at 110 Celsius, no fresh air and I am wearing helmet and body armour. It was like a pressure cooker.

The Warrior was narrowly missed by an RPG, tipping it sideways as if it was a toy.

I said to my commander, Cpl Si Gower, 'That cheeky fucker just fired an RPG at us, mate.' I tried to bring the gunner [Matt Lethbridge] on to the target, but I couldn't. That's when I knew the effects of the heat were starting to kick in. It was horrible, I could see this man reloading, but could not explain where he was, my brain was slowing down. Bang, shit, he has fired again, whoosh, it went over our heads and into the building behind us. How can I explain where he is? Then suddenly I see a load of tracer fired from another road straight into the position the RPG man was in. Target destroyed.

Drummer Melville was soon involved in helping evacuate men who had keeled over with heat exhaustion. Although he had drunk eight or nine litres of water he kept blacking out; his head was pounding and his speech was slurred. He was jolted awake by a burst from the chain gun: Matt Lethbridge had hit an RPG man the second before he fired: 'the target fell and the RPG just skimmed along the road'.

It came over the net 5, 4, 3, 2, 1. Go, go, go, the assault on the building had begun, and we were relocated to give the assaulting platoon all-round defence. We moved off. 'Si, I can't see, help me, everything is blurred.' I was driving blind using my commander's eyes, and we got to our new position unscathed. Damn me, we are an awesome crew.

After a wearying delay waiting in the heat, for a decision from higher authority, the company stood poised to assault, its men (Drummer Melville at last amongst them) dropping from heat exhaustion. Hallam Scaife's 4 Platoon was detailed to spearhead the attack, and when the word came he ordered Private Bishenden, who had never driven a Warrior before and was replacing a man evacuated because of the heat, to make an entry with style:

He got it perfectly on line, moving between the car and the lamppost, jinking right just at the last moment to bring us straight on to the wall. The Warrior shook as we passed straight through two eight-foot-high breezeblock walls. We

Opposite: Politics Iraq style: ammunition and RPGs
recovered from the OMS

Above: Small arms in the OMS building

were in, the dismounts quickly debussed and moved towards the main building. We moved back out on to the
street, as the rest of my platoon started to dismount from
their Warriors.

The building was cleared without opposition, and was found to
be full of weapons. 'The CO of the Cheshires arrived,' remembered
Lieutenant Scaife, 'and was as elated as the rest of us that we had
seized the enemy's HQ, and a sizeable amount of their weapons
with it.'

It took until dawn, with a steady drain of heat-exhaustion cases,
to remove the weapons from the building. RPG teams pushed in
to try their luck, and Private Andrews was splashed with shrapnel.

An RMP liaison officer
deploying to a contact in a snatch

Eventually, after dawn, Support Company of The Black Watch arrived to take over and the company trundled back to camp. Relief was now combined with muted elation, and Corporal Dax Pett was declared winner of the battle-damage competition when an unexploded RPG warhead was removed from the front armour of his Warrior. The following days were 'a little surreal'. Many local people offered their congratulations, and attacks on coalition forces stopped almost immediately.

Hallam Scaife had bittersweet memories of the company's tour in Basra.

> It is over for us now, and many soldiers are choosing to leave the army. They believe that they have seen what they joined the army to witness, and they never want to go through that again. Who can blame them? There is little time to dwell and self-congratulate now, as we are busy training, ready to return next year.

CHAPTER 7

Looking Back, Looking Forward

O N 22 OCTOBER 2004 The Welsh Guards formally assumed responsibility for Al Amarah, and the last of 1 PWRR left Iraq. But Matt Maer had long recognized that there were real disadvantages in taking the battle group home immediately. Experience in the Falklands suggested that troops who had been exposed to the risk of sudden death found it easier to get back into 'the world' if they had some time for decompression; time to relax, to talk things over with their friends, and to put their experiences into perspective. Air travel has many virtues, but sea journeys do at least provide time for this process to take place. The 1 PWRR battle group had grown very close during the tour, but as soon as it returned to the UK relationships would change for ever; the subunits from the Lancers and The Royal Welch would all return to their parent regiments. People needed time to say goodbye, time to say thank you, time to grieve.

There had originally been some prospect of getting the battle group to Cyprus to wind down together, but sadly it soon became clear that this fell, administratively, into the All Too Difficult category. Instead, thanks to what Matt Maer called 'the single most outstanding piece of staff work I have seen,' they were given the opportunity to spend a few days at the large US base of Al Udeid in the Gulf state of Qatar. Although Al Udeid did not enjoy all the advantages of Cyprus, it did provide the opportunity for officers and men to relax, and to allow themselves the luxury of thinking about the future without tempting fate. 'A great many of those we have slated as REMFs really pulled this one out of the bag,' said one battle group officer.

Matt and I had agreed that the last thing the battalion wanted was to celebrate its return to the UK in the traditional way, with parades – 'drums beating, bayonets fixed and colours flying' – through a selection of the towns of which the regiment holds the freedom. It was not that we did not value our relationship with those places from which so many of our soldiers come and upon whose continuing support our successful recruiting partly depends. But the brief stand-down in Al Udeid could not conceal the fact that everyone was very tired; there were the usual administrative chores that had to be completed at the base at Tidworth, and early the following year the battalion was moving, lock, stock and barrel, to Paderborn in Germany. If parades are to be held, they must be done well, and somehow the battalion was in no mood for a flurry of drill and rehearsals.

Instead, when it returned from Al Udeid we got the whole battalion – and as many wives and families as could make it – together in the gym at Tidworth, where, on his last day with the battalion, Padre Fran Myatt held a drumhead service. Each of the companies gave a presentation, with PowerPoint splashed on to the wall, dealing with its exploits in Iraq. It is easy to forget that, for most of those involved, so much of what had happened there was parochial. Soldiers knew what their multiple or their platoon had done, and had a fair idea of the activities of their company; but other companies were another country, where things were done differently. Not dissimilar was the distancing from events felt by the families, for whom terms like Danny Boy and Waterloo, Pimlico and Hammersmith, meant little. Wives and children, though, would be living with husbands and fathers for whom these operations would, one way or another, always be present, and the more they knew of the context the better they might understand their implications.

It would take some time for campaign medals to be issued – on my visit to the 2nd Battalion in Iraq in mid-2005 I presented some actually earned two years before – and there would be no operational honours and awards list until the late spring. Companies had been asked to vote for comrades whose contribution had been particularly well received, and I presented a symbolic handful of privately obtained campaign medals, wholly unofficially, to those nominated by the sternest of judges, their peers. It was a way that we, within the tribe, could thank at least a small proportion of the many who needed thanking. Here, too, was an opportunity for families to look around the barracks, to meet people who had featured large in a loved one's life over the past few months, and to enjoy a good lunch.

The battalion then departed on an extended Christmas leave. It returned to barracks in the New Year to set about moving to Germany, a task that was completed well before the first anniversary of its deployment to Iraq.

In mid-March, when 1 PWRR had barely established itself in Paderborn, the operational honours list for the period of its deployment was published. It was headed by Private Johnson Beharry, who was awarded that most highly prized of gallantry decorations, the Victoria Cross, for his bravery in Al Amarah in May 2004. He was the 1,351st man to win the VC since its inception in 1856. Although he was the first member of the PWRR to be so decorated, he joined the fifty-seven VC winners who had belonged to the regiment's predecessors. This was, in itself, remarkable, but what really set the seal on the battalion's achievement was the award of Conspicuous Gallantry Crosses, the new all-ranks 'second level' gallantry award which replaced the old Distinguished Conduct Medal, to Sergeant Broome of C Company and the recently promoted Sergeant Thompson of B, and seven Military Crosses (instituted as an officers-only award in 1915 but now available to all ranks). Two members of C Company 1 RWF also received Military Crosses. There were two Distinguished Service Orders, for Matt Maer and James Coote, an MBE for Sergeant Major Norman of Y Company, a Queen's Commendation for Valuable Services for Toby Walch, and sixteen Mentions in Dispatches.

The decorations were presented at two investitures at Buckingham Palace in May, and on both occasions the Haberdashers, our affiliated City Livery Company, gave the newly decorated members of the regiment and their immediate families a delightful buffet lunch at their hall. It was a good opportunity for everyone to relax after the excitement of the morning. However, I felt a powerful undertow of emotion, because we all knew that there were three members of the battle group who could never share our pride, and that at least fifty officers and men would carry the scars of the tour, physical or mental, with them to the grave. The point was silently emphasized by David Bradley, who was there with his wife Lara to congratulate the soldiers of his company and his brother officers.

We last saw Major Bradley arriving wounded at Camp Cherokee in Basra, where the medics of 1 RHA had set up a casualty room to handle the sudden influx of broken bodies from B Company. He tells us:

> A quick and efficient medic started to cut off my body armour and ask about my wounds. Unknown to me I had a large cut on my right jaw. He asked if my teeth were OK and I remember, with great trepidation, moving my tongue around my lower jaw expecting to find smashed teeth and a hole through to fresh air. The prospect of facial recon-struction and eating through a straw for months was very unappealing. As with all situations there were comedy moments. Sgt Pike came to talk to me: 'Sir, I've checked the family jewels and everything is OK.' 'Thanks, Sgt Pike,' I replied, 'but I'm actually more concerned about my hand.' Having said that, every soldier is concerned about his man-hood and I was grateful to be told it was all there . . .
>
> All of us [CSM Barnett, LCpl Drewery, LCpl Phillips and Pte Tallack] needed further medical attention and we were transferred by wheeled ambulance to the medical squadron at the [Shatt Al Arab] Hotel. I remember seeing the doctor who I normally talked to at battle-group-orders groups looking down at me on the table and asking how I felt. I do not remember much pain but I remember saying 'Right, I have had enough now, doc, just knock me out.' I am not sure if they did but I remember being taken to the helicopter. Having talked to the IRT nurse that looked after me, she said I was pretty angry at that stage. Apparently my last words before losing consciousness were 'You need to sort me out so that I can go back and kill those fucking bastards!'

At Shaiba he was operated on by Czech surgeons who made a radical incision into his chest to remove the assorted fragments of RPG and rifle, some of which were perilously close to his heart. Then he had a massive haemorrhage which would have killed him, had the surgeon not created enough space in the chest cavity to deal with it. Indeed, during the lengthy process David 'flat-lined' twice – his vital signs disappeared and the monitor registered a flat line rather than the regular heartbeat blips – but was revived. After the operation, to be sure that he was not in a coma they brought him round. He was being flown back to the UK, a nurse told him, but would need his helmet for the helicopter transfer to Basra Airport.

> I remember worrying about finding it for a short while, before thinking: 'How the hell am I supposed to know where my helmet is? I've just been blown up and I'm lying in hospital, you find it.' Having thought that, I then went on to think: 'But I need my helmet for the transfer. Knowing my luck I will have survived an RPG strike only to die in a helicopter crash, great.' After that there was nothing until I woke in Birmingham four days later.

Lara Bradley reflected:

> It is never easy being the wife of a soldier. The upheaval of moving home, packing, unpacking, changing schools, finding new jobs, the emotional turmoil for the children and the loneliness caused by the long periods of absence from the husband and father. However, I met, fell in love with and married a soldier who loves and lives for his job. As a soldier's wife you have to try to hold on to and focus on the positive aspects of life you and your family will live with. I have enjoyed meeting new people, making new friends, adapting to new environments and living in different places, and do believe some good can be gained from these experiences, for all the family.

Although she found the meetings for wives and families before the tour 'informative, positive and reassuring', she had experienced 'niggling worry and doubt' about Iraq from the start. She tried to push it to the back of her mind for the sake of their two young children, Philippa and Alexander, and both her job in a local school and contact with other army wives and children helped provide 'reassurance and support'. But listening to the news became 'almost an obsession'. On 9 August she returned to Tidworth after two relaxing weeks away, switched on the television for her children while she unloaded the car, and saw, from a 'breaking news' clip, that B Company had been in contact in Basra.

She spent the rest of the day 'as if walking on eggshells', constantly looking through the window, always ready for a phone call:

> Finally at 7.30 p.m. my worst fears were realized when I glanced out of the sitting-room window to see a blue car draw up and Capt Wells and Sgt Kendall Tobias emerge and walk down the path towards the house. Life at that point becomes rather a blur. The only information that was then available was that David had been critically injured in an incident in Basra and was in surgery, having suffered injuries to his chest. I feel numb writing this now. Nothing in life can ever prepare one for the overwhelming shock, fear and horror that I felt. Life changed for our family in a matter of moments. I have never felt so out of control or helpless. The chilling realization that I might never see him again was more than I could bear. Fortunately I had the support of a very good friend who had come to stay for the night and took control of the situation, asked the important questions and contacted our families, who arrived during the evening . . .

Lara was updated during the evening as more news became available. 'A night of no sleep and unimaginable anguish' followed. The next day, 10 August – their eighth wedding anniversary – she spent clutching David's anniversary card, which said how much he was looking forward to his imminent leave, 'and praying harder than I have ever prayed in my life'. There were more visitors that morning, including her parents, who took the children back home on a 'special holiday'. 'I had to be strong in front of the children,' she remembered, 'and I did not want them to hear the news until I knew more.'

Bob Wells came to say that David was in a critical but stable condition and would be flown home later that day, and in the afternoon Lieutenant Colonel Hay phoned from the medical centre at Shaiba to tell her as much as he could. The news of Private Lee O'Callaghan's death had now been made public. 'I kept thinking of the utter horror his family would be going through,' she wrote, 'and my heart and soul went out to them.' Late that night she was told that David's plane was in the air, and slept for the first time in two days.

Early on the 11th, Sergeant-Major Ken Furie drove her and her in-laws to Selly Oak Hospital, a large Victorian building close to the centre of Birmingham, the first UK destination for all serious casualties from Iraq. She knew that the plane had touched down at RAF Brize Norton: 'I remember the look of relief on my mother-in-law Janet's face when she heard this. She said: "Today is a good day . . . he's home and he's alive."' Somehow Lara Bradley expected that he would open his eyes and talk to her as soon as she arrived; she remembered how 'the loneliness is wearing but the hellos are always like meeting all over again'.

> Not this time. My illusions were shattered shortly after arriving when I was handed a black plastic bag containing what I was told were his belongings. What the bag actually contained were his bloodied uniform, boots and other possessions, which had been on him at the time of the attack.

When she saw her husband he was unconscious, hooked up to electronic monitors, his face and body swollen, covered in blood and orange anaesthetic paint.

David had a number of operations on his hand, eye and chest, and on 12 August he was transferred to the Queen Elizabeth Hospital in Birmingham for another operation 'to open up his chest, stop any small areas of bleeding, check for any other pieces of shrapnel and then close his chest cavity, rewiring his rib cage at the sternum'. His eyelids started to flutter on the 13th as Lara, his parents and his sister talked to him, and on the morning of the 14th, Lara's birthday, he was conscious when she arrived.

The next few weeks were a switchback, with each day bringing its highs and its lows. There were times when 'the mourning for the loss of one of his soldiers and having left his company was at times overwhelming for him'. Lara was now living in a room in a nearby block, 'comfortable and functional, with a shared kitchen and television room', but as Dave fought his way back she was allowed to spend the night in a chair by his bed, trying to get some sleep when she could.

> This was not easy on a busy ward, the noises and alarms from each machine and monitor were ceaseless, and the human sounds of others in pain and discomfort were at times almost too much to bear. However, the need to be near to David during this time was of greater importance to me.
>
> I never ceased to be amazed at the level of care that he received whilst on the units. He was monitored twenty-four hours a day in twelve-hour shifts by a range of competent and dedicated nurses and doctors, who kept me informed at every point as to what was happening. The competence and skill of all in the hospital, from surgeons, doctors and nurses to cooks, cleaners and volunteers, cannot go without mention.

On 18 August David had a pedical graft, which involved attaching his right hand under the skin on his stomach, where it would remain for three weeks. During this time the stomach skin would replace the skin that had been lost when the RPG exploded. His right index finger was amputated, and its bones were used to repair the rest of the damaged hand. Progress was slow and faltering, but each day brought tiny steps in the right direction. Feeding tubes were withdrawn as he began to eat again, and therapists encouraged him to move his limbs and take deeper breaths to improve the oxygen levels in his blood. Eventually Lara judged that it was the right moment to tell their children what had really happened:

> I will never forget their faces as they ran towards me on their arrival. They both looked so grown up. So much had changed in our lives that they were unaware of as yet . . . We were taken to a room in the Critical Care Unit and

David was brought in in a wheelchair. Children have an amazing resilience and propensity to adapt to situations, and although their shock was evident in seeing their once strong daddy confined to a wheelchair they were busy chatting in moments. It was, however, an incredibly moving moment for us all when our three-year-old son said: 'Daddy when I fall over and bang my knee, I will be a brave soldier like you.'

David was eventually well enough to return home on 6 October. When I met him at the Haberdashers' Hall six months later he looked so well that I instinctively reached for his wounded hand before I remembered what I was doing.

A good deal of responsibility had fallen on the battalion's welfare office at Tidworth. Some of it was familiar. Under the direction of Captain Chris Wright – forbidding in appearance, but wholly committed to sustaining the battalion's home front – the office helped families with a myriad of problems. Captain Wright explained:

Many of the wives could not drive and Tidworth is no sprawling metropolis. Its high street contains a chemist, a NAAFI, an arts supply shop, a strange two-storey shop selling furniture and pornography, a tyre centre and two takeaways (one of which was boarded up). The wives needed to be able to get into Salisbury or Andover to do most of their shopping and the welfare office provided coaches at least once a week. Pregnant wives needed to be taken to hospital for scans and health checks while their husbands were away. The army always tries to ensure that the father will be brought back for the birth of a child, but this could not always be guaranteed. And so the office had to be prepared to take women in for the birth . . .

There was a host of normal issues that the family had to deal with . . . Pipes burst and power failed from time to time. Christine Waugh was to deal with much of this sort of business . . .

... there would be a Sunday lunch where the wives could bring their children and chat with each other while the children ran riot on the battalion's bouncy tiger, or attacking the clown. These were not only attended by the wives but by a few girlfriends and their children as well, not normally well looked after in the army system, for a variety of reasons. As R and R kicked in some of the soldiers came to these too.

Most operational tours produce a trickle of casualties:

Someone does their leg in on a run, someone breaks their ankle taking up a fire position, someone runs themselves into the ground, someone gets slightly burned by a petrol bomb (usually in training) and someone gets sick with a reaction to local food that they were told not to eat but did anyway. Telic IV had all these minor incidents (Brooksie broke his ankle leaping over an open sewer and found himself in the ops room at Abu Naji for four weeks), but there were lots and lots of serious injuries. Twenty-five per cent in C Company – 50 per cent in 8 Platoon. There were bullet wounds, grenades, RPG fragments, WO1 Potter broke his neck when he was picked up by the blast wave of a rocket impact (though he carried on working for nearly a fortnight before he went to the medics to have it checked out), and of course there were Sgt Llewellyn's appalling burns. Whereas a handful of individuals would normally return [home] for illnesses and injuries . . . across the battle group and B Company fifty men were aeromedded to the UK.

Wounded soldiers arriving at Brize Norton were met not just by the duty driver but by a familiar face from the battalion. The more seriously wounded, up at Selly Oak Hospital, were visited regularly, 'with Cuddly Ken [Sergeant Major Ken Furie] doing two or three minibus runs a week and picking families up from as far afield as Portsmouth (Barry Bliss) and London (Pte Brown, shot in the ankle)'. When the wounded were released from hospital the welfare office would call them back for outpatients' appointments and checkups. Some of the wounded went directly from Selly Oak to the Armed Forces Rehabilitation Centre at Headley Court, near Leatherhead in Surrey, and they too received regular visits.

Chris Wright went out to Iraq for a month to ensure that welfare issues were being dealt with properly in theatre. While there he made extensive video recordings in both Abu Naji and Basra; these were edited into a presentation given, mid-tour, to families at Tidworth, and those who wanted them could get copies of the recordings of their husband or father. Chris could scarcely have known it, but he had already been an inspiration to David Bradley. When Major Bradley first saw his own mangled hand in the turret of his Warrior in Basra, he thought of 'our families officer, Captain Chris Wright. He lost his ring and middle finger in Northern Ireland as an eighteen-year-old private soldier, but still made it up to RSM and a late-entry commission. I looked at my hand and thought "It's bad, but it's not that bad . . ."'

All of the 1st Battalion's casualties were out of hospital by the end of the year, but as I write, in the autumn of 2005, several are still receiving treatment; some will make a full recovery, but others will not. More broadly, the experience of Basra and Al Amarah in 2004 changed the lives of most of those who served there, whether or not they were wounded.

However, we must beware of black and white judgements, for I detected no consistent effect. Several soldiers told me that they had always looked forward, with uneasy anticipation, to combat, and were glad to have experienced it; but once, they thought, was certainly enough. CSM Falconer of C Company observed:

> I have discussed this with others, that I have spent my army career quietly hoping to go into battle with my men. Now that I have experienced it (and will soon have the T shirt) I will be quite happy if I never fire another round in anger. After all, nobody runs to war!

Rather fewer said that they were eager for more, but all were prepared to accept it as part of the job. The number of soldiers leaving the army after the battalion's return rose above its pre-tour level, but it was a trickle rather than a flood, largely reflecting the fact that some soldiers had deliberately chosen to stay on so as to complete the tour and had always intended to leave when it was over.

A surprisingly large number were ambivalent about the way that Iraq had affected their lives. One officer told me that when he was there he tried to do his job to the best of his ability, but realized that his wife and children were actually the most important things in his life. Within just a few weeks of his return, though, he longed for the excitement and danger of Al Amarah, and wished that he was back there – perhaps, as he admitted wistfully, just so that he could wish he was back home again. Corporal Wesley of The Queen's Royal Lancers acknowledged that his first thoughts on hearing that he was going to Iraq

> were slightly reserved, as I was due to be married towards the end of the year. It was a time of mixed emotions as I was torn between staying at home with loved ones and the prospect of missing front-line action for the second time [his squadron had not deployed to Iraq with the rest of the regiment in 2003] . . . During the tour I experienced a lot and have only touched the surface. It has developed me both as a soldier and a person and has made me appreciate everything I have back home.

Trooper Boon wrote that he neither enjoyed not regretted his experience, but 'I think that now I'm a stronger person for going. To be honest, when I sit and watch the news I sometimes wish that I was back there, doing my bit . . . Iraq made me want to stay in the army as it's what it's all about.'

I grow impatient with a few politicians who maintain that soldiers are 'economic conscripts', who join the army simply because there is no alternative employment, only to be sacrificed on the pyre of governmental miscalculation. It is a simple truth that most soldiers join the British army in the expectation of going on operational tours and, as far as the combat arms are concerned, most of them actually hope to see action. The 1st Battalion was 'up for it' in a sense that was almost palpable. I happened to be visiting the 2nd

Lance Corporal Pearce provides cover

Battalion when the news arrived that it too was destined for Iraq. There was delight – there is no other word for it – that it was going to share some of the 1st Battalion's experiences and would not be the regiment's poor relation. The CO, who already had a distinguished operational record, was visibly vexed to be handing over command, albeit on promotion, before the battalion deployed. And, across the board, officers and men looked forward to the personal and professional challenges that the tour would provide.

In part, the appeal of danger is enshrined in the male psyche, and many young men see combat as the ultimate challenge. In part, too, it reflects the desire of professionals to see just how good they are at their job, and to test their skills in the toughest environments. For Private Bosch of 7 Platoon, whose reflections on his experiences in Iraq might surprise anyone tempted to make glib assumptions about the intellectual capacity of private soldiers, the personal and professional challenge fused into one:

> The search for yourself leads you on many paths through
> your life. Some are long and hard, while others are as short
> as a heartbeat. But the moment you think you have found

yourself, the search starts all over again. For as you find yourself you change and become a better man. You push yourself like an athlete to reach your limit, and then start again to find your next. No amount of training can prepare you for war. Like an Olympic sprinter, I can train my whole life, but I only know its true value the second I cross the finish line. Did I win? Did I lose? Did I do my best? Without the training and hard work you won't be out there in the first place. Training puts you where you can be used. It shapes you into what you were made for. In the same way you work a piece of metal into a blade, training shapes you into something more useful . . .

And then it happens, your first contact. You come face to face with the demon inside you. Fear and anxiety grips you and squeezes the very life out of you. This is life and death. This is where a man stands up and faces his destiny. This is what you have been training for. This is what you were born for. You were born to be a warrior. You were born to be strong and courageous; to be a man. And with that the demon turns and runs. The fear and anxiety disappears and your senses sharpen into a knife's edge with which you take control of yourself and lunge forward. You look round and you see the eyes of the men next to you. You grow strong with the confidence you see in their faces. For a split second, you almost feel sorry for the foes that stumble in the way of a force like this . . .

But a man is more than just a warrior, and war is more than just fighting battles. After all, we came here to keep the peace. 'To build a bridge between two nations,' as my friend Andy always says, peace being the one thing we have been wishing for for so many weeks. How do you get this peace? . . .

Peace starts with you, a soldier, walking the streets, talking to the people. Bringing your world to them. To give a little bit of who you are and what you know so that they may have a better life. This is something you cannot train for. The life you live in the battalion is the one that shines through you. As you give, you also receive. What you get back is what changes you. You end up like the hobbits in J. R. R. Tolkien's *Lord of the Rings* trilogy, unable to tell others what you have experienced. The only ones that understand you are the people who were there with you. The ones who have seen what you have seen and experienced what you have experienced.

In the heat of battle most soldiers regard their adversaries as ciphers: anonymous figures to be dealt with as expeditiously as possible. Combat 'is really very clinical when you're involved,' thought CSM Falconer.

You identify the enemy, place the sight on to him, pull the trigger and he is gone, but you don't think about it because you are still taking incoming fire. You move and start the process again, it is you or them at the end of the day and we all want to go home. What happens in the future when the images are played back through our minds only time will tell.

Most soldiers in contact killed to stay alive, and some went further, gaining professional satisfaction from outmanoeuvring or outshooting their adversaries, even if the consequence of this success was the death of another human being. Some found it impossible to shoot youngsters, even if they were trying to kill them. Trooper Ken Boon

used to think that I would be able to shoot and kill somebody but when it came to it on Yellow Route I couldn't. We were escorting an ITN news crew when we were blast-bombed, and we took cover behind a wall. Then a young lad in his early teens threw a grenade at me, I could have shot him easily but instead I took cover because I can't kill a child that had probably been told to throw it. Luckily it never went off and I was very shook up after that.

Feelings about Iraq and its inhabitants were rarely clear-cut. Soldiers on operations are usually too caught up with the pressing concerns of the moment to muse about the *casus belli*: they see a campaign through the microscope of their own experience, not the wide screen of broadsheet newspapers or worthy journals. However, many in Iraq were intellectually and emotionally seized by what they were doing, and whatever their views on the wisdom of going to war in the first place (an issue discussed far less often than one might expect), they genuinely hoped to make a difference. Captain Steve Brooks admitted:

> One of the big mistakes I made was allowing the men to watch Michael Moore's *Fahrenheit 911* on DVD in the middle of August while on QRF at CIMIC. I watched horrified as the anti-Telic propaganda poured across the screen, wondering whether I should make a stand and turn this possibly damaging docufilm off. I didn't, and the room was silent as the credits rolled. I thought I might need to say something to reassure the men as to the justice of their plight, but was rendered impotent as the youngest member of the multiple (Pte Barclay of A Company) stood up and said simply 'That was shit.' All the others nodded in agreement and went to discuss something more relevant over a fag.

He went on to affirm:

> I have found that soldiers are simple people and in general are apolitical – not amoral. As such I deployed to Ulster to stop children having to walk to school between picket lines under a hail of missiles, to Kosovo to prevent ethnic cleansing of a population, and to Iraq to secure democracy for a people who deserved the right to it. By looking at the basic scars of Saddam's regime I know that we were doing right by the common man. Yes, some suffer, as did we, but it was the necessary evil ... No one can doubt the misery and persecution of the Marsh Arabs in the south, and by freeing them we allowed them the ability to lash out at us – which some did.

Captain James Rands went further:

> The battalion were excited to be going to war and as professional infanteers we had waited some time to get the

chance for a proper operation. This sense dulled some of the debate about whether we should be going. This was not the invasion and so a lot of the moral and political questions were now irrelevant. Should we invade Iraq? Too late, we already have and now we're occupying it and we have a moral and legal duty to create security, law and order, aid a transition to self-government, and so on.

The big debate was not whether we should be going – that was already answered – but rather, what we should be trying to achieve. Myself and JD sat in the Red Shield [Salvation Army café] in Tidworth one morning talking about it. There was an orthodoxy that the Muslim world had one way of doing things and we had another, and that for us to impose our way upon Iraqi society was arrogant and morally wrong – who were we to say that British society with its drunkenness and teenage pregnancies was inherently better than Iraqi society?

This is so much bollocks. Before we had deployed, an Iraqi giving us cultural education had told us a story. Some British soldiers in Basra had chatted to a little girl of about twelve . . . This was apparently an amiable chat. There's no suggestion that there was anything lewd or undignified in the conversation. The girl's father was angry about her talking to soldiers and so he beat her – badly. The soldiers saw the bruises and found out what had happened. They reacted by finding the bloke and giving him a substantially more competent beating. The man, feeling that he had been humiliated and emasculated, decided to rectify the situation by slitting his own daughter's throat. This apparently restored his honour.

The storyteller used this to draw the lesson that we should not talk to the local children as their fathers would be forced into taking drastic action and that would be upon our heads. JD and I both drew the lesson that Iraqi society was fundamentally rotten to the very core and that it needed to be changed. Politically I am left-wing, and I think JD is too. I've never understood why the liberal left cannot find it in itself to condemn nasty, vicious, ignorant little bastards like the girl's father . . . For God's sake, some things are just plain wrong . . . And what was the point of invading the country and getting rid of a vile dictator if we allow a vile dictator to rule each household because we feel we have to respect their differing cultural values?

Captain Yates, who may have come to the argument from a different political perspective, felt that, despite efforts to improve cultural awareness, it was unrealistic to expect

a joyful multicultural confluence . . . What soldiers will do is to respond humanely to persons in distress, or who wish to help themselves – however, as well as being humane, they are also human.

On one occasion a local pestered a soldier for a bottle of drinking water from our coolbox. Eventually he convinced him, claiming he had a sick young child at home and the water would be for the child. Shortly after, the soldier caught the individual washing his feet with it. Bearing in mind that bottled drinking water was relatively precious to us as well – the heat of the day, the constant nervousness of a patrol, and the frustration of being pestered and distracted – exasperation and anger doesn't come near it. It takes only one or two instances like this for all Arabs to become tarred with the same brush, and most soldiers would have at least one or two similar stories to tell. The perception of ingratitude would gradually become reinforced and eventually a given truth, after which all the evidence would confirm the soldiers' outright resentment of the civilian population.

Equally, standing for hours in the heat of the day, faced with a crowd jabbering in a foreign language, demanding handouts, jobs – with urchins trying to steal items from one's webbing, and throwing stones – I expect would try the patience of the most fuzzy Islington leftie. Then returning to camp, to find things stolen by the locally employed civilians.

Ancient and modern: a recce platoon patrol on the Tigris

This is the soldier's experience of Middle Eastern culture, after months of which it's hardly surprising that some might jump to conclusions that more delicate souls might call racism. We were not dealing with an educated, representative sample of Arab culture, but a section of society that was generally looked down on by the rest of Iraq as backward and provincial. Just as psychologists describe abused children, this seems to be a common symptom of dictatorships: the loss of a sense of dignity and self-worth, grabbing what one can, with gratification and comfort such a rare commodity that deferral is unthinkable, and any means to achieve it is permissible. Community, truth and justice are just concepts soiled in the mouth of one's abuser. Such people are difficult to love, so the cycle continues. In some senses the Mahdi army were the only locals who got our respect – they didn't beg and scrape and steal, but fought (often bravely) for what they believed in. On the other hand, a visit to a local sheikh brought out one of the strong points of the local culture. The sheikh insisted that the soldiers guarding the Land Rovers received the same hospitality as the negotiating officers, and all were treated to inedibly large meals, and unfeigned and universal hospitality.

Trooper Martin:

My thoughts about the locals were split between disgust at the way they lived and how that was the best they could do and they never tried to improve the state of rubbish that they grew up in. I also felt sorry for the people that couldn't help it and didn't know better, especially the children, but some of them were terrible, they'd throw stones at you in the street and swear at you. The older people would try and stop them with considerable force sometimes. I didn't agree, but that was their way.

Corporal Wesley found the relaxed approach of the potential police officers he was training extraordinarily hard to deal with. 'The

Iraqi people were less than proactive,' he thought, 'they seemed to think manual labour was a Spaniard! Trying to teach them how to be a police officer was difficult to say the least.'

Some relationships diminished dignity on both sides. On a recent visit to Basra I visited the First World War Memorial to the Missing, commemorating British and Indian soldiers killed in Mesopotamia who have no known graves. (It was moved, with surprising care, during Saddam Hussein's time.) The multiple escorting me crisply secured the area, and although there is no sign of habitation nearby, we were immediately surrounded by urchins with the inevitable Saddam banknotes for sale. British soldiers are now not allowed to give beggars anything other than bottled water. In any event most of the multiple was too busy covering us against bombers or snipers, and there was always the chance that the children were a set-up designed to make us lower our guard. The chief urchin, a tough, self-confident girl of about twelve, with bare feet and wearing a grubby blue dress, eventually accepted a bottle of water when it became clear that no money, rations or sweets would be forthcoming. As we left I saw her hurl it, with silent fury, on to a heap of similar bottles.

Many of my correspondents reserved their real dislike not for the Iraqis who were trying to kill them, but for the Arab news media whose misreporting whipped up popular resentment. Steve Brooks admitted:

> I could understand the Iraqi fury at the perceived 'targeting' of places of worship. If some bugger had rocked into my local parish and threatened our local church where I and all my family had been baptized, confirmed and gathered to worship our God I too would have a sense-of-humour failure. Al Jazeera and the other propaganda machines worked wonders in reeling up anti-coalition force emotions and actions under this sacrilegious slur. However, in all my time we gave a generous, if not utterly unconditional, demilitarized zone around the main mosques in Al Amarah, especially worth noting since we saw armed activity constantly in the area and had numerous reports of heavy weapons (including the offending mortars) being

WO2 Falconer searching a suspect

cached there. As such I feel we treated the faith with utter respect throughout.

He became increasingly concerned at the plight of some children whose families lived in a prominent alleyway near the Pink Palace:

> It was always sad to see children with nothing; at one stage I had made up boxes of our extra rations to throw off the roof [of CIMIC House] to children, but stopped upon seeing a flier being distributed around town with a picture of a sweet wrapper on it saying that it was poisoned and had been given out by coalition forces to kill children. How do you fight that?

The coverage of the battle group by the UK's media was, as Matt Maer put it, 'varied'. The events of the first Mahdi army uprising, for instance, went largely unreported. Opinion in the battle group was divided as to whether this was the result of cock-up or of conspiracy, with the balance firmly on the side of the latter. 'It would have been politically embarrassing at the time for the UK government to admit that we had a company that had taken 25 per cent casualties, were suffering dozens of attacks a day, and [that] things were not going smoothly a year after the liberation,' suggested one officer. In its final 'celebratory tour-ending morale edition' the battle group's scurrilous newssheet *Tigeris Tales* (its tone so very like the trench newspapers of the First World War) ran the headline 'Blair Finally Admits War in Iraq':

> After seven months of war-fighting in Al Amarah, nearly nine hundred contacts and hell knows how many bloody mortars into CIMIC House and Camp Incoming, comfy in his office in No. 10 the Prime Minister has finally admitted that it might be just a tiny weenie bit more dangerous in Iraq than he had said in the past.

By this stage, however, the press coverage had improved, and on 28 July James Coote emailed to report that *Sky News*, the *Sun* and the *Sunday Times* had all visited Al Amarah. They were more interested in the fighting than in the work of reconstruction – 'It is, however, good to see some accurate . . . reporting at last!'

The absence of news early in the battalion's tour was a mixed blessing. Although there was a marked feeling that the public knew nothing of what was really going on in Iraq, at least families were initially unaware of just how dangerous it really was. 'I was pulled between the need to tell the truth as to what was going on and [the fear of] creating an air of alarm,' admitted Matt Maer.

> After [Operation] Waterloo I sent back an open letter which was to be published in the *Families' Newsletter,* telling those left behind how we had dealt with it and how proud I was of what we were achieving. What I did not want was hype which would add to an already strained situation. The second factor was that I, and indeed it appeared everyone else, was unsure as to how long the uprising was going to go on for and how severe it would be. Thus I did not in April wish to set the tone for a tour which could spend the next five months in stultifying boredom. However, once it

became apparent that what we were engaged in was not a
one-off, and was going to continue for a reasonable period
of time and was involving acts of heroism and stoicism, I
wanted greater coverage. Basically I wanted to have my cake
and to eat it!

Once journalists did appear at Abu Naji, Matt Maer found them

knowledgeable, courteous and well informed. Not once did
the end result of their endeavours cause me, the battle
group or its members any embarrassment. They generously
recognized the endeavours of the soldiers and never once
set out to trip me up with difficult questions. They were fair
and actually fun to have with us. We generally had media
visitors who spent a couple of days or more with us; a result
of our isolation as much as anything. This method worked
well. It gave those visiting the chance to see the picture in
the round, to really understand what we were trying to
achieve and get to know us as an organization and individuals on a better basis . . .

While it was not the fault of any of the media who came
to see us, if anyone's fault at all, I was depressed as the
summer progressed at the lack of focus on Iraq compared
to other events, particularly *Big Brother* and Euro 2004. Both
of these saw the media seeking heroes . . . the former in a
false 'reality' situation. It jarred in its contrast to the very
real 'reality' the soldiers were facing, really heroically across
Iraq, every day.

It may be that this lack of media focus was one reason why soldiers
became so keen on making their own CDs of the tour. And certainly,
I would never have felt inclined to write this book had I believed
that the British public had any real means of discovering what was
being done – whether it liked it or not – on its behalf in Maysan
province that blazing summer.

Even the best of the reportage (the *Sun* certainly put C Company
squarely in the public eye) failed to reflect the conviction, across the
battle group, that there was never any intention of seeking what

might once have been termed a military victory. Force was a means to an end, and ultimately the solution must be Iraqi, not British or American. I noticed a quote from T. E. Lawrence on the wall of the operations room in divisional headquarters in Basra: 'Better the Arabs do it tolerably than you do it perfectly.'

Major Chris James took over command of C Company from James Coote in late August when the latter returned to the UK to get ready to go to Cambridge University, where he had a place to read for an MPhil. He greeted the reduction of violence in mid-September with enthusiasm, not because it was evidence that the battle group was 'winning' the war, but because it enabled the troops to change their approach:

> This has presented an excellent opportunity for us to reduce our hard-fighting profile and take a more soft approach in the city, aiming to turn the fighters' loyalty. Most of the success in this area will come from recent significant increases in funding to allow more security-sector reform, where we recruit and train the Iraqi Police Service and the Iraqi National Guard. The most significant impact will be made in employment and business-creation schemes, which will help the economy, but most importantly it will take the large numbers of 16–25-year-olds off the streets, where the temptation to pick up an RPG is all too high.

It remains to be seen whether it will be possible for the coalition, working alongside indigenous security forces, to bring about a situation in which an Iraqi government can preside over a stable state without, on the one hand, a descent into civil war or, on the other, the reimposition of authoritarian rule by a new Saddam Hussein. There are certainly no simple solutions, but it seems to me that the rapid withdrawal of coalition forces, in response to a drawn-out campaign with a steadily rising toll of casualties, as well as to attacks like the 7 July 2005 bombs in London, would not simply accelerate the descent into anarchy in Iraq itself, but would encourage precisely those international terrorist groups that coalition leaders sought to deter in the first place.

Whatever the rights and wrongs of the initial decision to intervene, the coalition's task would have been easier had it been better placed to make the transition from war-fighting to peace-making; to siphon off at least part of the disaffected youth of the country by prompt and effective business-creation schemes, and by a much improved ability to finesse the transition from the 'hard' security associated with armed forces to the 'soft' security in which the police enjoy primacy. In 1933 King Faisal I of Iraq, whose Hashemite dynasty had been established by the British in the wake of their occupation of the former Turkish provinces in the First World War, declared:

> There still is – and I say this with a heart full of sorrow – no Iraqi people but unimaginable masses of human beings, devoid of any patriotic idea, imbued with religious traditions and absurdities, connected by no common tie, giving ear to evil, prone to anarchy, and perpetually ready to rise against every government whatsoever.

In at least one respect things have changed a little, for there is often a sense of 'Iraqiness' which would no doubt have delighted Faisal. But the British-inspired constitution never succeeded in integrating 'all elements of the population under a democratic formula'.

Given the fragmented state of Iraqi society, in which religion and resistance to foreigners are often the only unifying factors, the coalition's postwar task was never going to be easy, and when the history of our times is written perhaps the greatest indictment against the coalition's policy-makers will be that they paid insufficient regard to Clausewitz's assertion that 'the first and most far-reaching act of judgement that the statesman and commander have to make is to establish ... the kind of war on which they are embarking; neither mistaking it for, nor trying to turn it into, something that is alien to its nature'. Coalition misjudgement would be easier to forgive if the condition of Iraq in the immediate aftermath of the overthrow of Saddam Hussein had come as a surprise to those who knew the region well. But it did not.

Although this is no more a book about military theory than it is about politics, as I said at the outset I am drawn to using the term 'postmodern war' for what went on in Iraq in 2004. On the one hand, to deny it the title 'war' when 1 PWRR indulged in bouts of high-intensity military action using armoured vehicles, automatic weapons and an AC-130 gunship would be absurd. But on the other, the existence of rigid rules of engagement, the episodic character of combat and the constant interlacing of violence and negotiation – and the recognition, start to finish, that the solution must eventually be Iraqi – place the conflict beyond the 'modern war' of armoured arrows on desert maps. In his seminal book *The Utility of Force* General Sir Rupert Smith, who commanded the British 1st Armoured Division in the first Gulf War, affirms that what he terms 'industrial war' no longer exists: we 'are now engaged,' he says, 'constantly and in many permutations, in *war amongst the people*'.

What should we make of the performance of 1 PWRR in its first major experience of postmodern war? First, my own brief view of Iraq, together with the self-imposed task of sifting through the personal accounts on which this book is based, suggests that however postmodern the conflict, most of its lessons are ancient. The bonds of mateship linking men in the back of a Warrior were adamantine. Private soldiers wanted to tell me just how good their mates were. Private Sewell concluded:

> It's been a privilege to serve under the command of the NCOs and officers in 8 Platoon and C Company, not to mention the rest of the lads. I will never forget the time spent in Iraq. I'd like to say a special thanks to the crews of W20, W21, W22 and W23 for keeping me alive during my time on the ground. Finally I would like to say a massive thanks to the platoon and particularly Private Sullivan for keeping me smiling when times were bad and morale was low. He was always there ready to crack a joke or say something funny when it was most needed.

Private Hills, also of C Company, wrote: 'I will never forget this tour or forget the men I served with. I leave the army in January [2005] feeling proud of the regiment I served in and how professional it really is.' Private Tatawaga of the MILAN Platoon thought that 'the most important thing I learnt was teamwork and trusting your comrades'. For Drummer Matt Lethbridge of B Company the tour had a particular significance:

> The date was May 2nd 04, my twentieth birthday, which was great. The day started with a bang at two in the morning. I was lying in my bed thinking about why I am here today, when I could be having a nice cold beer surrounded by people who actually care that it is my day. Then it happened, the biggest explosion I had ever heard. Everyone jumped out of their beds and put their helmets and body armour on and sat on the floor – everyone except me. I went straight under my bed. Cpl Si Gower, my team commander, then asked my mate Mel [Drummer Luke Melville] 'Where's Lefty?', everyone was looking around for me and then Mel started laughing and pointing at my bed space. All they could see was my feet hanging out from underneath my bed.
>
> Cpl Gower then told me to come out, it's only a mortar and the QRF had gone to find the firing point. I got out and said to the boys that it must have been my present from those bastards, as it was the first time we had been mortared. Happy birthday me.

Six days later Private Pedley of B Company found himself in a major firefight:

> Communications as usual were crap, and I found myself as a runner between the vehicles and the dismounts. On the ground for me things were a bit over the top, with rounds landing around me, and I was pinned down beside Captain Reid's Warrior when the 30mm cannon went off.
>
> Well I enjoyed it to the max, and will do it any time in the future.

Commanders had no doubt that theirs were simply the best men in the world. Corporal Si Gower was proud of just how well his team worked in Basra in that same action on 8 May:

> We got to Yellow 5, which is a large four-way junction. I was going straight across, heading south-west, it was at this time

that my driver, Drummer Luke Melville, shouted 'Fuck me, Si, they're shooting at us.' At this point I did not see them and replied 'Who?' Mel then gave me a proper indication, just in time to see the warhead leave the launcher. 'Cheeky bastards,' I said as I pulled my rifle from the turret. At this point, all the training that we all think we will never need kicked in. Mel drove the vehicle to the firing point, my gunner Drummer Matt Lethbridge was to bring the turret to bear on the enemy, I was trying to send a contact report and LCpl Arran Jury (Jules) was getting the top cover back up, scanning their arcs. It took us only a few seconds to be in the position that we needed. At this point I saw the RPG man was manoeuvring away, however he insisted on turning round and engaging us, this was the last mistake he made . . .

Si Gower was hit soon afterwards – 'it was only part of a bullet, so you will have to ask other people how it feels to be shot, as for me just a small bit fucking hurts a whole lot'. Helped from his turret back at camp, he was treated by Lance Corporal John Drewery – 'a person that I have been friends with for the last eighteen years'.

As some sort of summary I want to say that once the contact started all the troops involved worked extremely hard and very well. They did their jobs with a small amount of guidance from me. All the lads were very young but worked to the best of their ability and produced the goods. As a commander who has been in the army from the dawn of time, I would never change my job and I would never change my men.

Captain Robbie Hicks of A Company was no less appreciative: 'The men in my command were all outstanding and I could not imagine or hope for a better command.' Sergeant Craig Brodie of C Company, writing just after Operation Hammersmith when his 9 Platoon had been in action for eight days – he 'slept like a baby for nearly twelve hours solid' when he got back – declared: 'I will always remember with pride how well the platoon coped and more importantly how well each of us did in what was an extremely intense period of fighting.' For CSM Falconer of C Company, small-group cohesion, pride and confidence were fundamental:

> The sight of men jumping out of the Warrior with incoming fire hitting the vehicles yet still no hesitance to go forwards is because of the self-belief in their ability, and the knowledge that the only way to stop the incoming fire is to fire back and close with and kill the enemy. Even when, in the last contact that day, or within the last few hours, you had taken casualties, with the right approach and control the soldiers were and still are more determined to get the job done . . .
>
> The training behind the scenes had an effect; we all knew what to do, how it was to be achieved. But more important than this was the build-up of confidence that the soldiers had in the system and themselves.

Captain Charlie Curry was delighted by what he saw of Y Company as he re-entered CIMIC House after his first patrol:

> As we got back in, the few trusted local policemen that still worked in the compound were applauding, patting the boys on the back and calling them 'great warriors'.
>
> They were. To most of them the fighting of the last hour or so was nothing more than routine, and it was a routine they were getting pretty sick of. Most had been in far worse contacts over the past few months. Yet they were still motivated, professional and keen to beat the enemy. That attitude never slipped in all the time I spent with Y Company, despite their natural concerns over what was going to happen and the sustainability of the base. Much of the credit for it must go to CSM Dale Norman, who worked unceasingly, never got stressed and held the company together when the real OC was away.

Justin Featherstone argued that his close relationship with CSM Norman went to the very heart of the company's ability to withstand over four hundred separate attacks, sustaining twelve casualties in the process.

> After every contact the CSM and I would gather every soldier involved in the cookhouse. We would then debrief them and get every soldier to give his own account if necessary. The teams would then go away and mull over the events and their emotions, discussions which commanders ensured continued over the tour. I remain convinced that this unloading, and my banning of any soldier going back to Abu Naji for forty-eight hours after any heavy engagement, was instrumental in ensuring we had only three instances of combat stress. WO2 Norman and I were no different. We shared what became termed 'DVD time'. During tactical pauses we would watch a DVD on his laptop and take the time to reflect on recent events and discuss our prevailing feelings, with unflinching and disarming honesty that would surprise anyone who had not shared similar experiences; such a friendship was critical in enabling us to function over such a tumultuous period.

Although my prime concern is with the PWRR, it would be wholly unfair not to point out that intense pride and confidence applied to other cap-badges within the battle group. A Royal Welch Fusilier concluded, after a period holding CIMIC House in August, that 'the feeling amongst the multiple was very good as this had bonded us together and we felt very proud of what we had achieved'. Lieutenant MacAvan felt that his time garrisoning Broadmoor [the British-held Iraqi prison at Al Amarah] was challenging, with punishing heat, cramped living conditions, constant guards and regular patrols:

> We maintained our vehicles, our weapons, and our bodies under the most demanding of circumstances. Most importantly of all – we maintained our spirit, our morale. We left Broadmoor satisfied at a job well done, with smiles on our faces. That is the biggest testament to the work of the commanders and the tenacity of the men I can think of.

His CSM was no less satisfied: 'We had trained hard; we had very good commanders and young Fusiliers with fighting spirit.' The Queen's Royal Lancers had also enjoyed a very successful tour, and for Trooper Ken Boon it was Matt Maer's concluding speech at Al Udeid that caught his mood: 'At the end of the tour the CO gave a speech which made me feel so proud and made the whole tour worth doing.'

Humour was a great help; there were times when, had people not laughed, they might have cried. Most military humour does not translate easily, but Steve Brooks's account of life in CIMIC House gives a flavour of it:

> With Y Company being older, longer serving and therefore the most cynical, part of the battle group humour was particularly fatalistic. The natural choice obviously is *Blackadder*, of particular significance as the soldier sees himself hard done by by the sardonic Blackadder. His less than proficient peers are the witless Baldrick, and the dash and doubtful-do of Lt George is perfect for ridiculing the commissioned officers. The two main protagonists of this were Cpl Chris Mulrine and Sergeant Clint Eastwood (fire controller turned water engineer). Chris would slope around crying 'Deny everything, Baldrick' or 'Don't forget your stick, Lieutenant' at the most inopportune moments, and on special occasions (usually on the eve of one of the big ops) he could be found muttering to himself 'Fine body of men . . . about to become fine bodies of men' and 'Ice cream in Berlin in fifteen days, or ice cold in No Man's Land in fifteen seconds.' His timing and application of quotes were carried out with understated style and panache.
>
> Clint was less discreet; he would fanfare his arrival into any room by crying 'I feel fantastic' and the occasional 'Good morning, Darling,' mimicking the fictitous General Melchett and Captain Blackadder addressing Captain Darling. He also got into the habit of referring to me as 'the

Major Justin Featherstone and Tigris

ship's cat', which conjured up in my mind images of a cool, calm and stylish creature strutting the deck of the good ship Y Company untouched by the chaos and the carnage and revered by the crew. Unfortunately he later told me that it was rhyming slang for twat.

There were times, even in the midst of battle, when men laughed out loud. Witness this snippet of conversation between two tank commanders during a difficult operation in Al Amarah (which sounded funnier then than it does now):

> Hello, Delta Four One, this is Delta Zero Bravo, what's that on your gun barrel? Over.
> Delta Four One, a market stall. Over.

This being the British army, there was a good splash of sentimentality. A mongrel bitch known as Tigris, badly beaten and her tail cut off by locals when she was still a puppy, had become a semipermanent fixture at CIMIC House before Y Company arrived. Justin Featherstone describes her regime:

> She was fed scraps from the cookhouse and took up residence in my Corrimec. Soon she was regularly following

Dog's dinner: Tigris in the cookhouse at CIMIC House

the patrols by day and night and was involved in a number of major contacts. Sometimes she would stray away and run with the feral packs of dogs for a few days, but always returned to my bunk to sleep by day. In August, I tied her up for most of the time, fearing the locals would kill her out of spite, and she spent a number of nights with the 51mm crew on the rooftop.

Her presence was not universally welcome. One soldier complained that she wedged her head under his smock during a contact, leaving him in a dangerous atmosphere riddled with tracer and doggy breath. Steve Brooks reckoned that

> there was a secret underground movement to terminate her with extreme prejudice. The movement was not short of volunteers after the siege of August saw meat a scarce commodity in the cookhouse; almost daily, however, a huge platter of carnivorous delights piled high was walked through the lines of tables full of soldiers and placed before Tigris the dog. How she survived I do not know.

When CIMIC House was handed over the only humane thing to do was to shoot her, for dogs are unclean to Iraqi Muslims, and Tigris did not help matters by 'her pathological hatred of all Iraqis, whom she would attack with great gusto, apart from my Lebanese general duties LEC and Abbas, the fourteen-year-old cook-hand'. Justin mentioned his cruel dilemma to his wife Claire, working as a captain in the media operations branch at divisional headquarters. She in turn mentioned it to Tom Newton-Dunn of the *Sun* – and 'Tigris, dog of war' became a celebrity. The RAF flew her to Basra and on to Kuwait, where she was hidden for two days in a US base that was officially a dog-free zone. British Airways generously flew her to Heathrow free, and the *Sun* paid half her quarantine fees while Justin paid the other half. Happily, Tigris 'survived quarantine and now terrorizes Sandhurst – a rather odd dog amongst black labs and spaniels. She is still very badly behaved but is improving daily and remains one of the most loyal dogs I have ever owned – as well as being infamous.' Justin is now teaching leadership at Sandhurst, a round peg in a round hole.

It will long have been obvious that there is a comfortable informality within the introspective world of a rifle company. The outlines of the army's policy about terms of address are clear enough. Officers and warrant officers are 'sir' to their subordinates, while NCOs are addressed by their rank by their seniors and juniors alike. Policies for the use of first names amongst officers vary between units, but generally all from second lieutenant to major are on first-name terms except in formal circumstances. The complexities grow as we hack into the cultural jungle. Commanding officers are usually 'colonel' in the mess but 'sir' where greater formality is demanded, and more senior officers may either be called by their rank (in the comfortable way of the cavalry) or 'sir' at all times (in the crisper rulebook of the Foot Guards.)

However, on operations, though a battalion like 1 PWRR preserves the hierarchical function, it relaxes the outward form. Nicknames were universal: see the specimen list of the admiring and the amusing, the obvious and the unintelligible, in my dedication to this book. Officers and NCOs used them widely down the chain of command, and privates employed them more guardedly upwards, sometimes as far as platoon sergeant. Junior officers were generally called 'boss', certainly by their own NCOs and sometimes by privates, and there were moments when deference was not the order of the day. On one occasion, under fire, Lieutenant Ben Plenge found himself waiting for his gunner, Lance Corporal Butler, to clear a stoppage on the chain gun:

> He is a skilled gunner, and can do this as fast as anyone, but it still takes a few minutes to do it properly, and under those circumstances it seemed like an eternity. While he cleared the stoppage I traversed the turret slightly, and on to another position by Green 9. I used the manual fire switch on the back of the 30mm cannon and sent some HE crashing into the side of a building 200 metres away. I had not, however, told LCpl Butler that I was going to do this and it scared the shit out of him. 'Fucking hell, boss, tell me before you do that!'

Using nicknames like this was something of a status marker, reflecting personal familiarity, length of service and experience in Iraq. There was nothing surprising in a senior Tom calling his platoon commander 'boss', but a recent arrival would think twice about it until there came the magic moment when it was suddenly so natural. Who called whom what revealed the ability of soldiers to know when informality was appropriate and when it was not, and for all the starchier concerns of somebody of my generation, familiarity never bred contempt and liberty never slid into licence.

Major Featherstone was struck by the confidence and mutual regard that characterized his soldiers, and cites a striking example.

> Having deployed by assault boat, we were returning on foot from ... a patrol in the area of Red 14 when we were ambushed from three positions. A blast bomb exploded immediately to my right and an RPG passed between me and Private Somers, followed by fire from only 50 metres to my front and machine-gun fire to my multiple's rear.

As the other multiples reacted by going to higher ground, I sent the contact report and assaulted with Private Somers, who was armed with an L96 sniper rifle. It was only after we got to the front edge of the enemy's ambush position that Somers calmly told me: 'I think we had better stop here for now, as the others haven't followed us, I think your PRR is fucked.' After forty minutes of sporadic engagements, the patrol extracted and I had time to reflect that Somers had continued to follow me into the assault, although he probably realized well before I did that the others had not heard the command; it was such examples of bravery and trust that marked the tour on a daily basis.

The solid common sense displayed by most soldiers on operations in Iraq led Matt Maer and many others to the conclusion that the achievement of 'the PlayStation generation' was the real eye-opener of the tour. The average age of the battalion was about twenty-one. Taking the salute at passing-out parades and talking to proud families afterwards had already shown me the unwisdom of making conventional assumptions about family structures, for most young soldiers nowadays come from complex, non-nuclear families. Before they began their military training nobody had said 'no' to them as if they meant it; trainers were the universal footwear, and many, deprived of male role models, ran in the wolf pack of their mates. Yet the same characteristics that might have made them such a liability in city centres on Saturday nights worked here to their advantage. They were quite capable of putting their shoulders to the wheel if they were shown where the wheel was. They responded well to brave and thoughtful leadership, with officers and NCOs taking on the roles of fathers or elder brothers.

Yet there is a darker side. No account of the British army in the early years of the new millennium can escape the related issues of bullying within the training organization (the Deepcut scandal being its most notable example) and trials for 'war crimes' in Iraq. While General Mike Jackson maintains that such cases reflect the action of a minority of rotten apples in an otherwise sound barrel, others take a very different view. In February 2005 Professor Joanna Bourke wrote an article in the *Guardian* affirming: 'From Surrey to Basra, abuse is a fact of British army life.' She cited several examples of recent lapses, and argued from these that 'it is plausible to assume' that abuse is far more widespread. 'The ethos promoted by army life and that accepted within civilian societies will always differ,' she concluded. 'What we have been seeing in Iraq, however, is the complete divorce between the two.'

In part she is uncontestably right. The army's ethos, with its emphasis on commitment, self-sacrifice and mutual trust, has few parallels in civilian life. The men of 1 PWRR risked their lives for one another day in and day out. These qualities are fundamental to military success, and in preserving them an army has not simply a right, but a duty, to be different. Moreover, there are serious questions to be raised about the degree to which some aspects of modern society, such as its litigiousness, its culture of blame, its quest for short-term gratification and its fragmentation, can be extended into the armed forces without effectively destroying them. Thus far a difference between the standards of military and civilian societies should not be lamented.

But of course, Professor Bourke's argument was intended to assail not the constructive aspects of the military ethos, but some of its uglier consequences. She argued that the inculcation of unquestioning obedience, the 'macho' culture in training, and the racial stereotyping of opponents were all likely to fuel abusive behaviour. There is no doubt that such abuse sometimes occurs: indeed, from time to time the members of almost any army in almost any conflict lapse from accepted standards of permissible behaviour. The key questions concern the degree to which such lapses occur, and the steps that are taken to prevent them. How far, in short, is it plausible to extend specific cases, as Joanna Bourke does, to assume a generalized culture of abuse?

During their training British soldiers are taught about the law of armed conflict, and are subject to rules of engagement which define the circumstances in which they are permitted to use lethal force. The latter are taken extremely seriously. Indeed, I was told that during Operation Pimlico, in the midst of what was evidently a substantial firefight, a military police officer ran about urging soldiers to fire only aimed rounds. It was not a popular move. Breaches of both the law in general and these specific rules occur in two broad sets of circumstances. In the first, men overreact in the stress of combat, perhaps by using more force than the situation warrants, or by engaging individuals who have not in fact made themselves liable to attack under the rules of engagement. In Iraq, for instance, shooting an insurgent who had been involved in an ambush, but had jettisoned his weapon before running away from the ambush site, would have breached the rules. Shooting him if he had retained his weapon, however, would not. In cases like this it is very hard to judge the culpability of an individual soldier, who is compelled to make a quick decision when his own life may lie in the balance.

I am perplexed that we seem eager to bring the full machinery of the law to bear on such men, sometimes even when an initial investigation suggests that there is no case to answer. The prosecution of soldiers under these circumstances sends wide ripples throughout the military community, and it is perhaps the one area where most soldiers feel that they are not being properly supported by their own chain of command.

The deliberate mistreatment of prisoners is quite another matter: here the soldier is usually at little risk, and rarely acts in hot blood, although the memory of recent acts by the prisoners or their friends may fuel his resentment. But a minority of soldiers may too easily imagine that it is absurd to behave with studied correctness towards men they regard (often not without cause) as torturers and murderers; they may believe that they are helping their own cause by giving prisoners 'a hard time', and they will be inclined to interpret a nod and a wink as a veiled order to behave badly.

The question of the prosecution of British soldiers for misconduct in Iraq generates a good deal more heat than light. It is inevitably politicized. On the one hand some of the army's traditional supporters complain that senior officers have failed in their responsibility to their men by permitting such prosecutions to take place: on the other, some of the war's critics suggest that the inhabitants of southern Iraq are being brutalized by the British. Yet in fact there is not the massive number of cases sometimes identified. By autumn 2005 over 80,000 British soldiers had been sent to Iraq, and there had been 184 investigations of all types. Of these, 100 related to shooting incidents, and of the total 162 had been dismissed, with no further action taken. Five cases await trial, another five await a decision by the Army Prosecuting Authority (its equivalent to the Crown Prosecution Service), and four are still being investigated. If the army fails to take action when there seems a case to answer it is damned from one direction; yet if it seems too zealous in its investigations it is damned from another.

Both in action and out of it the direction and example of leaders are vitally important. Many commentators argue that, for all the narrowing of the gap between commissioned officers on the one hand and NCOs and men on the other, it is an officer's key obligation to exercise moral responsibility and to ensure the legal behaviour of his subordinates. In this respect, arguably more than in any other aspect of professional training or competence, officers remain fundamentally different from those they command. However, the changing conditions of war have made the practical exercise of such responsibility increasingly hard, with small groups of individual soldiers out of sight of officers and thus able to overreact with little real prospect of detection. Most soldiers in Iraq acknowledge, however, that as the ultimate solution must be an Iraqi one, the alienation of the civilian population is counterproductive, and my own experience and research suggest that the overwhelming majority recognize the importance of restraint.

But the abiding truth remains. Adherence to civilized standards, even in the face of an enemy who never hesitates to play the butcher, is the responsibility of officers, of the moral climate that they create and of the judgement they exercise. Often they are forthright in identifying moments when it is hard to enforce restraint but, at the same time, essential to do so. I have little doubt, for instance, that C Company would happily have punched local heads (or worse) after the petrol-bombing of Sergeant Llewellyn. This is not because its members were fundamentally thuggish, but because the agonizing wounding of a brave and popular man, in circumstances where the infliction of legal retribution on his attackers was impossible, left them feeling bitter and frustrated. The company did not overreact, because its commander and his senior subordinates insisted that the rules be obeyed. It is often harder to curb the aggression of the tough and self-confident young men who make up combat units in professional armies than it is to inspire it; officers need to pay at least as much attention to the reins as to the spur.

Where some commentators misjudge the army is in their assessment of the mood and climate within its different units; they allow specific examples to speak for all. While it may be that in some military groups, as Joanna Bourke suggests, 'sensitivity, understanding and compassion are routinely derided', this is no more a universal truth than it is to maintain, say, that most male teachers are paedophiles or most bank clerks are given to peculation. Many professions pose particular challenges, and offer particular opportunities for lapse; the army is no exception.

Soldiers are trained to exercise lethal force when required to do so; the process does indeed inculcate collective values, and aggression and loyalty are highly prized. But military virtues often show vices on the reverse of the medal. Focused aggression can become mindless belligerence, and small-group loyalty can become amoral clannishness. On operations like those currently under way in Iraq the opportunity for overreaction or downright abuse presents itself from time to time, and some yield to a temptation fuelled by frustration, fear and resentment. This is a hazard inseparable from conflict, and no army is wholly immune from it. Yet if the British army's response must be a strenuous and continuing effort to ensure that standards are defined and maintained, so too society ought to recognize what it asks its soldiers to do, and to reflect on the circumstances in which they do it. Soldiers deserve more than to be drenched in the flash-floods of public emotion, all heroes when an awards list hits the front page, all villains when news of a court-martial breaks. Most are at least a little bit of both, and sometimes the difference between the two is less than we might think.

The regimental system, as we saw at the outset, has its strengths and its weaknesses. One of its strengths is its ability to gel the loyalty that becomes focused at the small-group level – those powerful bonds linking men in the back of a Warrior, for instance – into a bigger, broader sense of identity. In the case of 1 PWRR in Iraq this sense of identity was almost tangible. Yet the battalion's success was due to more than simply an amalgam of rousing nickname, regimental forebears of undoubted distinction, sense of common regional identity, and many (though by no means all) relationships within the chain of command, reflecting long and close personal friendships. Training, in both the general and the specific, was fundamental to success; weapons and equipment (with the notable exception of radios) were effective and inspired confidence; and, while key personnel could not expect to be popular all the time, I know of no significant lapses in courage or competence within the battalion. The rightness of the cause was seldom debated; the decision to intervene had been taken two years before, and even those who questioned its wisdom generally found, in the abundant evidence of Saddam's abuse, a *casus belli* that engaged their emotions.

Most soldiers I encountered in 1 PWRR were suspicious of politicians, though not in any party-political sense. Indeed, it is unwise to make conventional assumptions about the army's political affiliations – it may be conservative but I doubt if it is Conservative. Soldiers in Iraq often felt that politicians were buffeted by short-term pressures while they, in contrast, faced situations demanding long-term solutions. They thought that most politicians, like the public they represented, had little grasp of what soldiering was really about, and, in the case of Iraq, had misjudged the medium-term problems that the army faced.

Many soldiers have spent their careers squeezed between the rock of repeated deployments and the hard place of defence cuts, and have become cynical about the extent to which buzz-words like 'network-enabled capability' will genuinely promote their effectiveness. The names of a succession of defence reviews – 'Front Line First', 'The Defence Costs Study', 'Options for Change', 'The Strategic Defence Review' – have betokened many things, but more servicemen or a reduction in military-strategic appetite have rarely figured amongst them. Soldiers in Iraq were especially galled by the fact, as one captain put it, that 'the sun is hot, the rain is wet, and comms are shit'; by the sense that effective communications might be considered in some way an optional extra in a combat zone.

*

Public approval is hugely important. Members of 1 PWRR emphasized just how much they relied upon the support of family and
friends, and once the fighting in Al Amarah appeared in the news,
warmly appreciated the many unexpected letters that appeared from
members of the public. But there is an underlying fear that while
the public currently has a binocular view of Iraq, able to separate a
generally high regard for the army from growing disapproval of the
war, the continuation of the conflict against a back-cloth of more
courts-martial risks making this a monocular view: bad war and bad
warriors too. The initial under-reporting of the 2004 uprisings did
not help, and many men observed just how difficult it was to explain
to civilian friends that they really were fighting a war when there
seemed no evidence of the fact in newspapers or on television.

All the members of 1 PWRR who deployed to Iraq in 2004, in
common with their comrades in other units, risked their lives to a
greater or lesser extent. The majority were called upon to kill their
opponents, and there are a handful who, in the course of literally
dozens of contacts, have killed often. Most of them seem to have
experienced little difficulty in coping with the essential paradox of
soldiering, of being both victim and executioner. But to withstand
the twin burdens of risk and blood-guilt they need a mainspring that
goes beyond the cohesion of the small group, regimental pride or a
professional challenge. Ultimately they need to believe that they are
doing it for the rest of us, and a government that does not understand this does its uniformed servants the cruellest of disservices.

To the soldiers at Camp Abu Naji, politicians and senior officers
were necessarily remote figures, but there was a gentle derision of
those outside the immediate military group, spreading like ripples
from the observer's own vantage point. Visitors to the camp were
particularly suspect. *Tigeris Tales* contained details of a spoof award
available to those who, like me, flew in to discover how bad things
really were and flew out again as promptly. Stars on the medal
denoted an overnight stay, experience of the dreaded D and Vs, or
even going out on patrol, though the newssheet drily observed that
none of these had so far been awarded. REMFs – and I am certainly
one – were universally derided. Sergeant Andrew 'Murph' Murphy,
a member of the Territorial Army's Royal Yeomanry who had been

mobilized for a six-month tour in Iraq and spent much of his time acting as intelligence officer in CIMIC House where he became a very well regarded figure, gleefully reported a conversation he had overheard while attending a conference at Basra. Steve Brooks reported:

> He saved the story for when it was all going Peter Tong in CIMIC, and said that he had overheard two REMFS ... talking about Al Amarah. One had turned to the other and said: 'I was at CIMIC when *the* RPG attack happened.' The other nodded and looked suitably impressed. Wankers.

The presence of so many Territorials in Iraq highlights another problem of perception. To some regulars, Territorials are knows as STABS (stupid TA bastards), while Territorials respond with the acronym ARABS (arrogant regular army bastards). Over 11,000 Territorials have served in Iraq or Afghanistan over the past three years; some have been killed and others have earned decorations for gallantry. Yet public perception has not moved on much from primitive *Dad's Army* stereotypes, and the character in the television comedy *The Office* who spent much of his spare time doing military training did not shed much lustre on real Territorials.

Y Company had its own integral multiple of Lowland Scots Territorials, as Captain Charlie Curry tells us:

> We had ownership of them from the start of their mobilization and they were trained centrally by the battle group prior to deployment. We had teething problems as we whittled down those not physically or mentally tough enough for the job at hand; they were first to admit that not all those mobilized were suitable and there were jobs [available for these] around the battle group. What remained was a very well motivated multiple commanded by Sgt Steve Cornhill and supported by Cpl Steve Marsh and LCpl Sven Wentzel. These regs would assist in the integration of the multiple on ops, and eventually step back to allow the TA ranks to take the leash. It is worthy of note that other TA soldiers wound up in company HQ and in other multiples within the company. One such individual

was Cpl 'H' Hogarth who went into the company signals detachment and manned the ops room throughout the tour. He was always ridiculed by other net users for his thick Scots drawl . . . However, he was a fantastic operator, could effectively run the ops room alone and could fix anything he turned his hand to – a top lad.

Experience ranged from a number of years' regular service (including tours of Ulster) and a long stretch in the TA, to, in the case of one junior soldier, four weekends and a two-week battle camp . . . prior to mobilization. This man was a member of the multiple I took command of during August in CIMIC House. He had been in the QRF which responded to the contact at Yellow 3. He had subsequently become one of the most contacted soldiers in the battle group – and was mentally fatigued. I personally feel that we used that young man to his utter limit on the very minimum of training and investment – and he performed well. After mobilization he is entitled to one session with a community practice nurse. He comes from a poor area of Scotland. He will not return to a camp full of individuals who have endured the same experiences, and by his own admission, will probably leave the TA as soon as he gets his first [annual tax-free] Bounty to avoid subsequent mobilization. If, and when, he has any problems how will they manifest themselves, and who will care for him? Where is the duty of care in this case? It is one aspect that all of those in Y Company agreed on – that the TA appeared to have been used and then thrown away. They watched our backs – who would now watch theirs?

Sergeant Murphy agreed with much of this. He had spent nine years as an infantryman in a fine TA battalion, 5th Royal Anglian, before leaving when his job was relocated. He re-enlisted when a squadron of Royal Yeomanry was raised not far from his home. 'This was an opportunity for me to stamp my personality on a unit,' he wrote, 'and to help raise their standards to those of my old unit.'

In January 2003 he was delivering Land Rovers to the Croydon

TA Centre when he heard that a comrade had been mobilized. When he phoned home the postman had not yet arrived, and he was enjoying a greasy-spoon breakfast when his wife telephoned with the news. 'Sure enough, there was my nasty letter.' He reported to the Reserves Training and Mobilization Centre at Chilwell near Nottingham 'to go through the sausage machine of medical and dental examinations, kit issue and paperwork to turn me into a mobilized TA soldier'. He was first informed that he would be going as a troop sergeant to D Squadron of The Queen's Royal Lancers south of Basra, and so 'I told my family that this was one of the safer areas and that it sounded like the bulk of violence was coming from Al Amarah.' But just before his pre-deployment training at Catterick in North Yorkshire finished (where he was 'more acclimatized for Norway than the desert'), he heard that he was going to Al Amarah as A Squadron's intelligence sergeant. He then moved down to Lydd to train with the rest of the battle group: 'The directing staff were quick to point out that there was quite a lot for them to fit into a short exercise, and that on real operations we shouldn't expect a contact every time we went out of the gate of the base. Oh, how we laughed about that one later in the tour!'

A week's leave at home was 'very much overshadowed by the coming separation', and then he found himself at the movements centre at South Cerney near Cirencester, 'to be shunted from pillar to post for a day or so. Unfortunately the RAF will not accept passengers who have not been buggered about for at least twenty-four hours before flying.' When he reached Shaiba he

> spent seven days getting acclimatized, getting to grips with some of the new equipment we were being issued and getting to know the people of A Sqn QRL and the way they worked. Though the welcome from the QRL was equivocal in some areas, I wasn't ever made to feel anything less than a solid team member by my peers, nor did I feel that I was less capable than any of those regular soldiers with whom I was to work.

He spent much of his time working with Y Company, and was 'quite lucky in some respects, in that most people seemed to think that I was from the QRL or the Intelligence Corps, therefore I didn't have to overcome any prejudice about being a TA soldier. That said, most of this prejudice is prompted by ignorance and was normally dispelled by exposure to the TA.' Here Trooper Ken Boon would certainly have agreed: 'At the beginning I thought that because they were part-timers I would be better than them,' he wrote, 'but they soon changed my mind. I would honestly work in any environment with them again, and I made some really good mates.'

If one problem for many Territorials was establishing themselves in an unfamiliar group at the beginning of the tour, another came at the end. 'We dispersed almost immediately,' wrote Sergeant Murphy,

> instead of being surrounded by people who had been through similar experiences. It has taken quite some time to get used to normal life again, and the process is still not complete a year on. I also suffered from a superiority complex, aware that I had done more and been through more than the vast majority of the army, but still being treated, by the regular army, as a fat old TA sergeant . . . It has affected me more than I would have expected, I feel sorry for these young lads who were with me on the tour, simply because their 'normality' has been more coloured by these experiences than mine has been.

In contrast, Charlie Curry thought that the men of Y Company, who had the opportunity to wind down together, 'are a lot more quietly confident now. It showed in the numbers who attended the potential junior NCO cadre in November.' He had expected 'a lot more internal trouble and problems with the police on our return. In all honesty I can't think of any major dramas in Y Company.' Another officer admitted, though, that

> on the second night back I got bat-faced in the mess, set off a fire extinguisher in the intelligence officer's room, got dragged home by my wife who was summoned abruptly from our married quarter, and was put shamefully, but somewhat reluctantly, to bed. The next morning I awoke

with a hangover that would have killed a civilian, and turned
to my wife to apologize. She simply said, 'I thought it might
have changed you. It's good to have you back to normal.'
God bless us – everyone.

Yet across the battalion there were minor dramas aplenty. For
some, the appetite for alcohol reappeared with the chance to sate it.
For others, relationships, wobbly before the tour but temporarily
preserved in the desperate hope that things would somehow
be different afterwards, collapsed soon after the warrior's return.
A handful of men failed the army's rigorous compulsory drug-
screening programme and have been compulsorily discharged, victims of a clash between the mores of civilian society and the hard
standards the forces set themselves.

Several officers sought to put the experience into the broader
context of military history. Captain Paul Hooker of the Mortar
Platoon recalled that Bryan Perrett's book on The Royal Hampshire
Regiment had concluded: 'If there is a point to be made the Hampshires will make it quietly, without fuss, and in the manner of a
regiment that never sought to be grand but was always great.' This
description, he thought, 'translates to The Princess of Wales's Royal
Regiment in every way'. Charlie Curry argued that it was important
to keep the tour in perspective. 'This was not a major campaign,' he
wrote, 'just another skirmish in our regimental history, one to be
proud of but not indulgent in. It sounds like a cliché, but to consider
what our forefathers endured and conquered before us should
receive even greater appreciation after such an experience.'

Much of this quiet pride came from being part of the thin red
line, a county regiment with no frills and no foibles, that just got on
with its job. Yet perhaps the tour will encourage us to be less obsessed
with elites, and to recognize that the army's lasting strength comes
from lads from mean streets and tower blocks, little towns and
smaller villages, who take an unreasonable pride in those tribal mark-
ings that mean nothing to outsiders; who form fellowships 'untold
by ancient lovers in old song'; who bear the brunt of complex and
sometimes unpopular campaigns in distant parts, and then, at the
end of it all, slide quietly back into the society that produced them,

with a tattoo here, a regimental tie there, and a catalogue of memories that lose nothing over the years.

These young men blithely trample on your illusions, for some of them will let you down (with drink and sex the most probable stumbling-blocks) when you least deserve it. But it is their stock-in-trade to rise to the occasion, and if they confound your optimism they will banish your pessimism too. They often have a skill-set that means little to potential employers – though I have met few middle managers with the ability of a good CSM – and share values that seem out of place in British society at the start of the twenty-first century. And yet the longer I have known them the more I agree with the Duke of Wellington, who recognized that, when push came to shove, it all hinged on what he called 'that best of all instruments, British infantry'.

Let me leave the last words to the men who bear the burden of infantry battle. 'Whilst we were fighting, to be honest, after the initial shock, your body just takes over; it's not until you get back and think about the goings-on that it hits you,' mused Lance Corporal Pearce of the recce platoon.

> Anyone who has not experienced it will never know fear like it, and you are not just scared for yourself but for your brothers around you. The adrenaline beats any booze-fuelled night in a club. The tour has been beneficial and I have not been found wanting. Friendships are now stronger and our soldiering skills better.

Lance Corporal De Villiers of the Sniper Platoon thought:

> The only time I have felt fear during a contact is when I can hear an RPG coming towards me and I have no idea where it will land. If there are rounds coming in my direction, my training takes over and my emotions switch off. I also have a lot of faith in my commanders to do the right thing. The emotions begin when I am out of harm's way . . . If an attack went well I am hyper and excited. If it went badly, I am angry and quiet. I would never wish for more contacts but I am glad that I have experienced what I have.

My priorities in life have changed and I have learned a lot about myself and grown as a person.

Lance Corporal Robson of B Company reflected on the aftermath of the fighting in Basra on 17 September.

Before everyone disappeared the OC called us in around his Warrior to give us the usual speech, well done, pat on the back, that sort of thing. But what he said: 'You worked well and hard, I'm proud of you!' stuck in my mind, and as I looked at the drained faces all around it rang true. The lads had worked extremely well, and hard, and I too was proud of what we had achieved and all the effort that was put in, down to the newest member of the company who had only been with us a few days ... We then all walked down to the room via the loading bay to clear our weapons. As I sat there on my bed I was thinking about all I had done on this tour. To be doing this type of operations just months after completing Junior Brecon just never occurred to me. I'm proud of my regiment and all I have served with. If I had to go to full-scale war, I would go with nobody else.

But few summed it up better than Private Bosch of 7 Platoon:

So where does all of this leave me? Have I become a man? Did my training prepare me mentally? I am left with the most profound statement I have heard about being who you are, and spoken by one of my childhood heroes, Popeye the sailor man. Whenever he wasn't sure what to do or felt inadequate, Popeye would simply say 'I yam what I yam.' Today I can truly say, I yam what I yam. I am a soldier in the best armoured infantry battalion in the world. I am a Tiger.

1 PWRR HONOURS AND AWARDS, IRAQ 2004

VICTORIA CROSS
    Private J G Beharry

CONSPICUOUS GALLANTRY CROSS
    Sergeant D C M Broome
    Sergeant T A Thompson

DISTINGUISHED SERVICE ORDER
    Lieutenant Colonel M P Maer MBE
    Major J C Coote

MEMBER, ORDER OF THE BRITISH EMPIRE
    WO2 D E Norman

MILITARY CROSS
    Major J B Featherstone
    WO2 D G Falconer
    Sergeant D A Perfect
    Corporal M R Byles
    Corporal S V E Robson
    Private T O'N Samuels
    Lance Corporal B Wood
    Lieutenant R G Deane (Royal Irish Regiment attached 1 PWRR)

    Fusilier D O Evans (843)
    WO2 M D Evans (454), both of A Company 1 RWF and part of the
    1 PWRR battle group, were also awarded the MC

MENTIONED IN DESPATCHES
    Private G Cooper, Private D S Crucefix, Private T J Ferguson,
    Corporal L S Gidalla, Corporal S J Gower, Private J D Hartnell,
    Captain R Hicks, Sergeant B L Kelly, Sergeant D Mills, Lance

Corporal J T Natumeru, Lieutenant W J Passmore, Sergeant
A P J Pepper, Lieutenant B U Plenge, Lieutenant A P Styler, Major
S C Thomsett, Cpl Mason (REME attached 1 PWRR). Three
members of A Company 1 RWF were also Mentioned in
Despatched

QUEEN'S COMMENDATION FOR VALUABLE SERVICES
Major R T Walch

JOINT COMMANDER'S COMMENDATION
Staff Sergeant C D J Angelo (REME attached 1 PWRR), Captain
M J Butlin TD, Major C A Curry, Private E B Danquah, Corporal
J W H Davison. Major J J M Driscoll, Private S F Ervin, Private
J C Fowler, Corporal P D Gorman, Corporal J J Green, Corporal
S A Marsh, Lance Corporal M Scott, Sergeant M T Pike,
WO2 M A J Wood

GLOSSARY AND INDEX

GLOSSARY

A&SH   The Argyll and Sutherland Highlanders.

AGC   Adjutant General's Corps   The British army's largest corps, formed in 1992 to bring together a number of its small corps (responsible for matters like pay, education and legal services). AGC-badged members of a unit carry out crucial administrative tasks, and their efficiency has a substantial bearing on morale.

AK (*Automatov Kalashnikov*)   Russian-designed assault rifle, its many variants the weapon of choice for many armed forces and insurgents across the world.

ally (also spelt alley, ali)   Soldier-speak for smart, cool or fashionable. A desert hat with a trimmed brim is ally; a large external pistol holster made of neoprene and velcro is not at all ally but worryingly *REMF.*

arms-plotting   The regular planned move of units between barracks according to the arms plot. This contentious practice is about to cease in its present form.

ATO   ammunition technical officer   Officer, warrant officer or *NCO* of the Royal Logistic Corps specially trained in the handling of projectiles and explosives.

Ba'ath Party   Arab nationalist movement originating in the 1930s, embodying the ruthlessness of both communism and fascism, with political organizations in both Syria and Iraq. The Ba'ath Party in Iraq seized power with the assassination of General Qassem in 1963, but it took some time (and the defeat of a counter-coup) to establish itself firmly.

Badge, the   Soldiers' nickname for a company sergeant major, a *WO2* who, in combat kit, wears a slip-on badge of rank bearing a crown. The major commanding the company also wears a crown, but a rather smaller one. In 1 *PWRR* the Big Badge was *WO2* Dale Norman, the soft-spoken and unshakable *CSM* of Y Company.

Basher 75   Radio *callsign* used by the *Spectre* gunship supporting 1 *PWRR* in Al Amarah.

battle group (BG)   Combined-arms force usually based on the head-quarters of an infantry battalion or armoured regiment, and commanded by a lieutenant colonel.

BATUS   British Army Training Unit Suffield   A training camp on the Canadian prairie, used particularly for training units for armoured operations.

blind   Mortar bomb, artillery round or rocket that fails to explode as intended.

Brecon   Small town in South Wales, for long the home of the tactics wing of the School of Infantry. Its famously tough courses now train both *NCO*s and junior *officers*.

C-130   Four-engined transport aircraft.

callsign   Prefix to a radio transmission, usually with a mixture of letters and numbers, thus 'Alpha Three Zero Alpha', that identifies the caller. The word now also does wider duty to mean a group of soldiers, as in 'Get a couple of callsigns down here soonest', or 'I could hear another callsign taking some stick.' During 1 PWRR's tour in Iraq the prefix N in a callsign denoted A Company; E was used by B Company, W by C Company and A by Y (Support) Company. Subsequent numbers identified platoons within companies, vehicles within platoons, and so on.

casevac   Casualty evacuation.

CASREP   casualty report   Radio message giving details of casualties using *zap numbers* to identify individuals.

CBA   combat body armour   Armoured waistcoat with slip-in slabs of armour to protect the heart area.

CGS   Chief of the General Staff   A senior general, and professional head of the army. General Sir Mike Jackson held this appointment during the period described in this book.

chain gun   7.62mm machine gun mounted, co-axially with the main armament, in the turret of the *Warrior*. Its name comes from a chain (resembling a bicycle chain) in the weapon's innards. Notoriously prone to stoppages, but heart-warming to friendly troops who heard its distinctive clatter.

Challenger 2   The British army's current main battle tank, originally developed as a private venture by Vickers Defence Systems and selected to replace the Chieftain in 1991. It mounts a 120mm gun with a computerized fire-control system giving a very high probability of a first-round hit, and is a well regarded vehicle.

chaplain   In the army, a commissioned minister of religion. Although chaplains wear *officers'* badges of rank, they are strictly speaking not called by officers' rank titles, but have their own parallel structure in which a chaplain to the forces class 4 (CF4) dresses as a captain and a CF3 as a major. The army's senior chaplain (the chaplain general) ranks as a brigadier.

Chinook   Twin-rotor transport helicopter.

CIMIC   Civil-Military Cooperation   In practice, a range of public works projects, in which military personnel provide liaison or supply expertise and project management.

CO   commanding officer   The term has legal significance for it defines a level of disciplinary authority, and generally refers to a lieutenant colonel commanding an infantry battalion, or its equivalent in other arms.

co-ax   Machine gun mounted on the same axis (co-axially) as the main armament of an armoured vehicle. In *Warrior*, the Hughes *chain gun* is a co-ax.

contact   A widely used word originating in the first radio report of an encounter with the enemy: 'Contact, wait out.' This could be amplified to give the type of weapon used, the quantity of enemy, the progress of the action, and so on. As a noun it means any hostile encounter. When used as a verb the implication of hostile action is always clear: one meets a friend but contacts an enemy.

COS   Chief of staff of a field formation or regional command.

CQMS   company quartermaster sergeant   The logistician at company level, holding the rank of colour sergeant.

CSM company sergeant major Warrant officer class 2, the senior non-commissioned member of a company, with a variety of administrative and disciplinary tasks. In an armoured infantry battalion, responsible for the immediate extraction of casualties.

CVRT combat vehicle reconnaissance (tracked) Family of light armoured vehicles (including Scorpion, Striker and Spartan) developed by Alvis in the late 1960s and early 1970s.

CWS Common weapon sight.

DCOS (universally pronounced 'dee-coss') The deputy chief of staff of a field formation or regional command, in practice its principal administrative and logistic staff officer.

de-Ba'athification A term adapted from 'de-Nazification', and thus in part a reflection of the desire to see the Iraq of 2003 as similar to the Germany of 1945, denoting the removal of Ba'ath Party officials from authority in Iraqi public life.

DfID Department for International Development.

dismount Noun referring to the infantrymen in the back of a *Warrior* or any other infantry armoured vehicle, as distinct from the crew of commander, gunner and driver. Dismounts can either fight from the vehicle, e.g. as top cover, or leave to fight outside.

double tap Two swift aimed shots, often used in the first seconds of a *contact* to get the opponent's head down.

DS directing staff The instructional staff at a military training establishment. 'The DS solution' to a problem is its textbook answer.

ECM electronic counter-measures In Iraq the term usually refers to an assortment of boxes of tricks designed to interfere with the detonation of *IED*s.

EME Electrical and Mechanical Engineer The senior *REME* officer with a unit, commanding its *LAD* (Captain Liz Sandry for 1 *PWRR*). A junior *officer* serving under instruction is known as the Emelet.

establishment The authorized strength of a military unit, broken down into individual 'line serials' justifying particular posts.

FCO   Foreign and Commonwealth Office.

flag day   The day on which a unit formally assumes control of an area of responsibility.

flap sheet   List of personnel participating in a particular operation: crucial to ensure that everyone is accounted for.

FV 432   Armoured personnel carrier with several variants, first produced in the early 1960s. The most recent of these vehicles date from 1972, and their continued survival as ambulances in armoured infantry battalions would be a matter for mirth were human lives not at stake.

GOC   general officer commanding   In the modern context, usually the major general commanding an operational division or a region.

GPMG   general-purpose machine gun   Belt-fed 7.62mm, used either in the light role with its attached bipod, or, in the sustained fire role, mounted on a tripod and equipped with a heavy barrel.

IED   improvised explosive device   Term covering a lethal variety of car-bombs, booby traps and so on.

ING   Iraqi National Guard   During the period covered by this book, the small force that had succeeded the disbanded Iraqi army.

IPS   Iraqi Police Service.

IRT   Incident Response Team   Follow-up medical assistance.

ISF   Iraqi security forces.

IWS   Immediate weapon sight.

LAD   light aid detachment   The *REME* detachment attached to a unit.

LAW   light anti-tank weapon   A 10kg anti-armour rocket fired from a disposable launcher.

LE   late-entry   Describes *officers* who have been commissioned after working their way through the ranks. On commissioning they receive back-dated seniority, which usually ensures that they materialize as captains.

LEC   locally employed civilian   Generally interpreters, kitchen hands, cleaners and so on.

LI   The Light Infantry.

LSW   light support weapon   A 5.56mm automatic weapon, similar to the standard *SA80* A2 individual weapon but with a longer barrel and a bipod.

MILAN   Elderly anti-tank guided weapon of French design, its name the acronym for *Missile d'Infanterie Légère Anti-char.*

Minimi   Belt-fed 5.56mm light machine gun purchased just before the Gulf War to remedy the deficiencies of the *LSW.*

multiple   Small unit usually consisting of three teams of four men or half a platoon, perhaps ten to fifteen soldiers.

NCO   non-commissioned officer   In the British infantry, lance corporal, corporal, sergeant and colour sergeant.

OC   officer commanding   Generally refers to the commander of a subunit, a company-sized organization.

officer   Member of the armed forces holding the monarch's commission. In the army, ranks begin with second lieutenant and proceed through lieutenant, captain, major, lieutenant colonel, colonel, brigadier, major general, lieutenant general and general. The rank of field marshal is now in abeyance.

OMS   Office of the Martyr Sadr. A local office of the political party founded by the Sadr family. Its military wing is the Mahdi army, a Shi'a militia.

OPTAG   Operational Training and Advisory Group   Permanent team established to give specific pre-deployment training to units going on operations.

OSD   operational stand-down   In-theatre leave.

phonetic alphabet   Used for spelling out letters over the air to avoid confusion. The current version is: Alpha, Bravo, Charlie, Delta, Echo, Foxtrot, Golf, Hotel, India, Juliet, Kilo, Lima, Mike, November, Oscar, Papa,

Quebec, Romeo, Sierra, Tango, Uniform, Victor, Whisky, X-Ray, Yankee and Zulu.

POL   Petrol, oil and lubricants (now officially replaced by FLAP – fuel, lubricants and associated products).

POLYGON   Civilian VHF radio used in Iraq where it generally worked better than Clansman in urban areas – but so, it was said, did semaphore. It was incompatible with the Clansman harness and its loudspeaker had to be taped to or held alongside Clansman microphones.

PRR   Personal role radio. Small individual radio carried by soldiers. Generally popular and effective.

PW   Prisoners of War.

PWRR   Princess of Wales's Royal Regiment.

QMSI   quartermaster sergeant instructor   Actually a *WO2*, and in an infantry battalion the senior member of its physical training staff. Also an appointment held by other warrant officers, including some *ATO*s.

QRF   Quick Reaction Force   Immediate reaction force kept at a very short notice to move.

QRL   Queen's Royal Lancers.

R and R   Rest and Recreation, the home leave to which soldiers in Iraq are entitled.

Rarden   30mm cannon fitted to the turret of *Warrior*. It can fire both high explosive and armour-piercing rounds.

RCO   regimental communications officer   Formerly known as the RSO (regimental signals officer), the *officer* (captain) responsible to the *CO* for communications within the unit and the commander of its signal platoon.

REME   Royal Electrical and Mechanical Engineers   Corps responsible for the maintenance, repair and recovery of vehicles and equipment. In the Iraqi context the unsung heroes (and heroines) of endless repairs and modifications in the most exacting conditions.

REMF   rear-echelon mother-fucker   Term of abuse, originating in the US army in Vietnam, applied by front-line soldiers to those they believe to be closer to the rear. The more elegant homegrown alternative PONTI (people of no tactical importance) has failed to catch on.

RHA   Royal Horse Artillery   Once artillery units designed to accompany cavalry, and thus sharing the mounted arm's traditional dash. Now a distinctive elite within the Royal Artillery.

RHQ   regimental headquarters   In the context of an infantry regiment, a home-based headquarters, run on a day-to-day basis by the regimental secretary and answering to the colonel of the regiment and his council. It is concerned with things like recruiting, regimental ethos and benevolence, and exercises no operational command. Confusingly, the term has tactical significance in both armoured and artillery regiments. What would be RHQ to the infantry is 'home headquarters' to the cavalry.

RMP   Royal Military Police   The army's police force. Once a corps in its own right, but now subsumed within the *AGC*, although it retains its distinctive red beret. In the way of police forces elsewhere, its members are not universally popular.

ROE   rules of engagement   Written rules, which vary between theatres of operation, governing the circumstances in which lethal force may be used.

rover group   Small mobile headquarters typically used by a *CO* when moving from place to place. Individual preferences vary, but it requires transport (two or three vehicles), communications and protection.

RPG   rocket-propelled grenade   Several versions exist, but the RPG 7, which entered Russian service in 1961, is the most common. It launches a 6.9kg projectile which has anti-armour and anti-personnel variants. It has a maximum effective range of about 300 metres against moving targets. The anti-tank round self-destructs at 920 metres, while the anti-personnel round goes more than 1,100 metres. Simple, popular and available in Iraq on a lavish scale.

RRW   Royal Regiment of Wales.

RSM   regimental sergeant major   The appointment held by the warrant officer class 1 who is a battalion's senior non-commissioned member.

RWF Royal Welch Fusiliers.

SA80 A2 The British army's individual weapon, a 5.56mm rifle with a fully automatic capacity, weighing just under 5kg. Its earlier version had a bad press, but in its present iteration this is a popular and effective weapon.

sangar Originally a Pushtu term for a stone breastwork, but now extended to mean a sandbagged sentry position.

2ic Second-in-command.

shirmarsh Distinctive Arab scarf, generally red and white, usually worn as a headdress.

SIB Special investigations branch of the Royal Military Police.

SLB Shaiba Logistic Base Major British logistic base area near Basra. This once had a poor reputation and was known as Shaibiza by the more warlike.

Snatch Armoured Land Rover, available in two types, both giving a measure of protection and enabling soldiers to operate as 'top cover' through its roof hatch.

SO staff officer Usually with a number and title attached, to give a precise indication of level and function. Thus a lieutenant colonel responsible for recruiting would be SO1 Recruiting, a major dealing with visitors SO2 Visits, and a captain on the planning staff SO3 Plans.

Sparrowhawk Airstrip near Camp Abu Naji, Al Amarah.

Spectre US AC-130 gunship, initially a Vietnam-era modification of the durable *C-130* transport aircraft. The AC-130H mounts two 7.62mm mini-guns, two 20mm guns, two 40mm cannon and a 105mm cannon. These weapons fire through the side of the aircraft's fuselage, and are guided by sophisticated fire-control systems.

stag Period of sentry duty, as in 'You're on first stag'. Also used as a verb, e.g. 'Staggering on half the bloody night'.

TA Territorial Army Reserve force of around 40,000 *officers* and men, its members now regularly mobilized for six-month operational tours of duty.

Telic   MOD codeword for the current operation in Iraq. A suffix denotes a specific iteration: the second Gulf War was Telic 1, and the deployment of 1 PWRR Telic 4.

TES   Tactical Engagement Simulation, incorporating both DFWES (Direct Fire Weapons Effect Simulation) and AWES (Area Weapons Effects Simulation).

TESEX   Tactical Engagement Simulation Exercise.

Tigeris Tales   The *1 PWRR battle group* newssheet, scurrilous and irreverent, though much of its 'humour' was fortunately intelligible only to insiders. Closely associated with Major James Coote of C Company.

Tigris   One of the two great rivers of Iraq, running through Al Amarah. Also a large and occasionally peevish bitch of uncertain parentage, adopted by Major Justin Featherstone of Y Company, currently living in Camberley and becoming more benign by the day.

top cover   Soldiers travelling with their head and shoulders out of *Snatches* or *Warriors* so as to observe hostile action and return fire.

tracer   Projectile whose trajectory is made visible by an embedded flare. It enables the firer to see where his rounds are going, and can be used by a commander to indicate a target with the command: 'Watch my tracer!' The expression can also be used conversationally as a warning of trouble to come. The balance between tracer and non-tracer ('ball') rounds in a belt of machine-gun ammunition is shown on the outside of the ammunition box. A tracer-rich mix is 1B1T, one ball to one tracer.

TRF   tactical recognition flash   Coloured flash, usually in regimental colours, worn on the sleeve of combat kit. Blue-gold-blue for the *PWRR*.

UGL   underslung grenade-launcher   A 40mm grenade-launcher that fits to the *SA80*. A popular and effective weapon.

VCP   vehicle checkpoint   Can be sudden ('snap'), temporary or permanent.

Warrior   tracked mechanized infantry combat vehicle   Powered by a Perkins diesel engine developing 550hp at 2,300 revs. Its turret mounts a 30mm *Rarden* cannon and a 7.62mm Hughes *chain gun*. Its crew comprises driver, commander and gunner, and there is (just) space in the back for seven dismounts.

WO   warrant officer   *Officer* holding an Army Board warrant, and thus ranking between officers holding the Queen's Commission and non-commissioned officers. There are two ranks of warrant officer: warrant officer class 1 and warrant officer class 2. They are more often known by the title of their appointment – for example regimental quartermaster sergeant or company sergeant major (both, in practice, WO2s) – than by their rank.

zap number   Individual code (e.g. Zulu One Four) identifying a soldier so that he can be referred to over the air without breaching security.

INDEX

Page numbers in *italic* refer to integrated illustrations